The History of Romney Marsh ...

William Holloway

Nabu Public Domain Reprints:

You are holding a reproduction of an original work published before 1923 that is in the public domain in the United States of America, and possibly other countries. You may freely copy and distribute this work as no entity (individual or corporate) has a copyright on the body of the work. This book may contain prior copyright references, and library stamps (as most of these works were scanned from library copies). These have been scanned and retained as part of the historical artifact.

This book may have occasional imperfections such as missing or blurred pages, poor pictures, errant marks, etc. that were either part of the original artifact, or were introduced by the scanning process. We believe this work is culturally important, and despite the imperfections, have elected to bring it back into print as part of our continuing commitment to the preservation of printed works worldwide. We appreciate your understanding of the imperfections in the preservation process, and hope you enjoy this valuable book.

HISTORY OF ROMNEY MARSH,

AND ITS ADJACENCIES.

BY THE SAME AUTHOR.

In Octavo, pp. 624, price Twenty-one Shillings

(ONLY 200 PRINTED),

THE HISTORY AND ANTIQUITIES

OF THE

ANCIENT TOWN AND PORT OF RYE,

WITH

INCIDENTAL NOTICES OF THE CINQUE PORTS.

THE SCITE OF THE CASTLE OF ANDERIDA.

THE HISTORY

OF

ROMNEY MARSH,

FROM ITS EARLIEST FORMATION TO 1837.

WITH

A GLANCE AT ITS ADJACENCIES, AND SOME REMARKS ON
THE SITUATION OF THE ANCIENT ANDERIDA.

BEING

AN ACCOMPANIMENT TO 'THE HISTORY OF RYE.'

BY WILLIAM HOLLOWAY.

Common Seal of Romney Marsh, A.D. 1665.

LONDON:
JOHN RUSSELL SMITH,
4, OLD COMPTON STREET, SOHO SQUARE.

MDCCCXLIX.

The famous Tacitus tells us that the Britons complained that the Romans wore out and consumed their bodies and hands, "In sylvis et paludibus emuniendis," that is, in clearing woods, and embanking fens, if I mistake not; for the word "emuniendis" must have a sense as well befitting paludibus, fens, as sylvis, woods; and therefore cannot (I presume) be otherwise construed.

DUGDALE ON EMBANKMENTS.

C. AND J. ADLARD, PRINTERS,
BARTHOLOMEW CLOSE.

DEDICATION.

TO

THE LORDS AND BAILIFF

OF

ROMNEY MARSH.

AND TO THE

COMMISSIONERS OF THE OTHER MARSHES AND LEVELS.

My Lords and Gentlemen,

In dedicating this Work to you, I do not presume to point out any of the duties of your respective offices, or to doubt for a moment of their proper and efficient execution. But being the administrators of laws of very ancient date,—of the laws which were the first to be framed for the regulation of any of the Marshes of the kingdom,—and being the conservators of a very extensive tract of rich and valuable land, which has, in the course of eighteen centuries, grown into existence, I thought if any additional light could be thrown on the early formation of the Marshes, and a succinct history of their rise and progress down to the present day could be traced out, it might not be altogether useless or unacceptable. I am not aware that any complete history of the Marsh has ever been attempted; but that such a work is desirable, no one, I think, can dispute; I only regret that its execution has not fallen into hands more competent to the task; and may I be allowed to hope that it may serve as a stimulus to others to complete the work which I have thus begun. In the hope of its meeting your favorable consideration,

I beg to subscribe myself,

My Lords and Gentlemen,

Your very obedient servant,

W. HOLLOWAY.

INTRODUCTION.

HAVING lately published a History of Rye, I had no sooner commenced this task, than I perceived the necessity of accompanying it with some account of the locality in which the town is situated. No one can stand on the rock which forms the basis of the town, and cast his eyes around it, without being struck with the peculiarity of the district in which it stands. The rich alluvial soil, of which the adjoining marshes are composed, is not of primæval formation; there was a time when they did not exist; and the surface which they now occupy was covered by the waters of the sea. It is for the purpose of tracing the retirement of the waters and the embankment of the land this work is undertaken.

As early histories of all kinds are mixed up, more or less, with much that is fabulous, so the early part of this little history is necessarily founded partially on conjecture; but I would fain believe the reader will not find more conjectural matter than the circumstances of the case have warranted the introduction of.

As this work has to do with the embankment of lands, and the changing courses of rivers, and not with the lives and characters of men, it cannot be expected to be so generally interesting as histories relating to the latter. But to those who love to trace the slow though certain

ENGRAVINGS.

		PAGE
Frontispiece	to face	*Title.*
Map of the Marshes	,,	1
Plan of the City of Anderida, and Castle	,,	36
Plan of the Castle of Anderida	,,	37
Map of Romney Marsh at the Conquest	,,	63
Grant of Edward I to Edmund de Passeleye, to authorise him to fortify his Mansion of Mote	,,	89.
Sketch of the Harbour of Rye and Winchelsea	,,	139

LE of OX

Wittenham Lovell

HISTORY OF ROMNEY MARSH.

When we consider the peculiar localities in the midst of which the town of Rye is situated, it must be apparent to everyone that, to the more full and correct understanding of our subject-matter, some preliminary observations on those localities are absolutely necessary. It must be clear to the most cursory observer, who ascends any of the high grounds in or about Rye, that there was a time when all that immense level, which is comprehended under the general appellation of Romney Marsh, with all the various recesses adjoining thereto, was one vast bay of the sea, over the waters of which the fleets and vessels of very early times navigated with the same ease that they now do in that of Rye or Pevensey. We shall find that this bay extended upwards of twenty miles at its mouth, that is, at the point where it joined the sea, or the British Channel, having Fairlight Cliff, in Sussex, for its western, and the high lands at Hythe, in Kent, for its eastern boundary; its greatest depth from a straight line drawn between these two points to Appledore being about six miles. But we will now proceed to a more close inspection of this great bay and its numerous smaller inlets, describing the general outlines of the country, so as to form a better idea of its general aspect, and thus be enabled to trace out its early history. With this preliminary remark the reader will more fully comprehend the history which is about to be presented to him.

We will, therefore, without further remark, proceed to delineate the outlines of the neighbourhood in as clear a manner as we possibly can, bringing the account down, by means of such aid as we can pick up by the way, from a period anterior to the arrival of the Romans, to the present year 1837. The better to illustrate our subject, I shall divide it under the following heads, viz.:—

I. The state of the district previous to and at the time of the arrival of the Romans in Britain, 55 B.C.

II. The changes which took place during the time the Romans remained in Britain, that is to say, from 55 years before to 488 years after the birth of Christ, being a period of 543 years.

III. The further changes from the time of the final departure of the Romans from Britain to the Norman Conquest, that is, from A.D. 488 to A.D. 1066, a period of 578 years.

IV. The changes which took place from the Conquest, in the year 1066, to 1334, when the course of the Lymen was altered by a succession of violent tempests, being a period of 268 years.

V. The changes which took place from the year 1334 to 1600, being a period of 266 years.

VI. The changes which took place from the year 1600 to 1837, being a period of 237 years.

VII. Conclusion and Summary.

SECT. I.

The State of the District previous to, and at the Arrival of the Romans in Britain, 55 B.C.

So little light can be seen through the dense mist which a lapse of nearly two thousand years has thrown around events which took place, or localities which existed at so distant a period, that conjecture must have much to do with all that may be said or written on the subject. But, nevertheless, the subject we have to deal with is one which, in spite of all these difficulties, is capable of being rendered more intelligible than many others, inasmuch as Nature has defined our field of examination by such strong landmarks as are easily traceable even at this distant day. The rich alluvial soil of which the whole of the marshes is composed, shows so clearly that its formation is owing partly to the debris of the adjacent hills and high lands, and partly to the deposit of various substances brought from distant coasts by the continual flowing of the sea, that any person, having the slightest knowledge of geology, will readily agree with us when we assert that there was a time when these marshes did not exist, and that where thousands and tens of thousands of sheep now peacefully and safely graze, there the inhabitants of the deep wandered below, while the Aborigines of the country launched their canoes upon the surface of the waters. The high cliffs which surround the marshes are another landmark to guide us in our path, still forming at this present day the boundary of the alluvial deposit, as they formerly did that of the flowing of the sea. Let the spectator place himself on the top of Fairlight Cliff, and cast his eyes in a north-easterly direction to the high land at Hythe, and he will see, as we have already mentioned, that the original mouth of the bay must have extended in this direction about twenty miles; from Hythe let us travel at the foot of the Kentish Cliffs in a westerly course, and we shall pass in regular succession the parishes of Lympne, Aldington, and Bonnington. From this last parish the cliffs trend towards the south-west, through the parishes of Bilsington, Ruckinge, Warehorn, and Kenardington, gradually sinking, until, at Appledore, the land is too slightly raised above the level of the adjoining marshes to deserve the designation of cliff. Passing round the south-western point of this place, the sea flowed up into a bay to the north of it, and which, by way of distinction, we shall call Appledore Bay; the waters then found a passage to the north of the Isle of Oxney, having Small Hythe on the right hand, when they soon after emerged into the Bay of Robertsbridge, and flowing westerly passed the parish of Rolvenden, where, meeting the peninsula of Anderida, they divided into two bays, the one on the north called Exden, and that on the south Robertsbridge Bay; the former flowed up a distance of five miles, having Rolvenden and Hawkhurst parishes on the north, and those of Hawkhurst, Sandhurst, and Newenden on the south; while the latter passed up to Roberts- bridge in Salehurst, having Newenden, Bodiam, and Salehurst parishes on the north, and those of Salehurst, Ewhurst, Northiam, Beckley, Peasmarsh, and Iden on the south. When the waters reached the eastern extremity of the latter parish, this bay had an embouchure of about three quarters of a mile into the great Bay of Romney, being bounded by Iden Cliff on the south-west, and Stone Cliff, in the Isle of Oxney, on the north-east. We must now follow the waters round Iden Cliff to the south-west by that of Playden, to the high land at the back of the town of Rye, underneath Leesam, when they made a short detour to the north, and then continued their course westward up the Bay of Udimore, having the parishes of Peas- marsh and Beckley on the north, and those of Brede, Udimore, and Rye on the south; when, reaching the eastern point of Cadborough Cliff, which is a quarter of a mile distant from the rock on which the town of Rye stands, the sea again flowed westward up the Bay of Brede, being bounded on the north by high lands in the several parishes of Rye, Udimore, Brede, Seddlescomb, Watlington, up to Battle, its farthest extremity west: and on the south by those of Westfield, Guestling, Ickles- ham, and Winchelsea; it passed completely round Winchelsea, making it an island, and then continued its course rather south- west, under the line of cliffs in the parishes of Icklesham, Pett, and Fairlight, again joining the British Channel at the south- east foot of Fairlight Cliff.

Thus, to recapitulate what has been said with a view to pre- sent a *coup d'œil* of the country as it was two thousand years ago before our readers, we shall find that, in the first place, there was one vast bay, which we shall designate by the name of the Great Bay of Romney, while there were five smaller ones, called by the several names of Appledore, Exden, Roberts- bridge, Udimore, and Brede; we shall have the five peninsulas of Appledore, Anderida, Iden, Cadborough, and Fairlight; the islands of Oxney, Rye, and Winchelsea; the headlands of Iden, Cadborough, Winchelsea, and Fairlight; and the various cliffs of Kent and Sussex; while the four rivers of Limene,

Exden, Brede, and Tillingham flowed into the several bays to which they were adjacent. We consider these bays to have been so many arms of the sea, differing in shape and size: of course, at high water the sea was much deeper than at low; but still we conceive the sea never receded so much as to leave their bottoms in any state but that of a soft loose residuum, through which these rivers wound their way to the sea. Supposing this to have been the state of the marine part of the district on the arrival of the Romans in this country, let us next consider what was the state of the continental part of it.

The hills were, for the most part, entirely clothed with wood; immediately at the back of Hythe commenced the great forest of Anderida, which extended westward through this part of the county of Kent, throughout the whole of Sussex, and into part of Hampshire, measuring, in length, one hundred and twenty miles, and in breadth thirty; taking in a part of Surrey. Lambard, in speaking of this district, says—"The Weald: Saxon Weald—a woody country." The Britons called it Andred —great, wonderful. The Saxons called it Andrederleag. Latin—Saltus Andred: the Chase of Andred. Properly speaking, it means the great wood or forest. "Now, then," continues he, "we are come to the Weald of Kent, which (after the common opinion of men of our time) is contained within very straight and narrow limits, notwithstanding that, in times past, it was reputed of such exceeding bigness that it was thought to extend into Sussex, Surrey, and Hampshire; and of such notable fame, withal, that it left the name to that part of the realm through which it passed, for it is manifest by the ancient Saxon Chronicles, by Asserus Meneuensis, Henry of Huntingdon, and almost all others of later time; that, beginning at Winchelsea in Sussex, it reached in length one hundred and twenty miles towards the west, and stretched thirty miles in breadth towards the north. And it is (in my opinion) most likely that (in respect of this wood, that large portion of this island which, in Cæsar's time, contained four several kings), was called of the British word Cainc—Latin, Cancia—and now commonly called Kent; of which derivation one other infallible monument remaineth even till this day in Staffordshire, where they yet call their great woody forest by the name of Kanc also.

"Touching the true limits of the Weald there is a diversity of opinions, some affirming it to begin at one place and some at another; whereas (in my fantasy) there can be assigned none other certain bounds thereof than such as we have before recited out of the ancient histories. For even, as in the old times, (being then a mere solitude, and in no part inhabited), it might easily be circumscribed; so since (being continually from time to time made less by industry) it could not long have any standing and permanent terms. And, therefore, whatsoever difference in common report there be as touching the same, forasmuch as it is now (thanked be God), in manner wholly replenished with people, a man may more reasonably maintain that there is no Weald at all than certainly pronounce either where it beginneth or maketh an end."

Although Lambard, in the passage above quoted from him, says it was difficult, even in his time (the latter part of the sixteenth century), to say what where the original boundaries of the Weald, yet we may venture to give those boundaries, partly from what he himself states (his statement being backed, as he tells us, by the ancient Saxon chronicles, by Asserus Meneuensis, Henry of Huntingdon, and others), as to its ancient limits, and partly from what may be gathered with regard to its present state.

Lambard says it extended one hundred and twenty miles in length and thirty miles in width. He asserts that it commenced at Winchelsea, in Sussex: agreeing with him as to its length and breadth, but differing from him when he says it began at Winchelsea, we think rather, as has been already said, that it commenced not far from Hythe, in Kent, and running westward, occupied the surface of the parishes of Lympne, Aldington, Bonnington, Bilsington, Ruckinge, Arlestone, Warehorn, and Kenardington on the summits of the Kentish cliffs, extending backwards into those of Sellinge, Kingsnorth, Ashford, Shadoxhurst, Woodchurch, Bethersden, High-Halden, Tenterden, and then on to Benenden, Biddenden, Rolvenden, Smarden, Marden, Newenden, Staplehurst, Goudhurst, Hawkhurst, Sandhurst, and Lamberhurst, which last place is partly in Sussex and partly in Kent. Now all these places lie in what is called the Weald of Kent to this day, and in many parts are still very thickly wooded, more particularly Kingsnorth, Shadoxhurst, and Woodchurch. The very names of a great many of them testify that they were originally built in the woods, as all those ending in *hurst*, from the Saxon word hurst, a wood; and those in *den*, from the Saxon dene, a woody place or valley. Somner, in his 'Treatise of the Roman Ports and Forts,' has the following: "Somewhat now of the name of Anderida, which still in good part survives in Andred, and did at least for and through many centuries of years after the Romans' exit. The Britons called it Coid Andred; the Saxons sometimes simply Andred; otherwhile Andred's Berg and Andred's Wald, which latter is now the only syllable left surviving in the place's present name, the Weald.

In Latin it is found of old sometimes called Saltus Andred; otherwise Sylva Andred; here Saltus communis, there Sylva regalis, and the like. Some have maintained that this Weald was a great while together in a manner nothing else but a desert, and waste wilderness, and not planted with towns or peopled with men, as the outsides of the shire were; but stored and stuffed with herds of deer and droves of swine only. Doubtless as in those days the whole Weald appertained to none but the king, acknowledging no private lord or proprietor, and thence was usually called Sylva Regalis, so in royal landbocs or donations, (for I find it in no other age,) wherein this or that prædium or possession, this or that farm, seat, or mansion out of the Weald, was given by the king to any person or place, in the nature of what is since termed a manor or lordship, it was the usual custom (for the better completing of the seat) to accommodate it, by an additional grant in the deed, with a common of pannage, a liberty for hog keeping or hog feeding in the Weald; yet not at large; but with a limitation usually, and with reference to such and such a part of it, one or more den or dens in their term, i. e. a woody valley or place, yielding both covert and feeding for cattle, especially swine. And scarce any ancient grant is there in either the Church of Canterbury's, St. Augustine's, or Rochester's registers, of any considerable portion of land from the king out of the Weald without the addition and attendance of such a liberty; for example, in those of Aldington, Charing, Liminge, &c. And Den-Bera for the most part; sometimes Weald-Bera was the usual word or expression by which such a liberty did pass and was conveyed. For an instance or two: in King Offa's grant to Christ Church, of Ickham, anno 791. 'Et in Saltu qui dicitur Andred, pascua porcorum in his locis, Dunwalingden, Sandhyrst, &c.' That is 'And in the chase, which is called Andred, feeding for hogs in these places, Dunwalingden, Sandhurst, &c.' In the gift of Lenham to the same place, by Kenewulf, King of Mercia, and Cuthred, King of Kent, anno 804. Thirteen Denberende in Andred. So the Saxon, which the chronicler of the place turns ' xiii dennas glandes portantes;' that is, ' thirteen dens bearing acorns.' In a grant of land about the river Limen, to Minster Abbey, in Thanet, by Ethelbert, son of King Withred, with his father's consent. 'Pascua porcorum in Limen-Wera-Weald et in Wy-Wera-Weald, &c.' 'Feeding for hogs in the Men of Limen's Weald and in the Men of Wy's Weald.' These were parcels, it seems (like as Burg-Wera-Weald elsewhere occurring was) of the Weald, where the men of these three laths, since called Shipway, Scray, and St. Augustine, were more particularly accommodated with the liberty of pannage."

"Pannage was the emolument rising from the feeding of hogs there, and fatting on the mast of the place, whereof tithe was in those days usually paid, as may be seen in many old accounts, as of Aldington Manor, and others taking notice of so much money received by the accountant for Pannage in Waldis deductâ decimâ. Particularly one at Charing sans date."

This quotation is introduced to show that we are correct in placing the commencement of the Weald quite as far eastward in Kent as Hythe, for Liminge is rather farther east than that town. It appears also that Allington and Charing were both in the Weald. Having thus cleared up this point, let us resume our journey westward from Lamberhurst, where we arrived in our supposed perambulation a short time since, and here, passing the boundary of Kent, cross over into Sussex, and enter upon Waterdown Forest, which extended from the stream which runs through Lamberhurst, and which forms one of the smaller sources of the river Medway, through the parish of Frant, to the borders of Ashdown Forest, which, in a direct line, contained the parishes of Hartfield and East Grinstead, when it joined Tilgate Forest, immediately beyond which lay that of St. Leonard's, comprehending the parishes of Balcomb, Worth, Crawley, Slaugham, Nuthurst, and Horsham.

At this latter place we enter that part of Sussex which is still known by the name of the Weald, and pass through the modern parishes of Slinfold, Billinghurst, Kirdford, Lodsworth, Easebourne, Midhurst, Woolbeding, Steadham, Iping, Chithurst, Trotton, and Rogate in Sussex, touching probably that of Petersfield in Hampshire, when, turning to the south southwest, beneath the hills which form the westernmost extremity of the Downs; the woody belt, though no longer known by the same name, passes on to Stansted Forest, which latter joins Havant Thicket, through which you pass to Bere Forest, and so on as far as Waltham Chase, near to the town of Bishop's Waltham in Hampshire.

Now, on a closer examination, we shall find that the district here marked out extends, as nearly as possible, to the 120 miles, the generally designated length of the Weald. From the eastern extremity of the Weald, near to Hythe in Kent, to the easternmost part of Sussex, near Rye, is full twenty miles; from the last-named point to the western extremity of Sussex, which is Stanstead Forest, is ninety miles, and from Stanstead Forest to Waltham Chase, near Bishop's Waltham, in Hampshire, is twelve miles. Between Hythe and Rye lies Romney Marsh, consequently the Weald never extended over this part, and therefore it may be objected that this measurement is not a very correct one, but, seeing that this great forest, as has been already shown, spread over the hills which lie parallel with the Marsh, the objection cannot be considered a very sound one. But however, to obviate the fear of it even, we will proceed in another way; we will go through the Weald itself as traced out in the foregoing pages, and the result will be as follows, viz.: from the eastern extremity near Hythe, to Lamberhurst, Sussex, is thirty-five miles, from the latter to Petersfield, in Hampshire, is seventy miles, and from Petersfield to Waltham Chase, allowing for the circuitous course the Weald here takes round the hills, must be full twenty miles. The two measurements, then, will stand thus, viz:

From Hythe to Rye	20	Miles
„ Rye to Stanstead Forest	90	„
„ Stanstead Forest to Waltham Chase	12	„
Total	122	„

From Hythe to Lamberhurst	35	„
„ Lamberhurst to Petersfield	70	„
„ Petersfield to Waltham Chase	20	„
Total	125	„

Thus we find the ancient account, which gives 120 miles as the length of the Weald, to be very correct, and that more particularly as it is said to have run into Hampshire, where we have traced it in the statement we have given above.

Let us now consider the width of the Weald, which is said by Lambard (from the Saxon Chronicle of the year 893) to have been thirty miles, and to have extended into Surrey. The Encyclopædia Londinensis, under the article Weald, says—"A woody tract of country in England in the south parts of the counties of Sussex and Kent, extending from Winchelsea to the top of Riverhill, towards Tunbridge." There are two errors in this article: first, the Weald extends over the North of Sussex, and not over the south; and, secondly, River Hill is beyond Tunbridge, as you pass from Winchelsea to it, and therefore Riverhill is not towards Tunbridge, speaking of it in relation to Winchelsea, but beyond it. This passage is quoted to show the breadth of the Weald, which, taking it from Icklesham, and not from Winchelsea, to the top of Riverhill, is upwards of thirty miles. We say Icklesham, which adjoins Winchelsea on the west, because Winchelsea never could have been in the Weald. If old Winchelsea be meant that stood at the very edge of Romney Marsh on the sea coast, where no forest then grew; if, on the other hand, New Winchelsea be intended, that, in its original state, was an island, and, at the time of its erection, the hill was a rabbit warren. Taking Icklesham as its commencement southward, we must cross the supposed Bay of Brede to Udimore, then the Bay of Udimore to Beckley, and, lastly, the Bay of Robertsbridge to Sandhurst, through Hawkhurst, Goudhurst, Lamberhurst, Brenchley, Pembury, Tunbridge, to the top of Riverhill. If another line be taken from the northern foot of the Downs through East Grinstead into Surrey, into which county it is said to have extended, we shall find its width here again to be about thirty miles. Farther to the west it does not appear to have been so wide.

Perhaps in thus taking a view of the whole Weald, and not confining it to the part more immediately connected with the subject we have in hand, we may be thought to have indulged in too discursive a flight; but as we were anxious to put upon record what little had come to our knowledge touching the present state of the Weald, tending to elucidate its ancient history, we trust we may be pardoned for having thus far deviated from the regular path. But let us now return to it.

The scenery around the various Bays, which then existed in this district, and more particularly around the smaller ones, must have been beautiful in the extreme. The hills, which bounded these bays, were clothed from their very summits to their feet with the foliage of a rich and extensive forest, while the sea at high water must have almost washed the trunks of the noble oaks and chesnuts which were indigenous therein. If any of our readers have stood on the quay at Southampton, at high water, and viewed the trees of the New Forest which grace the opposite side of the water, he may form some faint idea of the beauty of the landscape which we are thus feebly attempting to describe. The great Forest of Anderida was (at the time of which we are writing), comparatively speaking, a tenantless wilderness. The deer, the fox, (perhaps the wolf,) the badger, the hare, and the rabbit ranged with unrestrained freedom throughout its wooded slopes, its sombre dells, and its tangled thickets. The natives, the ancient Britons, had probably, here and there, not far removed from the outskirts, some habitations; for Cæsar and Strabo (as quoted by Camden) do both tell us that the houses of the Britons were seated in the midst of woods. The stillness of the forest, too, was sometimes broken by the wild and solemn orgies of the Druids, the priests of the country, who loved to choose such wild and sequestered spots to perform their devotional rites, with a view to make a deeper impression on the minds of their deluded votaries. Amidst the solemn stillness of the forest, might be sometimes seen to arise the smoke of their unholy human sacrifices. Here and there, on the borders of the bays, the rude inhabitants might launch their little barks for the purpose of fishing; and perhaps the canoe, which was dug up in the bed of the river Rother, in the summer of 1836, near Bodiam Castle, was one that was formed by the aborigines of the country, some two thousand years since the period of which we are now treating. For the amusement of such of my readers as delight in antiquities, we shall give the description of this canoe as we received it from Mr. James Elliott, who has had the superintendence of the deepening of the river Rother from Scot's Float Sluice to Bodiam Bridge, and who is a man of judgment, and from whom we have received considerable information. It was dug up at the depth of ten feet below the surface of the adjoining level; it was nineteen feet six inches long, three feet wide, and one foot three inches deep; it was formed of one solid tree: there was no difference between the stem and stern, each being equally pointed. At about equal distances from their respective ends were two raised ridges, running from one gunwhale to another, something after the fashion of the ribs of a modern boat, about three inches wide. At a short distance from the gunwhale, on either side, were two holes in each of these ribs, about the size of those in modern boats (which are used to put the tholes in, for the purpose of steadying the oars while rowing), not running parallel with the gunwhale, but in a line from this part to the bottom of the canoe, so that if an oar of any kind was passed between them, it must have worked at the stem or stern, and not at the side. When it was first discovered its shape was perfect; but on attempting to remove it, although great care was taken, it fell to pieces in consequence of exposure to the air; and it now lies in a corner of Bodiam Castle, a shapeless mass of decayed wood, unnoticed by every one, who does not happen, like ourselves, to know its history.

We have stated, in a former part of this preface, that four rivers flowed into these bays, the Rother, the Exden, the Brede, and the Tillingham; at low water these rivers wound their slow, irriguous way through the slimy mud, which was left when the tide retired, and found at various points their entrance into the sea. The Rother and Exden (uniting their streams to the westward of the Isle of Oxney) passed under the Kentish Cliffs to the eastward, and forming a delta with their various mouths, joined the English Channel between Hythe and Dymchurch, while the Tillingham entered the sea to the south or south-west of Rye; and the Brede to the south-east of the rock on which the present town of Winchelsea stands. Even at this early period, in all probability, the falling trees of the great Forest of Anderida, together with their branches and leaves, which were continually dropping, were already carried down the different streams; and, being deposited at various places, formed the basis on which the whole alluvial soil of the several marshes has since been raised. The bed of the Rother, which, within these few years, has been deepened from Scot's Float Sluice to Bodiam Bridge (a distance of fifteen miles), was found to be full of trees, many of them of very large dimensions; and this summer a large tree was sawn through, before a well could be sunk in some premises at the Land Gate in the town of Rye, situate where the sea formerly flowed.

Thus was this great work (the formation of Romney Marsh) commenced 2000 years ago, while the last finishing stroke may be said to have been put to it in the year 1833, by the Act of Parliament, which was passed in that year, to authorise the inclosure of the Salt Marshes immediately adjoining the town of Rye on the east, and others in the several parishes of Iden, Playden, Guldeford, and Icklesham.

Having thus premised what was thought necessary to show the state of this part of the country, previous to, and at the time of, the arrival of the Romans in Britain, 55 years B.C., we shall hasten on to the second head of our discourse.

SECT. II.

The Changes which took place during the time the Romans remained in Britain, that is to say, from 55 years before to 488 years after the Birth of Christ; being a period of 543 years.

ALTHOUGH the generality of writers are agreed as to the year in which the Romans made their first descent upon Britain, yet they are not all equally united in opinion, as to the spot on which they landed. Mr. Somner, with others, asserts that Dover was the place; while the very ingenious Mr. E. Halley (according to Kennett, in his 'Life of Somner') has fully demonstrated, from astronomical computation, the year, the time of day, and the place—the Downs—where Julius Cæsar made his descent. A third spot has been fixed upon by the learned Dr. Lempriere, viz., Lemanis, under the head of which he remarks: "A place in Britain, where Cæsar is supposed to have first landed; and therefore placed by some at Lime in Kent." Now the place, here called Lime, we suppose to be the same as Lym, or Lympne, near Hythe; and therefore it lies within the localities of which we have undertaken to treat, and is consequently a fit subject to be mentioned here. It is too notorious a fact to require to be recorded here at any great length, that the Romans subdued the Britons and made them tributary; for, though the Britons were undoubtedly brave, yet their courage, like that of all rude barbarians, was compelled to yield to the discipline of a more civilized race of people. Having conquered the country, the Romans immediately adopted those means of securing their conquest which were usually resorted to by them. From the earliest ages, to which any historical records reach, down to the present time, the more rude and undisciplined nations of the earth have been continually conquered by, and rendered subject to, those which have made greater progress in knowledge, out of which civilization, order, and discipline arise. But, although the result of the contests between the different nations, thus relatively situated, has always been the same, yet the mode of retaining the conquest afterwards has differed with different people.

There seem to have been several different methods adopted by conquerors for the purpose of subjugating a conquered people. We scarcely know whether the first kind is to be ranked as a conquest or not; but the system we allude to, is the one which was adopted by the Tyrians in the foundation of Carthage and Utica, in Africa. They were a commercial people, and they founded these towns, not so much, probably, for the sake of conquest originally, as for commerce; they were fortresses, built for defence, among a barbarous people, chiefly with the view of carrying on a beneficial trade with the inhabitants, producing, if not intentionally, at all events practically, their eventual subjugation. This same species of conquest has been exercised on the western side of Africa, by the British, at Cape Coast Castle, and at its most southern point, the Cape of Good Hope.

A second mode of conquest is one of extirpation,—the most cruel, the most iniquitous, and the most unjustifiable of all. This was the system which (to their eternal disgrace) was adopted by the Spaniards on the first discovery of America, where, in the lovely islands of the West Indies, a quiet and peaceable race of people were so utterly destroyed, that not a trace is left of their existence. This was the lust of avarice and of power exhibited in the most revolting forms, in which it ever appeared on the face of this unfortunate globe.

A third mode of keeping a people in subjugation, is that of exercising a moral power over them. This is the least exceptionable of all the powers that have ever been brought into play, and is the one adopted by the British towards the Hindoos, where one hundred millions of natives are kept in peaceable subjection by a mere handful of Europeans, with few soldiers, and still fewer fortresses.

The last system which I shall mention, is the one which prevailed among the Romans, and was adopted in Britain, as well as in other countries which fell under their power. The Romans were a warlike, an ambitious, and a great people; the inhabitants of the countries they conquered having been very inferior to them in the knowledge of the arts and sciences, were greatly improved by their conquests. The system they adopted was well calculated to spread those arts and sciences among a conquered people. They formed chains of fortified camps throughout the country, which were connected by means of paved roads; and Britain, being an island, had furthermore many castles or forts on the sea-coast. And this brings us to the point more particularly connected with our present subject, viz., the changes effected in the vicinity of Romney Marsh by the Romans, during the time they had possession of the country.

It is reasonable to suppose that the first step taken by the Romans would be that of securing a good harbour as a place of shelter for their shipping; and equally reasonable that this harbour should be defended by a fortress of some kind; and accordingly we find that they erected five forts or castles in Kent, and chose three harbours in the same county; the latter were those of Richborough, near Sandwich, of Dover, and of Lemanis; while the five forts were those of Regulbium, near Reculvers: Rutupiæ (Richborough, near Sandwich); Dover, Lim, and Anderida. The last two places are those which alone relate to our little history, and therefore we will proceed to speak of them.

Gildas, surnamed the Wise, a British monk, in the sixth century, and the most ancient British writer now extant, was born in the year 520 of the Christian era, and of course lived at no very distant period from the time of the departure of the Romans from England. He informs us that the Romans built several fortresses on the south sea-coast of Britain, at certain distances, to guard them against the Saxons. These were erected in the time of Theodosius the younger, who began his reign in 395 and died in 450; consequently, they must have been built not a great many years before the Romans departed. We will now proceed to discuss the question as to the site of Lim, which we certainly consider to have been the present Lym or Lympne. The river Limen (the modern Rother) rises on Argas Hill, in Waterdown Forest, in the parish of Rotherfield, in the county of Sussex; it passed, at the time of which we are speaking, through the parishes of Mayfield, Echingham,

Salehurst, when it entered the Bay of Robertsbridge and flowed down it to the westernmost point of the Isle of Oxney. It then passed round the north and north-east sides between it and Appledore, where it made a sudden turn to the eastward, and flowed at the foot of the Kentish cliffs, until it met the sea at Hythe. At a little distance above the modern Hythe, under the shelter of the high lands, lay the once celebrated Portus Lemanis, defended by the castle immediately above it. Camden, in his 'Britannia Antiqua,' says, speaking of Hythe— " This is one of the Cinque Ports, and has its name from the Saxon word hith, a port or harbour, though at present it can hardly answer that name, by reason of the sands heaped in there, which have shut out the sea a great distance from it. Nor is it very long since its first rise, dating it from the decay of West Hythe, which is a little town hard by to the west, and was a haven till, in the memory of our grandfathers, the sea drew off from it; but both Hythe and West Hythe owe their origin to Lime, a little village adjoining, formerly a most famous port before it was shut up with the sands that were cast in by the sea. Antoninus and the Notitia call it Portus Lemanis; Ptolemy, Limlo, Gr.; which, being a significative word in Greek, the librarians, to supply a seeming defect, writ it Kainos Limlo; and so the Latin interpreters have turned it into Novus Portus, Newhaven; whereas the name of the place was Limen or Leman, as it is at this day Lime. Here the captain over the company of Turnacenses kept his station under the Count of the Saxon shore, and from hence to Canterbury there is a paved military way which one may easily discern to be a work of the Romans, as is also a castle hard by, called Stutfall, which included ten acres upon the descent of a hill, and the remains of the walls, made of British bricks and flints, are so closely cemented with a mortar of lime, sand, and pebbles, that they still stand up against time. Though it is not a port at this day, yet it still retains a considerable badge of its ancient dignity; for here, at a place called Shipway, the Warden of the Cinque Ports took a solemn oath when he entered upon his office, and here also, on set days, controversies were decided between the inhabitants of those Ports. Some have been of opinion that a large river did once discharge itself into the sea at this place, because a writer or two has mentioned the river Lemanis, and the mouth of Lemanis, where the Danish fleet arrived in the year 893. But I fancy they are mistaken in the description of the place, both because here is no such thing as a river, save a little one that presently dies; and also because the Archdeacon of Huntingdon (an author of great credit) has told us that this fleet arrived at the Portus Lemanis without ever a word of a river; unless any one think (as I, for my part, dare not) that the river Rother, which runs into the ocean below Rhy, had its channel this way, and changed it by little and little, when that champaign tract, Rumney Marsh, grew into firm land." Thus Camden is clearly of opinion that the present Lympne (generally pronounced Lim) is the ancient Portus Lemanis established by the Romans, and Stutfall Castle the original fortress built by the same people for its defence. But there is one point on which Camden entertains some doubt as to the Rother (the ancient Lemanis) having ever emptied itself into the sea at this place. He acknowledges, at the same time, that "some have been of opinion that a large river did once discharge itself into the sea at this place;" to which, if we add that the nature of the sediment which was left, as the sea retired, would allow of the Lemanis flowing out in that part as easily as at any other, and that traces of the ancient bed of a river are still visible under the foot of the Kentish cliffs, we may, without drawing too largely on the faith of our readers, fairly conclude that here the Lemanis did, at a very early period, enter the ocean. But perhaps we are advancing faster than is necessary in this business; for after all it is probable, at this early period, that the sea itself flowed into this part of the great Bay of Romney of a sufficient depth to form a harbour at all times of tide; and the observations here offered may more properly apply to a period subsequent to the one we are now treating of. The river might have still flowed here in after ages; for, according to Camden's account, the harbour of West Hythe was not entirely stopped up till towards the middle of the fifteenth century. His words are—" in the memory of our grandfathers the sea drew off from it." Now Camden's work was published in 1586; and, allowing 100 years for the period he speaks of, we shall come back to 1486. In a map of Britain, in the time of the Romans, published by the Society for the Diffusion of Useful Knowledge, Portus Lemanis is marked at the spot we are now speaking of, at the mouth of a river flowing into the sea. We will add one more observation, which is this: although, when the Bay of Romney was altogether a part of the sea, a harbour might exist without the aid of a river; yet, when once the sea began to retire, and a deposition of alluvium took place, a harbour would not long remain open without a backwater to scour it out at low tide; and accordingly we find that the river Rother and the harbour have been synonymous on that coast, and that for ages the one has not existed without the other. When the Rother flowed out at Romney and Broomhill, there was the harbour; when it changed its course, and flowed out at Rye, then the latter town became the sea port; and we have no doubt we shall be able eventually to show that the Rother flowed out at Hythe, and that the final disappearance of a harbour there arose out of the diversion of the river from that part of the district. But of this we shall treat more fully at a subsequent period of our history.

In the additions to Camden, under the head of Kent, the following remarks are to be found, as given by his publisher in 1695, viz.: "The old causey, indeed, between Canterbury and Lemanis does still in part remain, and is called Stonestreet, being the common way into those quarters. It has a foundation all of natural rock and hard chalk, and the adjoining fields afford sufficient quantity of most lasting materials." Again: " Not far from Hythe is a most noble antiquity, now called Stutfall Castle, which (no question) was the ancient Portus Lemanis, though Mr. Somner alleges the contrary. He objects to the distance, because the Itinerary makes it sixteen miles from Canterbury, whereas Stutfall is but fourteen, wherefore he thinks there was a mistake in the librarians, and that, instead of XVI, it should be XXI, which would place it at Romney. But, to admit of no mistake in the librarians at all, if we set Lyme (as our author says) at the same distance from Canterbury that Dover is, which is fifteen miles, and the lower side of Stutfall Castle, where the port must be, near a mile below Lyme, as really it is, and allowing, too, that the Roman miles are somewhat less than the English, we shall bring it again in true distance XVI miles, without carrying it to Romney, which, in all probability, in those days lay under water, at least in spring tides; or, if not so, the Marsh certainly did betwixt Stutfall and Romney, which they could never pass, nor did they ever attempt it; for we find that the Roman Way ends here, as 'twas necessary it should, since it could not well be carried on farther through a marsh, or rather sea, eight miles together, for so far 'tis hence to Romney."

Lambard, in his History of Kent, published in 1576, has the following remarks, bearing reference to this part of our subject: " Whether there were at any time a harbour for ships at Shipway or Shipwayham (which lay between Hithe and Westhanger), as the etymology of the name giveth likelihood of conjecture, I dare neither affirm nor deny, having neither read nor seen that may lead me to the one or the other; only I remember that Robert Talbot (a man of our time, and which made a commentary on the Itinerary of Antoninus Augustus) is of the opinion that it was called Shepway, because it lay in the way to the haven, where the ships were wont to ride, and that haven taketh he to be the same, which of Ptolemy is called Kainos Limeen—Novus Portus; of Antoninus, Limanis; of our chroniclers, Limeen Mouthe, and interpreted by Leland to betoken the mouth of the river Rother, which now in our time openeth into the sea at Rye, but before at Winchilsey. His conjecture is grounded partly (as you see) upon the etymology of the name, partly upon the consideration of some antiquities that be near to the place, and partly also upon the report of the country people, who hold fast the same opinion, which they have by tradition from their elders. Indeed the name, both in Greek and Old English (which followeth the Greek), that is to say, Limen or Limene Mouth, doth signify a haven, whereof the town of Lymne adjoining, and the whole deanery or limit of the ecclesiastical jurisdiction, in which it standeth (for that also is called Lymne), by likelihood took the name. This haven, saith he, stood at first under a high rock in the parish of Lymne, on the which there was situate a strong castle for the defence of the port. There is extant also a fair paved causeway, some miles of length, leading from Canterbury toward the same port, and they of the town enjoy the privileges of the Five Ports, and do reserve a brazen horn and a mace, as ensigns of castle-guard and administration of justice, in old time exercised there. Finally they affirm that, the water forsaking them by little and little, decay and solitude came at length upon the place; for whereas, at the first, ships were accustomed to discharge at Lymne; the sea afterwards (either hindered by the sands, or not helped by the fresh water) shortened his flood, and caused the merchants to unload at West Hythe; neither did it yet ascend so high (that is, I presume, to West Hythe) any long season, but by continual decreasings withdrew itself, and at length compelled them to lay their wares on land at this Hythe, which now standeth indeed; but yet without any great benefit of the sea, forasmuch as at this day the water floweth not to the town by half a mile or more. These conjectures and reports be reasonable, but yet as I am sure that they be utterly at variance with that opinion which Leland would plant of the present course of the river of Rother (as we will show in Newenden, when we shall come to the place), so am I in doubt also what means may be found to reconcile them with the relations of Asserus Meneuensis, Henry Huntingdon, and our old Saxon Chronicles, all which seem to affirm that Appledore stood upon the water Lymen, which, if it be so, then I see not (the places considered) how this town of Lymne could ever be situated on the same river. Their words in effect be these: 'In the year after Christ 893, the great army of the Danes left the east part of France and came to Boulogne, and from thence, with 250 vessels, sailed into the mouth of the river Lymen, in Kent, which floweth from the great wood that is called Andred;

thence they towed up their boats four miles into that wood from the mouth of the river, where they found a castle half built, and a few countrymen in it, all which, together with the village, they destroyed, and fortified at a place called Apultree;' by which it may indeed, at the first face, seem that the river Lymen led from Appledore to the sea, and came not by Lymne; but yet, that I may say somewhat for Talbot, these words do not necessarily enforce so much, for that they be not, that they towed their ships up to Appledore, but four miles to the wood, and builded at Appledore, which they might well do, although they had come in at Hythe. To the which sense also the words of Asserus Meneuensis (which lived in that very time) do give somewhat the more place and liberty, where he saith, 'they towed up their ships four miles into the wood, where they threw down a certain castle half built, in which a few churls of the country were placed, and the town also, and they raised another stronger in a place called Appledore;' for these words 'another stronger in a place called Appledore' seem to import that Appledore was not the town four miles within the river's mouth, which they pulled down, but some other, which, as for the distance, might haply be Lymne, which we have in hand; so because there is no apparent memorial of any such course of the river, I will not affirm it to have been the same, but refer the decision of the whole controversy to the learned and inquisitive reader, that will bestow his labour to try and trace out the very truth."

Thus Lambard agrees with Camden as to the fact of the modern Lym or Lympne being the ancient Portus Lemanis; but he also has his doubts as to the question of the Lymen or Rother having flowed out at this spot, though he does not take upon himself to say that the river did not in former times there empty itself into the sea. The Greek word Limeen is literally a port. Kainos Limeen is New Port. The Romans most probably called it Portus, a Port—or Novus Portus, New Port— and so Antoninus, who was a Roman, designates it; but Ptolemy, the most celebrated geographer of antiquity, who was born in the year 70, having written in Greek, substituted the name of Limeen for Portus, and Kainos Limeen for Novus Portus. When Lym ceased to be a harbour, its successor was called by the Saxons simply Hith or Hythe, a port; and it was not until the modern Hythe sprang up that the original Hythe took the name of West Hythe, to distinguish it from the new town which lies a few miles to the eastward of it. Thus the harbour, under all its various changes in this part of the district of which we are speaking, has, for the last 1800 years, always borne the name of Port, whether in Latin, Greek, or Saxon, which latter is the great root of the English. All this simply proves that here was a port or harbour, but shows nothing as to the existence of a river, which we are now in search of. But our ancient chroniclers, according to Lambard, called this same place "Limene Mouthe," and which is interpreted by Leland to betoken the mouth of the river Rother. Now here we have very strong evidence of the Rother having flowed into the sea at Lym. Some may object that the term "Limene Mouthe," used by our ancient chroniclers, only means the harbour's mouth; but to this I would reply, that we have but one Portsmouth, whereas we have numerous ports taking their names from the rivers at whose mouths they respectively stand, as Ply-mouth, Dart-mouth, Ex-mouth, Fal mouth, Bar-mouth, and thus, we have no doubt, comes the name of Limene-mouth. The quotation already made from the Saxon Chronicles of 893, relating to the coming of the Danes from France, states that they sailed with 250 vessels into the mouth (not of the Lymen or port) but into the river Lymen. This river is described as flowing from the great wood that is called Andred, thus identifying it with the Rother, as this is the only river in this part which rises in the Weald, the ancient Andred. Further to show that one mouth of the river was at Hythe at that time (893), it is stated by some writers that the Danes towed their vessels four miles into that wood from the mouth of the river, which, according to the situation of the great wood of Anderida, as described in the former head of this work, would be at about this distance. And even Lambard himself, in the passage quoted from him, does not deny that the words of Asserus Meneuensis will fairly bear this construction.

We shall now proceed to notice the observations of Somner on the site of Lymeen. He was a man of great erudition, and of considerable antiquarian knowledge; he published a treatise on the Roman Ports and Forts in Kent. He was born in 1606, and died in 1669. Having mentioned Richborough (near Sandwich) and Dover as two of the Roman ports in Kent, the author continues thus: "Passing from hence (Dover) I come to the third and last of their Kentish ports—Lemanis, as called of Antoninus; of the Notitia, Lemannis; in the Pentingerian Tables, Lemarius. Concerning the situation hereof, various are the conjectures of our English chorographers, some placing it at Hythe, others at West Hythe, a third sort at or under Lim Hill; to none of all which the distance between it and Durovernum (Canterbury) in the Itinerary (to omit other arguments) will very well suit, being sixteen miles, which is more by two than that between Durovernum and Dubris, which is full out as great as this. But as there is not much heed to be given to the distances, these being (as some have observed) often mistaken, so am I apt to expect a mistake here of XVI I mean for XXI, the second of those numeral letters in the Itinerary, by an easy mistake of a V for an X, being miswritten; which supposed, the port (as to the distance) is easily found, and that indeed is Romney, or, as we now call it, New Romney, distanced much about so many Italian miles (21) from Durovernum or Canterbury, and so called happily to answer and suit with the Greek 'Kainos Limeen,' or the Latin 'Novus Portus,' as some have termed it; although I rather deem that epithet given it more of late to distinguish it from the other Romney, called Old Romney, which distinction I find used near 500 years ago. But be that as it will, Romney (either the Old or the New) seems to be the port of the Romans so termed, and that either from the Greek Limeen, a port, according to Leland, or from Limeen-Palus, a moor or fennish place, as the soil hereabout for many miles, far and wide, is none other, which Ethelwerd's Linneus Portus, and the old and yet continued writings of the parish and deanries' name of Limne or Limpne, seems more to favour. Romney, I say, as I conceive, was that Roman port Lemanis, which, although at present, and for some hundreds of years, lying dry, and unbestead of any channel of fresh water to serve it, yet had of old a fair and commodious river running along by it, and unlading or emptying itself into the sea, in those days nothing so remotely from the town, as (by the sands and beach, in process of time, cast up and inbeaten by the sea, and, for want of the fresh to repel and keep it back, stopping up the harbour) since and now it is. This river rising and issuing, or breaking forth, about what for the right name, Ritheramfield, we call now Rotherfield (a place in Sussex), and so passing under Rotherbridge (corruptly called Robertsbridge), is from thence called the Rother; but afterwards running and keeping on its course to Appledore, and from thence to Romney, called (as we said) Lemanis, and, serving the haven there, becomes from thence termed Limena, as the mouth thereof, where it falls into the sea, Limene Mouth. And thus may those be reconciled that are at odds about this river's right name; some calling the whole river Rother, others Limene, which former name occurreth not to me in any ancient record, whereas the latter doth, and that as high up as whereabout it first riseth. It was afterwards (from the port so called, to and along by which it had its course and current) named Romney, as shall be showed anon. Meantime, for better method's sake, I shall endeavour to assert three things: first, that there was such a river, one, I mean, of that name of Limene and Romney; secondly, that this river had its mouth at or by Romney town; thirdly, about what time and by what occasion it ceased running hither, and forsook its wonted channel.

"Now, as to the first, express mention is found made of it, by that name of Limene, in a charter or grant of Ethelbert, the son of the Kentish King Withred, about the year 721, whereby he grants to Mildred, the then Abbess of Minster, in Thanet, a ploughland lying by or about the river Limene.

"The first of these three questions, viz., that there was such a river, one, I mean, of that name of Limene and Romney, is the only one we have to deal with at present. Somner agrees with us that there was such a river as Limene, but differs as to its course and its mouth. But, before combating this part of his opinion, let us see what he says as to the situation of the fort of Limene: 'Advance we now (says he) to Lim, or Lim-hill, where, although we find nothing at this day of a port or haven, which (as I have showed) lay elsewhere, yet want we not sufficient vestigia and remains of a Roman fort or garrison, witness Stutfall Castle, that large circuit and plat of about ten acres of ground on the side, brow, or descent of the hill; of old, inclosed and fortified on all parts with a wall of the Roman mode and make, full of British bricks, lying by lanes at set and certain distances, but, by the edacity of time at this day, here and there quite wasted and gone, elsewhere full of gaps and breaches; not so much (it may be) to be imputed to time and age, as to a seizure of its materials in after times (when become useless as to the primitive institution and design) for building what, with Mr. Lambard I take it, arose out of the ruins of that fort, Lim Church, and that vast and sturdy structure by it, the archdeacon's castellated mansion. Here (within, I mean, that Roman fortress) the band or company of Turnacenses (so called from Tornacum, now Turnay, in France) kept their station under the Count or Lieutenant of the Saxon shore, and, by the advantage of that ascent on which it stood, very commodious it was in point of prospect.'

"Having formerly given you the derivation of Lim (the place of this quondam garrison), as to the name of it, I shall stay you here no longer than while I observe, that the place is likewise called Shipway, as the whole lath (formerly and of old called Lim-ware-Leth) is also now altered in the name of it, and called the Lath of Shipway, a name, I find, of good antiquity and continuance; witness the mention made of it in Bracton, lib. iii, c. 55, but with a mistake of Shipey there for Shipwey. The name seems to be of a mere English original, betokening the way of the ships; they rather, perhaps, fastened on this place as by the great advantage of the lofty situation, remarkable for prospect and discovery of naval vessels (whether inward bound or out) in their passage through the channel."

We have already given a quotation from the publisher of Camden in 1695, in refutation of Somner's opinion as to Romney having been the original port of Limene. It seems curious that Somner should, without hesitation, place the fort of Limene at Lim, and yet fix the harbour at Romney, eight miles distant. As there were both a fort and a port of Limene, it is surely reasonable that they should be placed near each other, the former having been, doubtlessly, erected for the protection of the latter; but how that protection could be afforded at a distance of eight miles it would be difficult to show. Our author seems to be possessed with the idea that as it was all dry land in his time at the foot of Lim-hill, so it was in the time of the Romans. This feeling is further evinced by him when he speaks of Shipway, which he is not willing to derive from its simple meaning, a way or road for ships, what in modern language we should style a roadstead, but from its elevation enabling it to command a view of the channel and of ships passing up and down it. The slightest observation would convince any one that the sea once flowed to the foot of these hills; that West Hythe close by was, as its name imports, a haven, and only ceased to be such (according to Camden) so lately as the latter part of the fifteenth century. Speaking of Romney, our author says: "Naval sea-ports or havens have a river, stream, or course of fresh water falling into them, for their better keeping open; so, doubtless, did this port some time participate of this commodity, and had a river, a fresh, a current running to it, and then discharging or shedding itself into the sea; and the same so-called (*from the several places by which it had its passage*) *Rother, Limen, and Romney.*" By these three names has this river been called at different times—Rother, from Rotherfield; Romney, from flowing out at Romney; and Limen, from its embouchure at the ancient Portus Lemanis. Thus does Mr. Somner acknowledge that the river was called the Romney from flowing out at this town; and if Romney, why should it be called Limen? Again, if its name of Romney was derived from the name of the town by or to which it flowed, why should not the name Limen be borrowed from its having flowed out at the port of Limen?

We will now proceed to consider the site of the fort and city of Anderida. Camden says:—" The Rother for some time divides Kent and Sussex. The Rother, on the Kent side, has Newenden, which I am almost persuaded was that haven I have long sought after, called by the Notitia, Anderida; by the Britains, Caer Andred; and by the Saxons, Andred's Ceaster. First, because the inhabitants affirm it to have been a town and haven of very great antiquity; next, from its situation by the wood Andred's Wald, to which it gave that name; and lastly, because the Saxons seemed to have called it Brittenden, that is, the Valley of the Britains (as they called also Segontium), from whence Sel-Brittenden is the name of the whole hundred adjoining. The Romans, to defend this coast against the Saxon pirates, placed here a band of the Abulci, with their captain. Afterwards it was quite destroyed by the outrages of the Saxons; for Hengist, having a design to drive the Britains entirely out of Kent, and finding it his interest to strengthen his party by fresh supplies, sent for Ælla out of Germany, with great numbers of the Saxons. Then making a vigorous assault upon this Anderida, the Britains that lay in ambuscade in the next wood did disturb him to such a degree, that when at last, after much bloodshed on both sides, by dividing his forces he had defeated the Britains in the woods, and at the same time broke into the town, his barbarous heart was so inflamed with a desire of revenge, that he put the inhabitants to the sword, and demolished the place."

In the additions to Camden, we find the following remarks touching the site of the ancient Anderida: "In all probability, in the Romans' time, the sea might come as far as Newenden, where Mr. Selden and our author have placed the city and castle of Anderida, erected here by the Romans to repel the Saxon rovers; the sea here in all ages having retired by degrees. I know Mr. Somner rather inclines to believe, that either Hastings or Pemsey, on the coast of Sussex, must have been the old Anderida, founding his opinion on what Gildas says concerning these ports and forts, viz., that they were placed 'in littore oceani ad meridiem,' that is, on the sea-coast towards the south; but I suppose this ought to be understood in a large sense, everything being to be taken for sea whither such vessels could come as they had in those days; in which sense, no doubt, Newenden might be accounted a sea-town, and liable to such pirates as the Saxons were, as well as either Pemsey or Hastings."

Camden, in a note, adds: "The inhabitants show the plot, where were situated the town and haven."

Lambard, speaking of the wood of Anderida, says: "On the edge of this wood (in Sussex) there stood some time a city, called after the same, Andredes Ceaster, which Ælla (the founder of the south Saxon kingdom), after that he had landed with his three sons, and chased the Britons into the wood, razed and made equal with the ground."

Somner, in his 'Treatise on the Roman Ports and Forts in

Kent,' has the following remarks on Anderida: "We are at length arrived at the last of the Kentish forts or garrisons, Anderida or Anderidos, where they placed the band of the Abulci, with their captain, which I should not unreasonably, methinks, have sought for, as all the rest (being designed for espial of sea-rovers at or by the sea-coast), so many miles within the land, and at that great distance from the sea, as where, by the direction of our best antiquaries, we are sent to seek it, namely, at or about Newenden, upon the banks of the Rother. Indeed (if we consider Gildas's words, 'In littore quoque oceani ad meridiem,' &c.), where in reason are we to expect the garrison in question, but by the sea-side, to the southward? Among the British cities reckoned up by their historians (whereof from thence a Catalogue in the Britan. Eccles. Primordia, cap. 5), Cair Persanel-Coit is one, by which the learned author (Archbishop Usher) there understands Pemsey, in Sussex, of old written Penvessel and Pevensel, to which (saith he) the addition of the British word Coit (wood) doth not ill suit; because (as he adds) the county of Sussex, in which it lies, is a woody county. True it is, that immanis sylva, that immense and vast wood, Andred, was not confined to Kent, but extended itself from the south part thereof quite through Sussex, into Hampshire. Add to this, what we have from Mr. Camden himself, concerning Pemsey. It hath had (says he) a fair large castle, in the ruinous walls thereof remain great bricks, such as the Britons used, which is some argument of the antiquity thereof. All this put together—a wealdish situation, with the remains of a castle, partly built of British or Roman bricks—can it seem unreasonable that Pemsey should be thought the place of the garrison we have in chase—Anderida? But if any one do more fancy Hastings than Pemsey, since it hath the badge of a quondam Roman fort or fortress, in that addition of Chester given to it by the Saxons, and can (as Mr. Camden affirms) show the ruins of a great castle on the hill, besides lighthouses to direct sailors in the night-time, and was thought fit to be made one of the Five Ports, I shall not dispute the probability of their conjecture and choice of Hastings. But if, rejecting both these and all but Newenden, the reader cannot think of any other place, the authority of such famous and learned lights and guides as Camden and Selden especially (who have pitched upon Newenden for the place) is, I confess, so weighty, that I shall not be unwilling to excuse him from refusing me his company in my travels to that double place in Sussex, to seek out this fort."

From Dearn's 'Weald of Kent,' published at Cranbrook, in 1814, we have extracted the following remarks: "Two spots are still pointed out in the parish of Newenden, which are said to mark the site of the Roman station and city, called by Pancirollus, Anderida and Anderidos, by the Britons, Caer-Andred, and afterwards by the Saxons, Andred or Andred Ceaster. The one called Castle Toll, and the other near it, on the north-east, is a piece of land raised much higher, round which appears to have been a double ditch, inclosing an area of about five or six acres."

The same author, in a note to the above, says: "When Dr. Plott visited this place in 1693, he says, in some MS. papers, that they were then very lofty, and he was informed by an ancient and sober countryman, who had often ploughed upon the hill, that both the mounts or tumuli and the valla were then at least four feet lower than when he first knew the place, and therefore no wonder if I found them much lower yet, when I visited this place."

"The site of the ancient Anderida," says Dearn, "has given rise to many conjectures and ingenious surmises; but the greater body of argument is certainly in favour of this place. Among the principal opposers of this conclusion are Mr. Somner and Archbishop Usher; while on the other side are Camden, Henry of Huntingdon, Selden, Lambard, with Drs. Plott and Harris, whose opinions have been almost invariably adopted by subsequent writers. By some it has been placed at Reding Hill; others have sought for it at Hastings; while Mr. Somner has taken much pains and exhibited an imposing but futile display of antiquarian knowledge to establish it at Pevensey." Dr. Harris says: "I think it appears plainly, by the charter of King Offa, mentioned by Twine, p. 102, de Rebus Albionicis, that Andred was in Kent." If this conclusion of the doctor's be correct, and there can be hardly the shadow of a reason opposed to it, there needs no further argument against the hypothesis of Mr. Somner, or of those who would place it at Hastings, as these places are not in Kent, but in Sussex. The distance of Newenden from the sea appears the most formidable objection with Mr. Somner, though he admits the probability of the sea having reached within six or seven miles of this place. That it did once flow up as high as Newenden, no one can consider as improbable who has the least knowledge of the country. Dr. Harris says: "We have very good reason to believe the sea did once flow up to this place;" presuming principally on the following passages from Gildas and Twine, the former of whom places Andred's Chester " in littore oceani ad meridiem," that is, on the south sea-coast; and the latter, (de Rebus Albionicis, p. 31), says that Romney Marsh was once " pelagus et mare velivolum," that is, a sea or expanse of water on which vessels could sail. The same author further says, that tradition hath always fixed Anderida here; that Henry of Huntingdon saith, this place used to be showed as such to passengers; that it is situated in the wood Andred, or the Weald; that the whole hundred bears the name of Selbrittenden, and that probably this town had the name of Newenden from its being built anew near the place of the old one. Hasted says, " it most probably took its name from its being raised on the site of some more ancient town, perhaps built in the time of the Romans, of whom there are many vestigia in and about this place."

The next authority that we shall quote on the subject of Anderida is Horsfield's ' History of Sussex,' published in 1835, at Lewes. He says, "The site of the Civitas Anderida has, for many years, exercised the ingenuity and conjectures of antiquaries. It is placed, by Camden, at Newenden, in Kent; by Somner, at Pevensey; by Gibson, at Hastings; by Baxter, at Chichester; by Dr. Tabor, under the Downs at Eastbourne; by Mr. Elliott, and a correspondent whom we shall presently introduce, at Seaford; and by the late Mr. Hayley, eminent in Sussex antiquities, at Newhaven. As we have no theory to uphold on the subject, and are desirous only to discover the truth, we shall not hesitate to give evidence *pro* and *con*, leaving it to the reader to determine the question according to the weight of testimony. Camden's location of the city at Newenden has long been abandoned. Chichester it cannot be, as that is indisputably Regnum. Hastings it can hardly be, since it is described by Henry of Huntingdon, who flourished in the twelfth century, as ' locus autem quasi nobilissimæ urbis transeuntibus ostenditur desolatus'—'A desolate place, formerly the seat of a very noble city, is shown to travellers.' Matthew of Westminster, who lived in the fourteenth century, repeats almost the words of his predecessor, implying that the city was destroyed and never afterwards rebuilt, and in his time was a scene of desolation. Hastings, at both these dates, was not only *in esse*, but advancing towards its climax of prosperity. Nor can it well be Pevensey, for at the times when the above-mentioned historians wrote, and when they describe the site of Anderida as one wide scene of desolation, the castle of Pevensey was in a condition of defence, and the town progressing towards greatness. The point of dispute would, therefore, seem to lie between Eastbourne, Seaford, and Newhaven. With antiquaries of the present day we believe the preponderance of opinion is in favour of Eastbourne. The claim of Seaford has not been before fully investigated. We shall, therefore, after stating the grounds on which Dr. Tabor has fixed upon Eastbourne as the locality of Anderida, offer some observations, with which we have been favoured, as to the probability of Seaford being the site of this undetermined Roman station, and conclude the subject with an extract from Mr. Hayley's MS. in favour of Newhaven.

"'In the year 1717,' says Dr. Tabor, 'a tesselated pavement, a Roman bath, and extensive foundations were discovered at Eastbourne Sea-Houses, about four miles from Pevensey, and a mile and a half from Eastbourne church.' This of itself would certainly prove nothing more than that a Roman residence of some splendour was formerly situated here; this might have been the case, without bearing out any opinion as to the site being that of a Roman city. The buildings in question might have been the residence of a military officer, without determining the site of Anderida. Dr. Tabor, however, in No. 356 of the 'Transactions of the Royal Society,' goes on to show that this was, in all probability, the site of that ancient fortress.

" The Saxon Chronicle states that, in the year 490, Ælla and Cissa besieged Andredes-ceaster, and slew all who inhabited it, so that not a single Briton survived; and Henry of Huntingdon, who compiled his history from the Saxon Chronicle, calls the city 'urbem munitissimam,' a strongly fortified city, and says that it was destroyed, and never afterwards rebuilt. Gildas has described the Roman fort of Andred-ceaster, as "in littore oceani ad meridiem"—" on the sea-coast, towards the south." These facts, added to the discovery of the extensive Roman remains, certainly afford no despicable evidence in favour of the claim of Eastbourne. Dr. Tabor supposes this part of the sea-coast to have been peopled by the Andes, a nation in Armorica, in Bretagne, from whom Anderida took its name. He concludes his learned essay thus: "Excepting the want of a navigable river, the spot of ground where this old town stood yields to none in the country for importance and pleasure. Nature has shaped it like an equilateral triangle, having each side half a mile in length. Towards the sea, on the southern side, it is fenced by a low cliff, of twelve, fifteen, and in some places twenty feet high. On the northern side is a morass, with a large rivulet of very good water. Between the west side and the Downs lies a small valley, by which advantage there was formerly a harbour, capable of holding a small fleet. The banks on each side of it are an evidence that it was sunk by industry; but by weeds and gravel from the sea, and by mould annually added, as is observable in valleys, it is now raised, so that it is never flooded but at high spring tides, when a strong wind forces the waves into it. This bank must have been a good security to part of the west side; but what other works there might have been to defend it from the end of the harbour to the morass cannot be determined, because the intermediate ground has been for several years in tillage. It is easy to imagine of what importance a town, fortified at this place, must have been in those days, when the only pass, by land, from the west to the east end of the county was through it; for other there could be none in several miles north, unless the land in that tract, which is still very oozy and soft, had been well drained.

"The following observations are from the pen of Mr. Charles Verrall, of Seaford, in favour of the claim of this place to be considered as the site of Anderida. After disputing the claim of Eastbourne, as set up by Dr. Tabor, partly from its not being a port,—whereas Anderida is styled Portus Anderida, or the Port of Anderida,—and partly from its distance from the great forest, which was three or four miles off, he proceeds to remark: 'The river Ouse, in the time of the Romans, made its exit at Seaford Cliff. On the north-west, a creek, which tradition says was navigable a very few centuries ago, and which, 1500 years since, was no doubt capable of receiving the largest ships of that age, separated the supposed city from what is now the parish of Bletchington, and, assisted by the high and steep banks, which arising from it would have been the foundations of the city walls, must have rendered it very secure on that side. On the south-east, a similar creek extended along the base of the hill, for a considerable distance, towards the farm of Chinting. Thus three sides of a square or parallelogram would have had water and steep banks to protect it from assault; and there would have been space enough on the high grounds between, on a small part of which Seaford now stands, for the erection of a city of considerable magnitude. In the great flood in November, we had an opportunity of seeing the above description completely verified; the bar of beach gave way before the storm, both at Bletchington and Seaford, and the two creeks being deeply flooded, the high banks of the ancient Anderida were, after the lapse of many centuries, again washed by the waters of the sea. Furthermore, on the hill above Seaford are the remains of an extensive Roman camp, and also of another on the opposite height, called the Castle Hill, at Newhaven. An extensive Roman cemetery has also been discovered on Sutton Farm, where have been dug up many sepulchral urns and vases. Another fact is the existence, in various situations around the present town, of ancient and often deeply-buried foundations. All these circumstances combined go far, I think, not merely to prove that neither Newenden, Pevensey, nor Eastbourne could have been the site of the ancient city, but that the claim of Seaford to that honour outweighs that of any other place.'

"The last hypothesis that we shall mention," says Mr. Horsfield, "is that suggested by Mr. Elliott, and which placed this long sought-for city at Newhaven or Meching, near the mouth of the river Ouse. Mr. Hayley adopts this opinion. After having considered the evidence for or against other places named, as being the site of the ancient city, and not being satisfied with those adduced, he proceeded to examine several Roman fortresses, established on other coasts for the like purpose as was Anderida, and under the same direction. Upon examination, they all appeared to him 'to be so placed, as most effectually to guard such passes where the way lay open into the country by rivers.' He then proceeds: 'Returning into Sussex with this general observation, I behold at Hastings *a poor small rill*, as Dr. Holland, with the greatest propriety, names it. The river at Pevensey is of very small consideration; the remains of its castle are, notwithstanding, full proof enough that the Romans were once possessed of, and held it.' Dr. Tabor owns that the place which he contends for, near Eastbourne, has no river; the want of which he would willingly set aside, even when he is stating the importance and pleasure of the spot. So that we are led, by what seems a necessary requisite in these places of defence, to fix ourselves at or near the mouth of one of the greatest rivers in the county, which, running down from the north, at the side of the Rape of Lewes, pours itself out into the sea at Newhaven. It may be added, too, that what has been urged as an objection by Bishop Stillingfleet, Dr. Tabor, and Mr. Gale to other places, that they were not then in such a state of desolation as both Henry of Huntingdon and Matthew of Westminster described Anderida to have been in their days, cannot be pretended to have force here. To the words of the foregoing historians, expressing the desolate site to have been well known, we will contrast those of Mr. Humphrey Llwyd, as clearly expressing it, in his time (200 years ago), to have been quite forgotten. 'Urbem Caer Andred et Andredecestre dictam, ab Ælla rege South Saxonum penitus eversam ut non ruinæ ejus jam cognoscantur'—'The city called Caer Andred and Andred-Ceaster, so utterly destroyed by Ælla, King of the South Saxons, that not even the ruins of it can now be recognised.' And though I place little dependence upon conjectural etymologies alone, yet I would not pass without mention this remarkable and unexpected concurrence, that Meching (the proper denomination of the parish at the river's mouth, but almost justled out and forgotten by the use of that of Newhaven, which has grown up in it), Mece, or Meche-yny, in the language of those very persons who desolated Anderida and gave it its name, is exactly expressive of 'Gladii Campus'—'the field of the sword,' and with the greatest fitness and propriety adapted to the place whose ill-fated inhabitants, as Henry of Huntingdon and Matthew of Westminster tell it, 'omnes ore gladii devorati sunt,' and 'omnes in ore gladii perierunt;' that is, 'all were devoured by the mouth of the sword,' or 'all perished in the mouth of the sword.'

"If at any time it were convenient or necessary, from the season of the year or for discipline, to draw the troops out from the spot, or, upon occasion, to support them with an additional force, there were two camps in the adjoining parish of Telscombe, whose form declares them to have been Roman works, and which therefore may, with great propriety and little presumption, be pronounced to have been 'castra æstiva,' 'summer camps,' to Anderida. When the Romans relinquished their government here and withdrew their forces, Anderida was left to the sole use and disposition of the Britons, a maritime town calculated for habitation and defence. And that the Britons maintained it in the latter view, both as a protection against invaders from sea, its original design, and as a stronghold against their enemies on shore, what has been told of its deplorable fate is a most affecting proof.

"It is admitted that the position here supposed of Anderida, is unsupported hitherto by the known appearance of anything Roman, but the relative situation of the camps at Telscombe; and it is left for consideration how far propriety to its end and design, agreement in likeness of situation with other, the same sort of establishments, and such conspiring circumstances in its behalf, as have been suggested, may embolden one to put forth the supposition, and recommend it to the attention of those who are more able, and have better opportunities to look out for that sort of proof, which we want to confirm it."

Hasted, in his 'History of Kent,' published in 1790, gives it as his opinion, that Newenden is the site of the ancient Anderida; but, as well as some others, mistakes the relative position of the castle and the city.

The 'Gentleman's Magazine,' for July 1836, contains the following critique on that part of Horsfield's 'History of Sussex' which treats of the site of the ancient Anderida: "Our author is inclined to place the site of Anderida at Seaford, about which ancient 'civitas perdita,' so much has been said and conjectured by topographical writers. The Saxon Chronicle, under date of 490, says: 'This year Ælla and Cissa besieged Andredes-cester, and slew all the inhabitants, so that not one Briton was left.' This utter destruction effaced even the memory of the spot from the land, and Anderida has become a locomotive, at the antiquary's command, as any other doubtful station of the Roman colonists. We think, however, there is little doubt but Camden and Harris are right, when they place this much-sought fortress at Newenden, in Kent—a harbour ruined by geological changes of the Rother, dividing, at this place, Kent and Sussex. Important vestiges of military works existed at this spot (of which we do not, however, speak from local knowledge). Hasted says, the manor was called, in ancient deeds, 'Andred;' and Harris tells us of a hill called Ander-Down at the place, of which Dimum or Dinas Andred is evidently the derivative. Neither etymologically nor locally can Pevensey (the Anderida of Somner), although a Roman fort, compete with this: for it does not lie sufficiently in connexion with the Weald to claim such distinction. We suspect that the station was called by the Britons Dinas Newydd Andred, whence Newenden; and we know how frequently Newydd was appended to rising colonies by the Britons; hence Newydd Much, Noviomagus, &c."

Holinshed, in his Chronicles, says: Ælla, the Saxon, erected his chief palace at Chichester, whenhe had destroyed Andred's-wald in 492.

Having thus placed before our readers all the evidence we have been able to collect both for and against Newenden being the site of ancient Anderida, we shall proceed to state our own opinion on the subject, and to show on what grounds we come to the conclusion that this is the identical spot on which this long-sought city stood; and for this purpose we conceive it will be necessary to prove the following propositions:

1st. What was the real nature of the place generally called the city of Anderida?

2d. That there was a city of the nature above described.

3d. That there was a fort.

4th. That there was a port.

5th. That it was situated on the southern sea-coast of England.

6th. That it was on the borders of, or in, the forest of Anderida.

7th. That Newenden possesses all these requisites, and that no other place, named as the site of the ancient Anderida, does possess them.

1st. What was the real nature of the place generally called the city of Anderida?

From the many ages which have elapsed since the destruction of Anderida by the South Saxons, strange and illusory accounts of it have come down to us; and as objects when seen through a mist appear larger than their natural size, so events which are concealed by the mist of time frequently assume a shape and form far exceeding their true dimensions, as we should discover, were we able to penetrate the darkness which surrounds them. Thus probably it is, that the city of Anderida, as it has been called, has taken a shape, a magnitude, and an importance far beyond what it ever really possessed. With the word city we associate the idea of size, of wealth, and of grandeur—of spacious streets and noble edifices; but whoever expects to find these in the spot dignified as the site of the ancient Anderida will, I conceive, be miserably disappointed. It has been called a city of the Britons; but in what sense do they understand it who thus designate it? The lover of antiquity, in his fond dreams, perhaps thinks its origin must be dated from a time anterior to the arrival of the Romans; but this cannot very well be the case, since we find by the account given by Julius Cæsar, that the towns of the Britons were at that time a confused group of huts, placed at a small distance from one another, generally in the middle of a wood, to which all the avenues were guarded by mounds of earth or with trees. If it is to be considered at all as a city of the Britons, it must have received this designation from the Saxons, who, on the departure of the Romans, found it in their possession. It was then known by the name of Andred's-Ceaster. Now, we have numerous places in England whose names terminate in Caster, Cester, and Chester, the root of which is the Latin word *castrum*, and which was given to them in consequence of the Romans having had either camps or castles on the spot. Thus we shall find that although, in the generality of instances, this termination implies the site of a castle erected by the Romans, yet it by no means follows that a city has invariably sprung up near to it. It was a Roman camp or castle; and, for the sake of protection, of trade, and of mutual benefit, inhabitants naturally flocked to its neighbourhood, and, according to its peculiar advantages, formed in its vicinity a village, a town, and in some instances a city; but whether it became a city or a town, or only a simple village, it still took the name of castrum or camp from the Romans; the Saxons changed the Roman castrum into Ceaster, Castre, Cestre, and Chester; and hence we have at this day Chester, the camp; Chichester—Cissa-Ceaster, the camp of Cissa, and many others, which will readily suggest themselves to every observant reader. And thus also we had Andred's-Ceaster, the camp of Andred, so called from its being in the great forest of Andred. The word Ceaster simply implies that here was formerly a camp of the Romans; the name does not necessarily designate the site of a city. The word city is thought by some to be derived from Ceaster; and hence they jump to the conclusion that every place which is honoured with this termination either is or has been a city.

2d. That there was a place of the nature above described.

So much has been written on the subject of Anderida—such difference of opinion has arisen as to its real site, that some may almost be inclined to think that no such place has ever existed, and that the city of Anderida is but the idle dream of the antiquary. But various as have been the opinions on the subject, and numerous as have been the spots fixed upon as its true locality, nevertheless there can be no doubt, that there was in the time of the Romans a place designated by them Anderida; by the Britons, Caer Andred; and afterwards by the Saxons, Andred's-Ceaster. Somner says, "that the Romans, having once the supreme command in Britain, had their forts as well as ports in Kent, is evident enough by that Notitia Imperii Occidentalis, that Roman office book, set out by Pancirollus, where we find the names of Dubris, Lemanis, Anderida, Rutupiæ, and Regulbium under that notion." Thus Pancirollus mentions Anderida, thereby marking its existence under the Romans; while the Saxon Chronicles record the fact that, very soon after the departure of the Romans, the Saxons, under Ælla, besieged, took, and utterly destroyed it. As it seems clear that Anderida did once exist, so it is equally evident that its destruction took place at a very distant period; and hence the difficulty which writers have found in tracing out its original locality.

3d. That there was a fort.

It appears that, even while the Romans held possession of Britain, the Saxons had already begun to make irruptions into the country, and that, to guard against these inroads and the annoyances consequent thereon, they found it necessary to erect forts on the coasts which were most exposed to their depredations; and accordingly Gildas says: "In littore quoque oceani ad meridiem, quo naves eorum habebantur, quia et inde barbarorum irruptio timebatur, turres per intervalla ad prospectum maris collocant," &c. That is, "On the southern sea-coast, where their vessels lay, and because on that part they feared the irruption of the barbarians, they (that is, the Romans) erected, at intervals, watch-towers to command a view of the sea," &c.

This evidence of Gildas is sufficient to establish the existence of a fort in the time of the Romans; while Hasted, quoting from Kilburne, says it was destroyed by the Danes in the year 892.

4th. That there was a port.

The quotation given from Gildas under the last head equally corroborates this proposition with that; for he tells us distinctly that the Romans chose the spots on which they erected their watch-towers for two reasons: one, because here the Saxon rovers were in the habit of landing; and the other, because here their own vessels held their stations, clearly implying that the towers were built on spots near to such parts of the sea as were convenient harbours for shipping.

5th. That Anderida was situated on the southern sea-coast.

Pancirollus having, as I have shown in my second proposition, established the existence of Anderida, Gildas's words, "In littore quoque oceani ad meridiem"—"On the southern sea-coast," are sufficient to point out the necessity of our looking for its locality on this part of the coast.

6th. That it was on the borders of, or in, the Forest of Anderida.

But little need be said under this head, as the Roman Anderida, the British Caer-Andred, and the Saxon Andred's-Ceaster, each and all must satisfactorily point to the origin of the name,—that it was the city of the great Forest of Anderida. As a further corroboration of this fact, I may here add that Lambard says: "On the edge of this wood there stood some time a city, called, after the same, Andredes-Chester, which Ælla (the founder of the South Saxon kingdom), after that he had landed with his three sons, and chased the Britons into the wood, razed and made equal with the ground."

7th. That Newenden possesses all these requisites, and that no other place, named as the site of the ancient Anderida, does possess them.

The antiquary who goes in search of the ancient Anderida, will in vain look for the lofty columns which still mark the site of Palmyra, the "Tadmor of the Desert;" in vain will he seek for the sculptured marbles which still point out the spot on which stood the city of Perseus; and equally vain will be his search even for the misshapen mounds which form the only remaining monuments of Babylon the Great. All the remains of the city of Anderida are a slightly raised platform, containing an area of about ten acres, and a vallum of about 280 feet in length. These are the only data on which we have to proceed in our investigation. We offer the following remarks with more confidence than we should otherwise feel warranted in doing, from the circumstance of our being well acquainted with the locality of which we are treating. We have been repeatedly at the house of the late worthy and hospitable proprietor (Samuel Bishop, Esq.) of the estate on which the spot in question is to be found. We have traced and retraced it over and over again, and are thus able to fix the true relative position, both of the city and of the castle, which neither Dr. Plott nor Mr. Dearne has done, although they have both undertaken the task. With these preliminaries, we proceed to our work.

At Lossenham estate, in the parish of Newenden, in the county of Kent, in that part where the river Rother separates it from Sussex, at the distance of ten miles from the town of Rye, are three fields, lying at the south-east extremity of the property, called Tolls—viz. Castle Tolls, containing six acres, on which the castle formerly stood; Barn Tolls, containing eleven acres, lying to the south of Castle Tolls; and Ten Acres Tolls, containing eleven acres, lying to the west of Barn Tolls.

In Ten Acres Tolls, a vallum, extending from north to south for 280 feet, is still visible, and a raised ground is traceable from the south end of this vallum, all round the Barn Tolls, back into Ten Acres Tolls, on the north again. These are the spots alluded to, we presume, by Dr. Plott, though, as we have before observed, there is an error in the relative positions of the city and castle, he placing the site of the city on the north-east, instead of that of the castle. Here we imagine was the city of Anderida, with the castle on the north-east angle. Adjoining to Ten Acres Tolls, on the south, is a marsh, called Well-Brook. The real contents of the ground on which we suppose the city to have stood are about ten acres, and the accompanying plan of the ground, copied from a map of Lossenham estate, taken by order of the late Samuel Bishop, Esq., in 1834, gives an exact view of the relative position of the ground in question.

1. Castle Tolls, in which is the site of the old castle.—2. The site of the castle of Anderida. The raised marks at the N.E. and S.W. corners indicate that here the ground is much higher than on the other parts of the mound, particularly that on the N.E., which was evidently the keep.—3. The Barn Tolls.—4. The Ten Acres Tolls.—5. The Well-brook.—6. Marshes.—7. The Exden river.—8. This line shows the remains of a vallum, still visible, running about 280 feet from S. to N., where it is lost.—9, 9. Here are evident indications of raised ground, with a slight continuation of the vallum marked 8, running round till it meets the moat of the old castle at the point marked 10.—10. The south moat of the castle.—11. The river Rother.

PLAN
of the
CITY & CASTLE
OF
ANDERIDA.

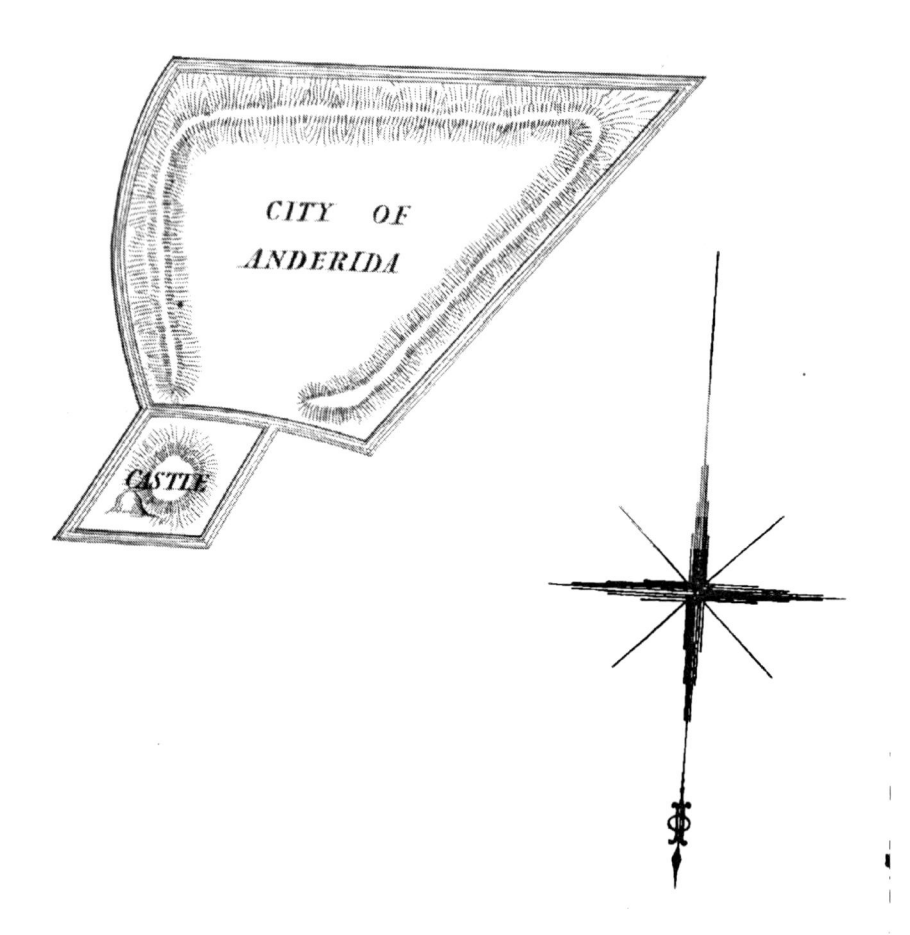

CITY OF ANDERIDA

CASTLE

On this plan we beg to submit to our readers the following remarks. A peninsula of high land runs for several miles from west to east, being bounded on each side by marshes, through which the Exden river flows on the north, and the Rother river on the south. In the early times of which we treat, the sea flowed to the foot of this peninsula, and the castle was erected on a hill, at that time almost insulated, and commanding a view of the water on three sides. The adjoining fields are called Barn and Ten Acre Tolls. Toll, in this part of the country, signifies a high ground, and the name may have been given to these pieces in consequence of their having been artificially raised. The Castle Toll, we are sure, has been so raised, and the vallum marked 8 in the foregoing plan also clearly indicates that some artificial works have at a distant period also existed here. Now Dr. Plott speaks in 1693 of having seen two mounds, which even then were much lower than they had been, and the lapse of nearly a century and a half, during many years of which period the plough has passed over the high ground and vallum on which I suppose the city to have stood, must, as a matter of course, have tended to level it still more; and the only wonder is, not that we find so little trace of what ceased to exist nearly 1400 years ago, but that we should discover any trace at all of it, as we do clearly in this piece of the vallum. Let us now once more place each part in its proper position. The castle itself occupied an area of about two acres at the extreme north-eastern point of the peninsula, and this area is still as visible as when the castle was first erected. The city of Anderida occupied an area of about ten acres, adjoining the castle, on the south, being only separated from it on this part by the moat of the castle. I shall here give a plan of the city and castle.

On the south-west side of the city is a brook or marsh, which goes by the name of the Well-Brook. Now it does not appear from anything I have heard or read on the subject, that any buildings have existed in this part of the peninsula; and therefore, if there has been a well in this brook, it may have been dug at the time of the existence of the city, for a name often remains for ages after the thing itself has ceased which originally gave rise to it.

We now come to consider the situation of the castle. I have already shown that it stood at the north-eastern angle of the city, at a point which, in the present state of the surrounding district, would not appear to be the most advantageous, but it must be remembered that, when it was erected, and many ages afterwards, the river Rother, soon after passing the peninsula, joined the Exden, when they flowed in one united stream round the north and east sides of the Isle of Oxney, meeting the great Bay of Romney at Appledore. This, then, would be the passage by which vessels, whether belonging to friends or foes, would enter the Bay of Robertsbridge, and hence an early sight might be obtained of all such vessels as did thus enter. The castle, jutting out into the Bay of Exden, would offer a good protection to such vessels as sought shelter there, where, in all probability, was the port. We are not to look for a harbour like that of Portsmouth or Plymouth, with a depth of water sufficient to receive ships of the largest burden: to show that here was, in ancient times, a port, it is not necessary that we should prove the existence of any such thing, for it must be recollected that the vessels then in use were but of very small size in comparison with those of the present day, and drawing but very little water. That a port might exist at this distance from the sea for such craft as were then in use, cannot, I think, admit of a doubt, since we find that in 22 Edward III, in the year 1349 (that is, nearly a thousand years after), complaint was made to the king by James de Echingham, that, by the erection of certain works near Newenden, "such ships and boats which had used to pass with victual and other things from divers places in these counties of Kent and Sussex, unto his manor of Echingham, through this channel, were then hindered, as also the destruction of his market town of Salehurst, situate upon the said river, and of his market there, which, by the course of that water, had been supported, and out of which he and his ancestors had used to receive tolls and commodities." Now Echingham is seven miles higher up than this part of Newenden, of which we are speaking, and if a harbour existed at the former, there can be no difficulty in concluding on the probability of one at the latter.

It now remains to show the contiguity of the city to the forest of Anderida, and this will be no difficult task; for Newenden is situated in the very midst of the Weald, and this peninsula was then clothed with oaks, as were all the adjoining parts; its very termination of den shows its locality—a woody valley or place yielding both covert and feeding for cattle, especially swine, while this is further confirmed by the adjacency of the several parishes of Rolvenden, Benenden, Biddenden, and Tenterden on one side, and those of Sandhurst, Ewhurst, and Hawkhurst on another, the Saxon *Hurst* meaning wood, and thus showing their peculiar situation.

Thus have I endeavoured to show that Newenden possesses all the points requisite to identify it as a site of the ancient Anderida. I do not think it was ever a city in the modern sense of the word; for I do not find that any foundation of buildings have ever been discovered on the spot. I conceive it was originally a Roman camp, defended by a deep fosse, and a high rampart of earth, which constituted a sufficiently strong fortification in those early days before the introduction of fire-arms. Here we find the traces of an ancient encampment, with a fort and a port, all lying contiguous to the great forest of Anderida. All the early traditions are in favour of this place, while, as Camden justly observes, the Saxons seem to have called it Brittenden (that is, a valley of the Britons), from whence Selbrittenden is the name of the whole hundred adjoining.

While thus Newenden possesses all the necessary identities, it will not be difficult to show that neither of the other places which have been mentioned as having a claim to this honour, viz., Pevensey, Eastbourne, Seaford, and Newhaven, does combine all the requisite elements. Pevensey possesses certainly the ruins of a large castle, the walls of which contain many of those thin tiles or bricks generally designated Roman, from their use having been first introduced into this country by the people of that nation; but whether Pevensey existed at the time the Romans held sway in Britain, may be a question; but even if it did, it is very certain that Pevensey originally was an island, separated from the main land by a bay of the sea, which, being now filled up by the alluvial deposit from the ocean, forms a fine rich tract of marsh land, known by the name of Pevensey Level. The breadth of this marsh cannot be much less than three miles, therefore Pevensey could not have been sufficiently contiguous to the great forest of Anderida to render it probable that it was the site of the city we have been in search of. If thus the claim of Pevensey cannot be maintained, still less can that of Eastbourne; for this place has no decided vestige either of a fort or a port, and from the forest it was still more distant than Pevensey. Seaford and Newhaven are both near the mouth of the river Ouse, and not far distant were two Roman encampments; but here the difficulty as regards the forest, the contiguity of which it seems absolutely necessary to prove, becomes greater than at either of the former places; for, while at Pevensey it was only three miles off, and at Eastbourne about five, at Seaford and Newhaven it could not have been less than seven or eight.

The next place I shall mention as belonging to this branch of our subject, is the Isle of Oxney, situate a few miles below the peninsula of Anderida. Whatever might have been its state on the arrival of the Romans, whether it was inhabited by the Britons, or whether it was a dreary and deserted spot at this time, it is pretty clear that the Romans took possession of it, for an ancient square altar was dug up here, having an ox in relief on each side; it had a basin or hollow on the top, retaining a blackness as if burned by fire, occasioned by sacrifices made on it. This relic I presume was of Roman workmanship, as neither the Britons nor Saxons were sufficient masters of the art of sculpture to execute it.

We now come to the last spot, and one of great importance in this work, viz. that on which Old Romney now stands. Before the Romans left Britain, a small island had made its appearance at this part of the Bay of Romney, a mere speck in the great waters; but a speck, small as it then was, that was destined to be the nucleus around which the debris from the high lands above, and the diluvial deposits from the sea, were to collect by little and little, until this island of the Romans, containing but a few acres of land, grew and increased to the extent in which we now behold it, when there are in Romney Marsh alone 24,000 acres, and in all the other marshes connected with it not less than 60,000.

Thus this little island, like the cloud which, on its appearance above the horizon, was no bigger than a man's hand, but which afterwards overspread the whole heavens, at length filled up the whole of the immense Bay of Romney, and the work, which was commenced by the Romans, probably in the fourth century, was completed by the Commissioners of Rye Harbour in the nineteenth.

As a proof that this island had made its appearance before the departure of the Romans, I may quote the following from Holinshed: "The shortest and most usual cut that we have out of our island to the maine is from Dover, altho' we find that now and then divers of them came also from Bullun, and landed at Sandwich, or some other places of the coast more towards the west, or between Hide and Lid; to wit, Romneie Marsh (which in old time was called Romania or Romanorum Insula—the Island of the Romans)."

The sea having begun to leave a small tract of land in the time of the Romans, in all probability these began to embank it against any future inundations, and this is the opinion of that very high authority on this subject, Dugdale, who, in his History of Embanking and Draining, has the following remarks, viz.: "Having now done with my observations of the most remarkable bankings and drainings in foreign parts, I come to England, wherein I do purpose to begin with Kent, in respect of its eastern situation, and in it, first with Romney Marsh, a spacious tract in that county, and more anciently secured from inundations of the sea than any other part of this realm, as may seem by the laws and constitutions for regulating its repair, which have been long ago made the rule and standard whereunto all the other marshes and fens in this nation were to conform. How long since, or by whom this fruitful and large tract (containing no less than 24,000 acres) was won from the sea, there is no testimony left to us from any record or historian that ever I could discover; which defect doth strongly argue that the first gaining thereof was a work of the greater antiquity. To attribute it unto the Britons (the primary inhabitants of this nation) or to the Saxons, who succeeded them, I dare not adventure; the first of these being a people so rude and barbarous, as they were not versed in any arts; and the latter so illiterate, for the most part, as that little of invention can justly be ascribed to them. That it was therefore a work of the Romans, whilst they were masters here, as it is the opinion of some learned men, so do I make thereof no doubt, considering to what a height, not only in learning, but in divers arts and sciences, that people were arrived, as by sundry testimonies we plainly find. Besides it is not only evident, from the credit of our best historians, that their several colonies dispersed throughout this nation were so excellently disciplined, that, for avoiding the mischiefs which idleness produces, they were always exercised in some fit and necessary employments, as those great and public ways, and other stupendous works made and raised by their skill and industry, do sufficiently show; but by the testimony of the famous Tacitus (an author of that time), who tells us that the Britains complained, that the Romans wore out and consumed their bodies and hands 'in sylvis et paludibus emuniendis,' i. e. in clearing the woods and banking fens, if I mistake not; for the word *emuniendis* must have a sense as well befitting *paludibus* (fens) as *sylvis* (woods), and therefore cannot, I presume, be otherwise construed."

Not being aware of any other changes which took place during the stay of the Romans in Britain, I shall hasten to the examination of the third part of our work.

SECT. III.

The further Changes from the Time of the final Departure of the Romans from Britain, to the Norman Conquest; that is, from A.D. 488 to A.D. 1066, a period of 578 years.

WE are now arrived at a period in our researches when, emerging a little from that dense mist which time had thrown over the events we have already attempted to record, we find some few beacons to light us on our path, though still it must be owned they are

"Like angels' visits—few and far between."

From the death of that great ruler, and still greater man, the Emperor Antoninus Pius, which took place in the year 161 of the Christian era, our most indefatigable and most eloquent of historians, Gibbon, dates the commencement of the decline and fall of the Roman empire. The mighty eagle, which for so many ages had spread his widely-extended wings over almost all the then known regions of the earth, began to wax weak and faint; his pinions no longer were able to sustain him in those vast and rapid flights he had hitherto dared to soar, while a dimness had come over his eyes, so that he could not now, as once he did, gaze unhurt on the sun in all his meridian splendour. Marking the diminished strength of their royal master, the lesser birds of prey began to hover around the outskirts of his vast domain, and to dare to feed on victims, from which the dread of the eagle's talons had for so many ages scared them away.

But to drop all metaphor—the Roman empire now began to decline, and the barbarians who hovered round its borders began to make incursions within those borders, and, growing bolder and stronger in proportion as their enemy became more weak and timid, they made advances into the very heart of the empire; and to guard against the dangers which threatened them so near at home, the legions were withdrawn from the more distant colonies, and the nations which they had hitherto kept in subjection were now abandoned to their own government. Britain, having been one of those distant colonies, was at a very early period thus abandoned by the Romans.

We have already seen that, even while the Romans yet remained in Britain, those bold marauders, the Saxons, made frequent inroads upon its coasts; it was therefore reasonable to suppose, that when the former had completely evacuated it, the latter should hasten to take advantage of their departure. Accordingly we find, that so early as the year 491, only three years after the Romans had retired, Ælla, the Saxon, had made himself master of the whole of Sussex, where he laid the foundation of the kingdom of the South Saxons, and in the latter part of the same year laid siege to the city of Anderida, or Andredswald; but meeting with great resistance from the Britons, who had posted themselves in the adjoining forest, they were at that time compelled to raise the siege. However, Ælla, being determined on making himself master of so valuable a place, in the following year sent into Germany for a reinforcement of his countrymen, when his three sons came over with a powerful body of men. With these he once more beset the devoted city; and having driven the Britons from their strongholds in the wood, they soon got possession of the place, when they razed the houses and the fortifications to the ground, and put all the inhabitants to the sword. Thus perished the ancient city of Anderida and its inhabitants more than 1300 years ago; and if the question be asked how it is we find no traces of buildings, my answer is, that the houses within the ramparts were all composed of wood; and if, as some historians relate, fire was introduced to aid the work of destruction, a few ages would suffice to obliterate all traces of its former existence. I say the houses were of wood, for of this material the dwellings of the people were at that time composed. The strong works of the Romans were confined to the castles which they erected, these were the only buildings of brick and stone; the houses were of wood. The houses of the Britons were of wood; and the houses of the Saxons, for many ages after, were of the same material.

But although the Saxons destroyed the city, they preserved the castle of Anderida. Having made themselves master of the latter, they, in all probability, placed a garrison in it, with a view to keep the refractory Britons in awe; and having so done, Ælla erected his chief palace at Chichester.

How long after the departure of the Romans the Britons retained possession of the castle of Limen, I am unable to say; but as Hengist, with his Saxon followers, fully established himself in the kingdom of Kent, previously to his death in 488, this castle had no doubt at that time fallen into the hands of him and his people.

We will now once more turn our attention to the little island which had made its appearance in the time of the Romans, and on which in due time was built the town of Old Romney.

And before entering further into its history, I shall claim the patience of my readers while I offer a few remarks on the origin of its name. Holinshed tells us it was called Romania, or Insula Romanorum—the Island of the Romans. Somner derives it from the Saxon Rumen-ea, the large water or watery place; while Harris thinks that Romney is but a corruption of Roman way. Not exactly agreeing with either of these writers, I shall state my reasons for differing from them. Harris's idea of its being a corruption of Roman way is not, I think, tenable; as it was but a small island in the time of the Romans, it was, of course, unconnected with the main land, and consequently could not have formed a way or road to any other place. Somner's derivation strikes me as not being correct, inasmuch as he gives a name which would be applicable to the water to a spot of land. Had he said the bay was so called, it would have been more reasonable; but even then I think he would prove to be wrong, as it is the land which generally gives the name to the water, and not the water to the land. Holinshed's name is only erroneous (according to my humble opinion) in one letter; had he written it Roman-ea, instead of Romania, he would have given the true Saxon name. The Saxons obtained full possession of Britain in the year 596, and gave names to almost all the places in this part of the country. This island having first appeared in the time of the Romans, and having been first embanked by them, it was very natural for the Saxons to name it, as I suppose they did, Roman-ea—Roman Island. This opinion will receive further corroboration, if we consider the number of islands which have been similarly named by the Saxons, as may be seen in the following catalogue, viz.:

Anglesey—Angles-ea. The Island of the Angles or English, they having fled there from the Saxons.
Athelney—Atheln-ea. The Island of Noblemen.

In Chichester Harbour we have three islands, viz.—

Thorney—Thorn-ea. The Isle of Thorns.
Fowl—Fowl-ea. Fowl Island, so called from the great number of wild fowl that formerly resorted there.
Pilsey—Pils-ea.

Passing eastward, we come to—

Selsey—Seles-ea. Seal Island, from the number of seals formerly resorting here.
Pevensey—Pevens-ea.
Winchelsea—Wind-chill-ea. Cold-Wind Island, and bleak enough Old Winchelsea must have been.
Oxeney—Oxen-ea. The Isle of Oxen.

Numerous other examples might be adduced, as—

Ramsey—Rams-ea. The Isle of Rams, having excellent pasture for them according to Holinshed.
Sheppey—Sheep-ea. Sheep Island.
Ely.
Mersey, E. and W.—Mers-ea. Perhaps Marsh Isle.
Osithe—St. Osithes-ea. The Isle of St. Osith.
Northeie—North-ea. North Island.

Enough has now, I presume, been said to establish the question as to the origin of the name of Romney, and when we consider the time that has elapsed since it was first so named, we cannot fail of being struck with the slight alteration it has undergone—Roman-ea—Romney.

Having thus made it apparent, I trust, that the spot on which Old Romney now stands was the first which emerged from the deep—that it appeared in the time of the Romans—that it was then an island, and was first embanked by these people—I shall now proceed to trace the gradual preservation of the remainder of the Marsh from the inroads of the sea, but shall first trouble my readers with two preliminary remarks. That at the time of which we are now speaking, viz., the latter part of the fifth century, the Limene river still emptied itself into the sea at or near to that part of the country where the town of Hythe now stands; and that the embankment of Romney Marsh was, in the first instance, carried on to the north and east of the island of the Romans.

The Saxons being in full and perfect possession of this part of Britain about the year 596, when the Britons had been subdued, they had time to turn their attention to the internal and peaceable arrangements of the country. And now it was, I imagine, that they proceeded to carry on those embankments which had been commenced by the Romans; for although Dugdale, as already quoted, speaks very slightingly of the abilities of the Saxons in these matters, yet he himself, in that branch of his subject, wherein he treats of the early embankments in Holland, says: "I find that the Saxons, whom my author (Bertius) calls 'aggerum exstruendorum peritos,' i. e. 'skilful men in making banks,' did exercise their industry in this kind here; the town of Saxenheim giving also some testimony thereof." Besides, if the Saxons did not execute the works, who could? They had possession of the country from this period, 596 A.D., to the arrival of the Normans in 1066, that is, for nearly 500 years, and at this latter time we know that the greater part (if not the whole) of Romney Marsh, properly so called, was embanked, as we shall be able to show in the progress of this work. Nor can it be objected to this that the Danes performed the work, for however much they might have annoyed the Saxons by their frequent and bloody inroads, yet it does not appear that they ever held this part of the country for any time sufficiently long to enable them to perform such works as these, which require quiet and peaceable possession to be carried into execution. Moreover we may add, that the names of all the places are so decidedly Saxon, as to preclude the possibility of a belief that any other people could have carried on the work, and completed it after the departure of the Romans from Britain. Strongly impressed with the truth of this opinion, I shall now proceed.

It was in the year 596 that St. Augustine first preached Christianity in England, before Ethelbert, King of Kent, at Canterbury, by whom the cathedral of this city was built. I allude to this fact, with a view to show the hope which now awaits us of finding some better guides than we have hitherto had to point out to us the path we wish to tread; for, after the introduction of Christianity, churches were founded and endowed with lands for their support, and the records of these transactions are among the oldest to which we can refer for information on the subjects with which we are now engaged. But we shall still have "to pick our devious way" without this aid for upwards of a century more, for it is not until the year 721 that any written document can be traced as having reference to our present task. It is this chasm in our history that we now have to fill up in the best manner we can. Taking Old Romney as our starting-point, we must suppose the Saxons to have carried on the embankments in this island, extending them to the southeast, until they reached the point on which New Romney now stands, and where an accumulation of beach took place, which formed a natural barrier against any further encroachments of the sea. It must be observed, that the embankment of Romney Marsh commenced generally on the sea side, and was then carried inland, and I have been told that this is corroborated by the slope of the banks being towards the main land, and not towards the sea; and thus it is, moreover, that Appledore Dowls, which lie at the back of the Marsh, are much lower land than that which lies on the coast. At the distance of about a mile, or something less, from Old Romney once stood the village of Hope; its chapel, which is now in ruins, is reported by traditionary lore to have been the first that was erected in Romney Marsh: it was called Hope, it is said, to express their wishes for the future prosperity of their newly-acquired home, and it was dedicated to All Saints, with the pious and sincere belief that if the inhabitants enjoyed their protection, they should have little to fear from any future inroads of the sea, which was the enemy they stood most in dread of. Thus I conceive that Hope, Old Romney, and New Romney all stood on the original island, which was the first formed and preserved in Romney Marsh. As we advance in our work, I think we shall find that several of the oldest places in the Marsh were originally islands. Romney was an island, Lyd was an island, as were also Ivy Church, Medley, Old Winchelsea, Guildeford, and probably Broomhill. But I shall not stop to discuss this point at present, it being necessary to proceed with other matters.

Under the second head of this work I have stated that the Romans built Lymne Castle on the side of the hill of that name, and that a port then existed at the foot of it. At what time the sea began to recede from the port of Lymne I am unable to say, but probably it was at an early period. Lambard tells us that the country people in the time of Robert Talbot, who wrote a Commentary on the Itinerary of Antoninus Augustus, had a tradition from their ancestors, " that the water forsaking Lymne by little and little, decay and solitude came at length upon the place; for, whereas at the first, ships were accustomed to discharge at Lymne, the sea afterwards (either hindered by the sands, or not helped by the fresh water) shortened his flood, and caused the merchants to unload at West Hythe." As the sea had now begun to recede at Romney, it is not improbable that a change also took place soon after at Lymne, and that West Hythe was one of the first places that sprang up in Romney Marsh after the Island of Romney itself. Independent of the desire of securing the land from the sea, there was the further inducement of forming a town at West Hythe, to insure to the inhabitants the trade of the river, which was formerly enjoyed by those of Lymne; these concurrent inducements will form a strong reason for the foundation of West Hythe at the earliest moment possible after the sea had deserted the port of Lymne; and if we are justified in supposing that the sea had already begun to recede from Lymne in the commencement of the seventh century, then are we also justified in supposing that West Hythe, at the same time, had its rise and commencement at the distance of something less than a mile to the eastward of it. Embankments must have been likewise carrying on in other parts of the Marsh during the latter part of the seventh, and at the beginning of the eighth centuries; but as we have at this latter date some few documents to guide us, we will leave the field of conjecture, and henceforth follow such instructions as they will be able to give us.

Somner, speaking of the river Limene, says, " that the name occurs in a charter or grant of Ethelbert, the son of the Kentish

King Withred, about the year 721, whereby he grants to Mildred, the then Abbess of Minster, in Thanet, a ploughland, lying by or about the river Limene." I quote this to show that, at this period, embankments must have taken place on the margin of the Limene, and consequently that West Hythe, as I have before conjectured, had, at this time, sprung into existence. The name of the Limene next occurs, he says, in a charter of King Eadbright, in the year 741, granting to the church of Canterbury " the taking or catching of fish to be had in the mouth of the river which is named Limene." Up to this time the river was called Limene, and its mouth was, in all probability, still near Hythe, for we shall find hereafter, that when it flowed out at Romney, it took the name of this place, and was called the Rumenea.

By the year 774 great changes had taken place, both as respects the land and the water in the district of Romney Marsh. Somner says: "Albeit the Rother (for that only is the now remaining name, though some call it Appledore Water) cuts or falls many miles short of Romney Port (after it is once got to Appledore, wheeling about and running into that arm of the sea or estuary, insinuating into the land by what, from that or some other current became so called Rye), yet had it heretofore a direct and foreright continued current and passage at Appledore, so from thence to Romney the old and new; on the west side whereof, meeting with the estuary, it presently disembogued and fell into the sea, which, in elder times, with so large and wide a mouth flowed up within the land there, that in the year 774 Lyd, both to the northern and eastern bounds thereof, is said to border on the sea; as witness the charter of King Offa, of that manor, given to Janibert, the then Archbishop of that tenour: "In nomine Jesu, Salvatoris mundi, &c., Ego, Offa, Rex totius Angliorum patriæ, dabo et concedo Janibert, Archiep. ad Ecclesiam Christi, partem terræ, trium aratorum, quod Cantianitè dicitur 'Three Sulinge,' in occidentali parte regionis, quæ dicitur Mersware, ubi nominatur ad Lyden, et hujus terræ sunt hæc territoria: mare in oriente, in aquilone, et ab austro terra Regis Edwy, nominant Dengemere, usque ad lapidem appositum in ultimo terræ, et in occidente et aquilone confinia regni ad Bleechinge." "In the name of Jesus Christ, the Saviour of the world, I, Offa, king of all the country of the Angles, give and concede to Janibert, Archbishop of the Church of Christ, a certain piece of land of three ploughs, called in the Kentish dialect 'Three Sulinge,' in the western part of the district which is called 'Mersware,' where it is known by the name of Lyd; and of this piece of land the following are the boundaries, viz.: the sea on the north and east, and on the south the territory of King Edwy. It is called Dengemarsh as far as the stone which is placed at the extreme point of the land; and to the west and north, the confines of the kingdom, as far as to Bleechinge." "From whence," adds Somner, "clear enough it is, that the sea, with a large and spacious inlet, arm, and estuary, in those days flowed in between Lyd and Romney, and was there met with the river Limen."

Thus we find that Lyd had, in the year 774, been called into existence, and it is also pretty clear that it must have been an island, and that it formed the western boundary at this point of the kingdom of Kent. Lyd originally stood on the shore, and its name, which, in ancient records, is written Hlyda, is from the Saxon word Ladian, to purge or cleanse, and hence Lade or Lode signifies the mouth of a river, as by its mouth it empties itself into the sea, and carries off the mud and filth, whereby it cleanses itself. From this derivation I judge that Lyd, at that time, was an island at the mouth of the river which then disembogued into the sea between it and Romney. The town of Lyd then stood on the sea-shore, though, by the accumulation of sand and beach since that time, it is now between two and three miles from it.

By this time, I imagine, the Limene had either entirely changed its course, and flowed out at New Romney, or that its waters were divided, a part of which still flowed out at Hythe, and another at Romney. The latter, I think, was most probably the case, as it is clear that Romney must now have been growing into repute; and it also seems that West Hythe remained a port for several ages after this period, which it would not have done had it been deserted by the river Limene so long before.

In the year 791 I find that Orgerswick had been preserved from the sea, for in this year the manor was given by Offa, king of Mercia, to Christ Church, Canterbury. Wick may be derived either from the Saxon Wic or Wica; the latter signifying a country house or farm, and the former a place on the sea-shore, on the bank of a river. In this instance I incline to the former; Wic, as the place in question, at that time must have been on the sea-shore, and thus we may infer that the lands then belonged to one Orger, and hence were designated Orger's Wic, now Orgerswick.

The sea seemed now to be fast receding from these parts, for I find that in this same year 791, the manor of Aghny, otherwise Agonhie, situate partly in the parish of Midley, and partly in Old Romney, was given to the church of Canterbury by Offa, king of Mercia. This parish is, in Doomsday Book, called Midelea, and is said to be two miles from Lyd, in Walland

Marsh. This place I suppose, too, was an island, as its name seems to imply, being derived from the two Saxon words Middel, middle, and Ea, island, literally Middle Island; and its situation was between the two other islands of Romney and Lyd.

Romney Marsh had now already become an extensive district, and could boast of containing many inhabitants who were known by the name of Merscware, and the country itself was designated Merscwarum. King Offa, in his grant of Lyd to the Archbishop, which has already been alluded to, calls it Merscware, while Ethelwerd, in 795, calls it Merscwarum. Camden tells us that, " in the time of the Saxons, the inhabitants were called Mersc-Ware, and for my part," says he, "I do not understand Ethelwerd (that ancient writer), when he tells us that 'Cinulph, king of the Mercians, destroyed all Kent, and the country called Mersc-warum, in the year 795;' and in another place, 'that Herbythus, a captain, was slain by the Danes in a place called Mersc-warum,' unless he meant this very marshy tract."

Merscware is formed from the two Saxon words, Mersc, a marsh, and Wer or Were, a man; and thus the inhabitants were simply called Marsh-men, and even to this day, they are, in familiar language, frequently thus designated.

It cannot have escaped the observation of my readers, that several grants about this time were made in the Marsh by Offa, king of Mercia, which circumstance may require some explanation. It appears that Withred, king of Kent, died in the year 725, and was succeeded by his eldest son Edbert, who enjoyed his kingdom in great tranquillity twenty-three years, which must have been to A.D. 748; and then the crown, by his death, without issue, devolved on his brother Ethelbert, the second son of Withred, who permitted his son Ardulph to partake of the regal dignity; and he dying in the lifetime of his father, the succession returned to Aldric, the youngest son of Withred, and the last lineal descendant of Hengist, the founder of the kingdom. Aldric's reign was continually disturbed by the restless ambition of his neighbours, each of whom were willing to add this reduced kingdom to his dominions; but the most formidable candidate was a prince at a more remote distance—Offa, the king of the Mercians, to whom this kingdom became tributary after the death of Aldric, which happened, according to Malmesbury, A.D. 794. This is Mortimer's history of the affair, and from it we gather that Offa had, at this period, obtained great influence in Kent. Now every one is aware that, at this time, the church had great power, and, in all probability, it was with the view to propitiate this power, that Offa, whose only title to the kingdom was that of conquest, made these grants of land to the church. And this seems to me to be the proper time and place to introduce some remarks on the great number of churches which are to be found in Romney Marsh.

Laing, in his 'Travels in Sweden and Norway,' has the following pertinent remarks: "The expense of building the cathedral of St. Magnus, in Kirkwall, in 1138, was provided for in the following manner, viz.: a great part of the lands in Orkney were held of the jarl by a feudal tenure, and, on the death of a proprietor, his heir had to redeem the land from the jarl. The jarl proposed to make the lands hereditary without payment of a fine, on condition of one mark being paid to him for each plough-gale of land. This was willingly agreed to by the vassals; and money was not wanting, says the Orkneyinga Saga, for carrying on the work. This information throws some light upon what has often puzzled the traveller in some districts in England, viz., the number of churches, as in Romney Marsh, in Kent, and in the fens of Lincolnshire, situated in very small parishes, and where there never could have been a population to require so much accommodation. In Kent, fifteen or sixteen churches may be seen within a space which altogether would only be a considerable parish in extent, and in some of the parishes there never have been above half a dozen families. But if it was a common practice in those ages for the feudal lord to impart to his vassals full hereditary rights to their lands, in consideration of a payment, which he laid out in pious uses, such as the building of churches, it is evident that the quality of the land and value of the right ceded to the vassal, would have more to do than the number of the inhabitants in determining the size and number of these parish churches; and it is precisely in the rich alluvial lands gained from the rivers and fens, in which the feudal lord had a title to the new land formed contiguous to his vassals' land, that the most of such parish churches as were evidently not erected with any reference to a population in the parish are found. In Romney Marsh, in Kent, a tract of alluvial land studded with churches, many of which are spacious, there are no indications that the tract has ever been so densely peopled as to require so many and such large places of worship. On the ground there are no traces of former inhabitants, no marks of the plough, no vestiges in the churchyards of numerous resting-places of former generations; the land, being gradually gained from the state of fen or marsh, could never have been cultivated so as to employ a large, resident, agricultural population. It must have been always, as at present, pasture land, thinly inhabited, and attached to the arable estates upon the clay ridge adjoining to and overlooking this marsh. The erection of so many churches in such a tract, has therefore probably been connected with the grants of the land, as it was gained from the water from time to time."

In the early ages of Christianity, the king and the nobles were uneducated, rude, and licentious; their word was too frequently their law, and, to obtain their ends, they were not very scrupulous about the means they employed. The only check upon their tyranny was the influence of the clergy, and, to conciliate them, they made frequent grants of land to them to be employed in pious uses; one of the chief of which was the erection of churches. Agreeably to this idea, we find, at this present day, that a great deal of land in Romney Marsh is held of the great Church of Canterbury (as it is styled), that is to say, of the cathedral of this city.

The observations of Laing, as to the number of churches in Romney Marsh, are well sustained, when we consider that in Romney Marsh, properly so called, and which does not extend to the westward of the Ree Wall, there are fifteen parishes, the contents of the whole of which altogether are but 24,000 acres, the greatest length of it not exceeding eight miles, and the width not averaging more than four.

I have already hazarded an opinion that the river Limene was divided into two streams, one flowing under the hills to Hythe, and the other out at Romney; and I am happy to find my opinion corroborated by that of Hasted, in his 'History of Kent,' who says: "The river Limene was, in very ancient times, a large navigable river, which, rising in Sussex, flowed down to the town of Appledore, on the northern or inland side of the Marsh, and thence, separating into two channels, one of which flowed south-eastward under the hills of Ruckinge and Bilsington, on that side of the Marsh under Limne Hill by Stutfall Castle, where the ancient Portus Lemanis is supposed to have been, into the sea by West Hythe; the other directed its course southeast from Appledore, across the Marsh to Romney, where it formed a haven or port, and emptied itself into the sea there."

Having now given a summary of all the facts that have come to my knowledge up to the end of the eighth century, I shall hasten on to the record of those of a later period, when they will probably be found to be more numerous, and better authenticated.

In addition to the grants already recorded, as having been made by Offa, I must not omit the Manor of Newenden, which was given to the monks of Christ Church, Canterbury, under the name of Andred, one additional confirmation of the fact of Newenden being the true site of the ancient Anderida.

The Danes effected their first landing in England in 787 A. D., and probably they paid an early visit to this part of the country; for Camden tells us, on the authority of Athelwerd, as already quoted, that one Herbythus, a captain, was slain by the Danes in a place called Mersc-warum, as I suppose towards the close of the eighth century; but be this as it may, it is quite clear that during the ninth they made several incursions into this district.

The next part of the Marsh of which I find mention made, is some land in the parish of Warehorn; for, according to Somner, a charter or grant was made in A. D. 820, by Egbert, the West Saxon King, and first king of all England, together with Athulf or Ethelwulf, his son, to one Goding, the particulars of which run thus, viz.: " Two ploughlands in a place, in English, called Werehorns, amongst the fens, and cost 1000 shillings, or 50 pounds of money; and these are the boundaries, on the east part it extendeth southward over the river Limen, into the South Saxon limits." On looking at a map of Romney Marsh, I think it is clear that a branch of the Rother at this time flowed under the hills to West Hythe, otherwise I cannot understand the boundaries of this land in Warehorn, as this parish does not extend over the Ree Wall, and consequently they cannot apply to this branch of the river; and, moreover, it still retains the name of Limen, which we shall find not to be the case, when once the stream was principally directed towards Romney. This name of Limen was still retained in a deed or grant, made by one Warhard or Warnard, a priest, to the monks of Canterbury, A. D. 830, and which is as follows, viz.: " One yoke of land, lying on the south side of Limen, and of the inhabitants called Lambeham, but belongeth to Bromham."

Ebeney is a small parish in the Isle of Oxney; it is bounded, according to Hasted, on the north and east by the river Rother, and on the south and west by a small rill, which separates it from the parishes of Stone and Wittersham, which, together with it, form, at the present day, the Isle of Oxney. From Hasted's description it is evident that Ebeney was originally an island of itself, and so its name indicates, being derived from Eben-ea—Eben Island. The situation of the church seems further to strengthen this opinion, as it stands on an eminence, and in winter was, some years since, frequently surrounded by water. In this place existed a priory at a very early date; for we find that Athulf or Ethelwulf, king of England, gave it to the Priory of Christ Church, Canterbury, in the year 832.

In 838 A. D. the inhabitants of Romney Marsh were, according to Hoveden, still called Merscware, or Marsh-men. They were also designated Limware, that is, Lim-men, men belonging to the district of the river Limen; and thus the whole lath was afterwards, and in Doomsday Book, called Limware-Lest and Limeware-Leth. Lim, Limen—Ware, Wer, Sax., men; Lest or Leth, Læthe, Sax., a part or division of a county; literally, the district of the men of the river Limen.

The next part of the Marsh which was gained from the sea seems to have been Burmarsh, written in Doomsday Book both Borchmeres and Burwarmarse. In the reign of King Ethelwulf, about A. D., 848, Edbald, his grandson, for the sum of 4000 pence, gave this manor to his friend Wynemund, who again gave it, with the land of Wyk, to the Monastery of St. Augustine for ever, where he had chosen himself a place of sepulture.

It has been mentioned, under a former head of this work, that the Isle of Oxney had been inhabited in the time of the Romans; we have lately spoken of the early establishment of a priory in Ebeney, and we now have to record an inroad of the Danes, who, in the days of King Ethelred, when almost all parts of the realm felt their fury, piteously spoiled and burnt Stone, which done, they departed to Sandwich. This must have taken place some time between A. D. 866 and A. D. 871.

The Danes now continually harassed the kingdom by their inroads, and we find that in the year 892, they sailed up the river Limen as far as Newenden, the ancient Anderida, and destroyed the castle. Thus, after a lapse of 500 years, or thereabout, fell the castle of Anderida, which was erected by the Romans; left by them in the hands of the Britons, wrested from these last by the Saxons, and finally captured and destroyed by the Danes.

We now come to the record of a remarkable event, not only as being connected with the history of this part of the country, but with that of the kingdom at large; it is the landing of the Danes at Appledore. Holinshed describes it thus: " About the 21 yere of King Alfred, an armie of those Danes and Normans, which had beene in France, returned into England, and arrived in the haven or river of Limene in the east part of Kent, neere to the great wood called Andredesley, which did contain in times past 120 miles in length, and thirtie in breadth. These Danes, landing with their people, builded a castle at Appledore."

Lambard, quoting the Saxon Chronicles, says: " In the year after Christ 893, the great army of the Danes left the east part of France and came to Boulogne, and from thence with 250 vessels, sailed into the mouth of the river Limen, in Kent, which floweth from the great wood that is called Andred; thence they towed up their boats four miles into that wood from the mouth of the river, where they found a castle half built, and a few countrymen in it, all which, together with the village, they destroyed, and fortified at a place called Apultree."

Of the fact here recorded there can, I believe, be no doubt; that the Danes visited this part of the coast in the year 893—that they passed up the river Limen—that they fortified themselves at Appledore—and that Alfred forced them to quit the country altogether—are matters mentioned by all our historians, and therefore not open to controversy. But there is one point on which there is room for discussion; it is this: where was the mouth of the Limen here alluded to? was it at Hythe, or was it at Romney? I have already given it as my opinion that the Limen had two mouths. West Hythe was at this time in existence, and here was one of its mouths. Romney was also now in existence, and to it was added Hope. Lyd formed an island to the south-west of Romney, and the sea passed between these two places, forming, in all probability, a second mouth of the Limen, and up this branch of the river it was, as I suppose, that the Danes passed; and to the discussion of this question I shall now proceed. Somner, speaking of the sea passing between Romney and Lyd, in A. D. 774, uses these words: " From whence clear enough it is, that the sea, with a large and spacious inlet, arm, and estuary, in those days flowed in between Lyd and Romney, and was then met with the river Limen, which of necessity must have a very large and capacious mouth or bosom to receive, as it did, a fleet of 250 sail, the number of those Danish pirates being no less, who, in the year 893, put in here, and towing up their vessels four miles within the land, even as far as to the Weald (which then extended eastward unto Appledore), there cast anchor, and destroying a fort or castle (as old and imperfect as ill-defended), built a new one, and kept their rendezvous there. For I can easily believe that however Appledore be distanced from Romney about six miles, yet so large a bosom had that estuary, and so high up into the land the sea then flowed (haply so high as that place in Romney Customal, written about Edward the Third's time, called Read Hill, whither the franchise from the entrance of the haven is said to reach), that Appledore was not above four miles from the river's mouth, some vestigia and remains whereof, that trench of large extent, both for length and breadth, between Appledore and Romney along the wall (from thence called the Ree Wall), by the diversion of the current at this day lying dry and converted to pasturage."

Thus Somner is clearly of opinion that this was the branch of the Limen by which the Danes penetrated to Appledore.

The distance of this mouth from Appledore, which, according to the Saxon Chronicles, was about four miles, is much more in accordance with this description than that at West Hythe; the distance of the latter from Appledore being twelve miles, while that of the former is not more than six from Romney, and only four from Read Hill, as already quoted from Somner.

It appears that the Danes passed unmolested up the river, which they probably would not have done had they passed up the Hythe branch, as Lymne Castle was then a place of strength, and would have offered some opposition to their progress. However, after all that can be said, I am free to confess that much doubt hangs over the subject. The Chronicles tell us that "the Danes towed their boats four miles into the wood of Andred from the mouth of the river, where they found a castle half built, and a few countrymen in it, all which, together with the village, they destroyed, and fortified at a place called Appledore." Now where was this half-built castle? It could not have been at Appledore, because it was at this place they built a castle, and fortified themselves. Could it have been at Kenardington? Dearn tells us, that "below the hill on which the church of Kenardington stands, and on the south-east, are the remains of some ancient fortifications of earth, with a breastwork thrown up, and a small circular mount; and in an adjoining marsh below it is another of larger size. These are supposed by Hasted to have been thrown up during the wars between Alfred and the Danes, perhaps about the year 893, when a division of them sailed up the river Limen, or Rother, and entrenched themselves at Appledore." If we can suppose Kenardington to have been the village alluded to, then the Danes must have passed up the Hythe, and not the Romney, branch of the Limen. But with such few landmarks to steer by, it is difficult to find the exact port we are in search of; thus much, however, we do know, that the Danes built a castle at Appledore, and maintained themselves there until driven away by Alfred, who found them encamped, in the spring of 894, near Appledore, when they marched hastily to Farnham, in Surrey, where Alfred gave them battle and defeated them, and finally, in 897, drove them out of his kingdom.

It is in the year 893 that we first hear of Appledore; and this being the case, I shall endeavour to give the origin of the name, as I have done with the other places which have already come under our notice; for although this may seem to some a very dry and unprofitable part of our business, I must take leave to differ from them, inasmuch as the origin of the name of a place frequently serves to point out certain ancient localities, which otherwise time might have entirely obliterated. Lambard says, "this place was called by the Saxons Apultreo; Latin, Malus; English, Apple-tree." With this derivation I do not agree, but rather prefer that given by Somner, who says "the soil is moorish, boggy, and fenny, such as our ancestors here at home, with some of their neighbours abroad, have usually called Polder, a word of Kilianus, in his Teutonic Dictionary turned 'palus marina, pratum littorale, ager, qui e fluvio aut mare eductus, aggeribus obsepitur;' that is, 'a marsh-fen, a meadow by the shore-side, a field drained or gained from a river or the sea, and inclosed with banks;' to all which qualities and properties our Appledore fully answereth, being a kind of mere, bog, or quagmire, bordering on the water, and often overlaid of it." To this I may add, that Polder is a word still used in Belgium and Holland in the same sense as is here implied. It appears too, according to Somner, that the Saxons were in the habit of prefixing At to their names of places, thus making Atpolder; and in process of time, the *t* being dropped, we have, as at present, Apolder, or Appledore. To show further the nature of the land about this place, there is at this day a low wet spot called Appledore Dowels, the latter word coming from Dole Brit, according to Camden, a low open plain upon the sea or a river.

To close our history to the end of the ninth century, I must now allude again to Romney, which Somner, speaking of the river, makes the following mention of: "In 895 A.D. it was, that the same river (that part of it at or near Romney town), in a grant of Plegmond, Archbishop of Canterbury, under the name of Romney appears thus: 'the land called Wefingmersh, beside the river called (Rumeneia, Lat.) Romney.'" Again he says: "The eldest mention I find of Romney is in that grant or charter of Plegmond, the Archbishop, in 895, A.D." To judge from the foregoing information, it appears that Romney, up to this period, was not a place of any note. All writers on the subject seem to agree that Romney was one of the first parts of the Marsh which was left by the sea; and Leland goes so far as to say, that "the very town of Rumeney, and two miles about it, was always by likelihood dry land, and once (as it is supposed) the sea came about her, or at the least about the greatest part of it." Old Romney was without doubt originally an island; its boundaries were increased at this time by the land where New Romney stands, by Hope, and by Orgerswick. From this period it probably began to increase in importance; for we find that a considerable (perhaps the larger branch) of the Limen now flowed in this direction, as it is now first recognised by the name of Rumeneia, that is, the Roman Water, from its passing by Roman Island, the literal name of Romney.

I must here close my information as regards the transactions of the ninth century, and proceed to those of the eleventh; for, however singular it may appear, I have not been able to discover the record of any single event connected with our history throughout the whole of the tenth. How this is to be accounted for I am quite at a loss to say; all I can do in this place is to record the fact as far as my researches have led me.

We are now approaching the close of the period marked out in the third head of our dissertation, being about to commence that century in the sixty-sixth year of which William the Norman made a conquest of England.

In the year 1006 Appledore is mentioned in the charter of King Ethelred; and in A. D. 1032, one Ædsi, a priest, having become a monk of Christ Church, made a grant of Appledore, with the consent of his master, King Canute, and his queen, to that monastery. As this grant is curious I shall insert it here; it is as follows, viz.: "Here appeareth in this writing how Cnut King, and Ælfgife his Lady, gave to Ædsi their priest, when he turned monk, that he might convey that land at Appledore as to himself most pleasing were. Then gave he it to Christ Church to God's servants for his soul, and he it bought that of the Covent for his days and Ædwine's with four pounds, on that contract, that men deliver every year to Christ Church three weights of cheese from that land, and three bundles of eels, and after his days and Ædwine's go that land to Christ Church, with meat and with men, even as it then inriched is, for Ædsi's soul; and he bought that land at Werhorne of the Covent, for his days and Ædwine's also, with four pounds; then goeth that land forth with the other after his days and Ædwine's to Christ Church, with the crop that there then on is; and he gives also those lands at Palstre and at Withesham, after his days and Ædwine's, forth with the other to God's servants for foster-land for his soul. This bequest he giveth to the Covent on this contract, that they ever him will well observe, and to him faithful be in life and after death; and if they with any unadvisedness with him this contract shall break, then stands it in his own power how he afterwards his own dispose will. Of this is for witness, Cnute King, and Ælfgife his Lady, and Æthelnoth Archb., and Ælfstan Abbot, and the Covent of St. Austine's, and Brihtric young, Ætheric husbandman, and Thorth Thurkills nephew, and Tefi and Ælfwine priests, and Eadwold priest, and all the King's Counsellors; and this writing is threefold: one is at Christ Church, and one at St. Augustine's, and one hath Ædsy with himself."

Hasted tells us that, A. D. 1036 Halden, or Halfden, one of the Saxon Thanes, gave Hythe and Saltwood, with all their appurtenances, in the presence of King Cnute, to Christ Church, Canterbury. It was a borough appurtenant to Saltwood Manor. This I suppose to be the first mention of the present town of Hythe, although it was not then arrived at that stage of greatness or prosperity to which it afterwards attained; for we shall find as we proceed that West Hythe was still in a flourishing state, and that it was made a Cinque Port in the reign of Edward the Confessor. That the place here mentioned is the modern Hythe is clear, from its being appurtenant to Saltwood, in which parish it is situated at this day.

Edward the Confessor began his reign in 1042; and as it appears that he had a survey taken of the whole kingdom, much useful information is to be gleaned from the records left by him. It was this king who (according to the generality of antiquaries) granted the first privileges to the Cinque Ports. The places then named were Sandwich, Dover, West Hythe, Romney, and Hastings. Of these, West Hythe and Romney are the only two with which we have to deal. Hasted, speaking of the former, says: "The particular times of the destruction of these havens (that is, Lymne and West Hythe), by the sea deserting them, has never been ascertained. That of Lymne was after the Romans had left this island; and it must have been during the time of the Saxons, perhaps in their earliest time here; for in the reign of Edward the Confessor, that of West Hythe was become of such resort and consequence, that is was esteemed as one of the Cinque Ports."

Thus had West Hythe quietly succeeded as a port to that of Lymne; it was probably at this time still partially assisted by the Limene, and had a large and capacious opening to the sea, forming, by the shelter of the cliffs on the north and east, a commodious and safe harbour.

Though the name of Romney does not appear so early as those of several other places, yet it must have been rising into eminence for some years past; as we find that New Romney had succeeded to Old Romney before the reign of Edward the Confessor; for, at the time of taking the survey of Doomsday, in 1080, there were 86 burgesses which belonged to the archbishop's manor of Aldington. Now as New Romney only is mentioned at the time we are speaking of, it is evident the latter town must have long before grown into note, and consequently adds considerably to the antiquity of the old town.

The inhabitants have a tradition that the old and new town were once connected, and this, I think, was most probably the case, for they both stand on the banks of the Limene, and as the mouth of this river, by the deposits from the land and the sea, was continually being transferred nearer and nearer to the English Channel, it became necessary that the buildings should follow after it, so that the port might be as near to the mouth as possible. This has been the case with this river from its earliest history down to the present time. Originally Robertsbridge, and even Echingham, were ports; to these succeeded Bodiam, Newenden, Small Hythe, Appledore, Romney, the whole of which have now ceased to be so. Then, in the time of the Romans, we had Lymne, then, in the Saxon times, West Hythe, and, finally, the modern Hythe.

In 1053, when Earl Godwin and his sons had been exiled by Edward the Confessor, they committed many depredations on this coast. Henry, the Archdeacon of Huntingdon, tells us: "That at such time as Godwin, Earl of Kent, and his sons were exiled from this realm, they armed vessels to the sea, and among sundry other harms that they did on the coast of this shire, they entered the haven of Rumney, and led away all such ships as they found in the harbour." Lambard, speaking of the Ness, says: "Neshe, Nesse, Sax., a nose—a nose of land extended into the sea. This cape lieth in Walland Marsh, south from Romney, and is of the number of those places that Earl Godwin afflicted in the time of his banishment." It would appear from this that there was then a place, a town or village, called Neshe. Lydd was at this time an island, and it seems that Lydd must have been merely the name of the island, and Neshe or Ness the name of the village or town then existing upon it.

Lambard moreover informs us, that Earl Godwin and his sons, in the time of their exile, fetched away divers vessels lying at road at Hythe, even as they had done at Romney also.

Blackmanstone had been saved from the sea in the time of the Confessor, when the manor was held by one Blacheman, from whom the place, I have no doubt, took its name, it having been called from him Blacheman's Tune, from Blacheman, the owner's name, and Tune, Sax., a place. Blacheman's Place or Town, since slightly corrupted into Blackmanstone. And here I would beg to remark that mistakes are frequently made as to the real meaning of many names of places ending in stone, as Bishopstone, Sussex, Kingston in Surrey, Orlestone in Kent, Ingatestone in Essex; some consider the original meaning to be Bishop's Stone, King's Stone, Orle's Stone, Ingate's Stone; whereas it is properly Bishop's Tune, Bishop's Town; Orle's Tune, Orle's Town; King's Tune, King's Town; Ingate's Tune, Ingate's Town. But the word here translated town must not be considered in the same sense as we now understand it, for it originally only simply meant a dwelling-place. Some noble or great man probably built a residence on the spot, which he called by his own name, and that name was afterwards retained, although he had parted with the property.

Eastbridge, which is in Romney Marsh, was the property of Godwin, Earl of Kent.

Newchurch is mentioned as having been in existence in Edward the Confessor's time.

Hope All Saints is in the manor of Honychild, and this manor was in existence at the Conquest.

Midley, in the time of Edward the Confessor, was worth sixty shillings. Doomsday Book says: "here is a church and ten acres meadow. Wood for the pannage of ten hogs."

Brenset is part in Romney and part in Walland Marsh. The canons of St. Martin, Dover, appear, by Doomsday, to have been possessed of lands in this parish.

St. Mary's, near New Romney, in Romney Marsh. The manors of Honychild and Blackmanstone claim over the greatest part of this parish.

Appledore possessed, at this time, a church, and six fisheries of three shillings and fourpence.

Newenden, under Edward the Confessor, was accounted part of the archiepiscopal demesnes held by one Leofric, as an appendage to Saltwood.

Approaching, as we now do, the close of this third branch of our work, it is necessary that I should sum up the substance of the changes which have taken place since the departure of the Romans.

At the commencement of the era of which we have been speaking, Romney (the Isle of the Romans) was the only spot of land existing in what is now called Romney Marsh. This was Old Romney, from which the sea receded towards the south-east, until it reached the point on which New Romney stands, and in all probability, as the sea receded, the houses were carried on in the same direction, and, in the lapse of time, when the new town had extended itself two miles from the old, it assumed the designation by which it is now distinguished from its original parent.

To the eastward of Old Romney, and adjoining to it, is the parish of Hope All Saints, which now had been added to the first acquisition from the sea.

Orgerswick must next be added to our list, lying north-east of Hope All Saints.

Blackmanstone, lying to the north of Orgerswick, was likewise rescued from the water by this time.

St. Mary's also, situated to the west of Orgerswick, I presume, was become dry land, as I find it lies in the manors of

Honychild and Blackmanstone, both of which were recognised at this period.

Newchurch, to the north-west of Blackmanstone, must be added to our list.

Now here let us pause a moment while we cast our eyes over the map, when we shall observe that our original island of the Romans has now been increased to a considerable extent, containing the several parishes of Old Romney, New Romney, Hope All Saints, Orgerswick, Blackmanstone, St. Mary's, and Newchurch. It was still an island, but now, instead of one, it contained seven parishes. I have met with no document to show me that Ivychurch was yet in existence; and as its name is from Ea, Sax., water, implying a watery place, I imagine it remained a wet, swampy spot for many years after the time of which we are now writing. Walland Marsh was still a sea, the water flowed between Romney and Lyd; there was a considerable influx of water at Dymchurch, which separated Burmarsh and Eastbridge from Blackmanstone and Newchurch, and joined the waters, which then covered Walland Marsh, by running round the north-east point of Newchurch, spreading over what is now the parish of Ivychurch, and passing between Old Romney.

While this accumulation of land was going on at Old Romney, the sea was likewise receding from Lymne; West Hythe, as we have seen, had sprung into life, and though, like Old Romney, it was doomed to give birth to a town which should finally supersede and eclipse it, still at this time it was in a flourishing state, as Edward the Confessor endowed it with the privileges of an original Cinque Port.

Burmarsh is situated to the south-west of West Hythe, and was now added to this part of Romney Marsh.

Eastbridge, west of Burmarsh, had also been rescued from the watery element.

These three parishes formed a peninsula, having the English Channel on the east, and the Dymchurch water on the south and west.

There had been other lands saved immediately under the Kentish cliffs, and which belonged to the several parishes which abutted to the Marsh. A branch of the Lymene probably still flowed out at West Hythe, serving to keep its harbour open.

Amid the waters which still flowed between Romney and Appledore appeared the island of Brenset. I call it an island, as I find no mention at this period of either of the adjoining parishes of Ivychurch, Snargate, or Snave.

Lyd was an island, lying to the south of New Romney; while Medley was another, to the south of Old Romney, and north-west of Lyd.

Thus we find that at this period there were four islands and one peninsula formed by the retiring of the waters; two islands, viz. those of Romney and Brenset, and the peninsula of West Hythe were in Romney Marsh; the island of Lyd was in Dengemarsh, and that of Medley in Walland Marsh.

The larger branch of the Lymen, now called the Rumenea, flowed out at New Romney, between that town and the island of Lyd.

SECT. IV.

The Changes which took place, from the Conquest, in 1066, to 1334, when the Course of the Lymen was altered by a succession of violent Tempests; being a period of 268 years.

SOMNER tells us, "That in the Conqueror's expedition for the conquest of England, some of his company, by mistake it seems, landed, or were put ashore, at Romney, and were rudely and barbarously treated by the inhabitants thereof; and of the revenge upon them taken by the Conqueror, after his victory and settling his affairs at Hastings, his chaplain Pectairensis, and, after him, Ordericus Vitalis, give us an account." He adds: "This, I take it, is the port in Doomsday Book called Lamport, and the hundred in which it lay, the Hundred of Lamport. 'In Lamport Hundred (so that book) Robertus de Romenel tenet de Archiepisc. Lamport,' &c. That is, 'In the Hundred of Lamport, Robert of Romney holds of the Archbishop, Lamport,' &c. Thus in the account of the lands and possessions of the Archbishop's knights, afterwards in that of the Bishop of Bayon, thus: 'In Lamport Hundred, Robertus de Romenel tenet de Episcopo Affetane, pro 1 solino se defendit. Idem Robertus habet 50 burgenses in burgo de Romenel,' &c. 'In Lamport Hundred, Robert of Romney holds Affetane of the Bishop; he is taxed at one ploughland. The same Robert has fifty burgesses in the burgh of Romney,' &c. It was since, and is at this day, altered into Langport, containing the town of St. Nicholas, &c., and as there was a double Romney, the Old and New, so, in the 14th year of Edward II, I read of an Old and New Langport."

Might not this Lamport (afterwards Langport) be a corruption of Landport, that is, the port at which goods were landed?

and as the old town of Romney gave way to the new, so the old Land Port gave way to the new Land Port.

According to some writers, New Romney (at the time of the Conquest) was in a flourishing condition, having in it twelve wards, five parishes, a priory of Priors Alien, and an hospital, and Sir Robert of Romney was then owner of the same. It had also a good haven at the west side of it.

Romney was now, in all probability, in its greatest prosperity; it is described as having five parishes; but the word parish did not then convey the same meaning it does in our days. It is derived from two Saxon words: Preost, a priest, and Scyre, a shire or division; thus implying the district allotted to each priest for the performance of his duties. Thus there were probably five churches, one of which, a fine old structure, with a beautiful arched doorway of the Norman order, is still remaining; the inhabitants also still point out two inclosures, which are said to have been the sites of churches, with their yards. If to these we add that of Old Romney, and I consider New Romney is a continuation of Old, we have four churches out of five. Shall I be considered as indulging too wild a fancy, if I hazard an opinion that Hope originally made the fifth? It is said to be the most ancient church in Romney Marsh; it is clearly on the original island of the Romans, and it is much nearer to Old Romney than this latter place is to New Romney. Hope is only one mile from Old Romney, while New Romney is two.

We have seen that, in the reign of Edward the Confessor, Blackmanstone was held by one Blacheman, who, I have ventured to suppose, was the first possessor of it, and gave it its name. It appears that, at the Conquest, this manor was wrested from the Saxon proprietor of it, and given to Hugo de Montfort, who had followed the Conqueror into England.

In the previous reign we have seen that West Hythe was constituted a Cinque Port; but now, in the reign of the Conqueror, the present town of Hythe was created in the room of Old or West Hythe; previous to which time it had been accounted within the liberty of these ports. This event marks the rapid change which was now taking (or more properly, had taken) place in this part of the Marsh. The sea had been gradually receding from the foot of Lymne Hill ever since the departure of the Romans; the Saxons had erected West Hythe, as more convenient for carrying on their commerce, at a distance of about half a mile to the eastward of Lymne; and now New Hythe had superseded Old Hythe, at a distance of more than a mile to the eastward of it. The new town was, like New Romney, a continuation of the old. The port of West Hythe was not entirely closed; but the water was become so shallow, that the vessels of largest bulk delivered their cargoes at the new port. The lesser branch of the Lymen brought but little water to its assistance, and that little was now every year becoming less and less.

In 1080 A. D., which is the date of Doomsday Book, I find that Newchurch had been added to our first island of the Romans, being situate to the north-west of Blackmanstone.

Soon after the Conquest, Hope belonged to the family of De Montford, to whom also was given Blackmanstone.

In addition to the fifty burgesses in the town of Romney, which were owned by Robert of Romney, it appears, according to Doomsday Book, that eighty-five belonged to the Archbishop's manor of Aldington.

I have stated that Robert of Romney had fifty, and the Archbishop of Canterbury eighty-five, burgesses in the town of Romney at the time of drawing up Doomsday Book, which was in 1080 A.D.—and here it may be well to observe what is the meaning of the expression that these two great men had together 135 burgesses in the town. Does it imply that they were the slaves or villeins of these lords, and that they held over them the power of life and of death?—or does it only imply that these burgesses were under their special protection? On inquiry, I think we shall find that the latter was the case. In the time of the Saxons, and afterwards of the Normans, the peasants who cultivated the soil were called villeins, that is, vile, low, base men; they were (like the serfs in Russia to this day) *adscripti glebæ*, attached to the soil, part and parcel of the estate on which they worked, and transferred with the estate, like cattle, from one owner to another; in short, they were slaves. There were in the earlier times only three classes—the king, the nobles, and the villeins. The king's power was but nominal—his strength lay in the jealousies and quarrels of his nobles among themselves; but whenever they forgot their rivalries, and united to check his power, he was weak indeed. It was with a view to check the arrogant power of the nobles that the king first established burghs, and endowed them with great liberties, immunities, and privileges, and among these one of the greatest conferred, particularly on the Cinque Ports, was that of giving freedom to the villein who fled from the country and settled within the precincts of a burgh. But still the power of the nobles, who were the owners of the soil, was very great, and they would not willingly consent to the loss of their villeins; it therefore was necessary to raise up some counteracting power to theirs; for it would have been useless to grant liberties and privileges and immunities to the burgesses, unless there was authority invested in some one to guard and protect and secure to them the full enjoyment of these liberties, privileges, and immunities. Accordingly, when a villein came to settle in a burgh, and claimed the privileges of a burgess, he placed himself under the protection of those who owned the property in the burgh in which he settled: he became the possessor of a house situated in the burgh, which belonged to some powerful man, such as probably at this time was Robert of Romney, and as was decidedly the Archbishop of Canterbury; they held their houses under these proprietors somewhat in the same way that copyhold tenants held their lands under the lord of the manor in which the lands were situate. The burgesses paid certain rents to the lord of the burgh, and he in return protected them in the full enjoyment of all their liberties, privileges, and immunities.

The next circumstance I have to record is one that took place in the reign of Henry I, that is, some time between the years 1100 A.D. and 1135 A.D., when Gaufridus, the Prior of Christ-Church, Canterbury, with his Covent, made and passed many grants of land at Appledore, in gavelkind, with this covenant and tie upon the tenants, viz.: "Et debent wallas custodire et defendere contra friscam et salsam; et, quoties opus fuerit, eas reparare et firmas facere, secundum legem et consuetudinem Marisci," &c., setting them but at small rents in respect hereof. The English of the above is this: "That the tenants engage to maintain and defend the walls against the salt and the fresh water; and, as often as there shall be need, to repair and strengthen them, according to the law and custom of the Marsh," &c. But Somner, from whom I borrow this, adds: "I shall not insist on this and many such like any further than to note, that the sea did much infest and endanger these parts with æstuations and irruptions in those days."

In 1168 A.D. Thomas à Becket, being at variance with Henry II, secretly took boat at Romney to go to Rome, but was driven back by a contrary wind. This fact serves to prove that Romney enjoyed a port at this time, and lying conveniently contiguous to the French coast, and he, the Archbishop, moreover, as has been already shown, possessing considerable property, and consequently influence also, in the town, was still further induced to make choice of this port for his embarkation.

Some time during the reign of Henry II, that is, before the year 1189 A.D., when he died, Ivychurch was rescued from that watery state in which I suppose it to have been at the time of the Conquest, about a hundred years before. I now find that during this reign the family of More, or De la More, was seated here, showing evidently that it must now have become a habitable place.

In this century, also, that is, during the reign of Richard I, we meet with the first mention of the Manor of Snave, which was held by John de Snave.

And thus at this time Romney Marsh, properly so called, was saved from the sea, with the exception of Snargate and Dymchurch, of which two last places I have not as yet met with any account.

I now pass on to a century which was fruitful in events affecting the places of which we are now writing. I allude to the thirteenth century, in the sixteenth year of which Henry III commenced his reign, and in his time Fairfield first comes under our observation, when the manor, together with the church, is mentioned as being part of the possessions of the Priory of Christ Church, Canterbury; but when they were given to it does not appear, and therefore I am unable to say more precisely when this place was first embanked from the sea. It lies in Walland Marsh, to the west of Snargate.

Though great part of Romney Marsh was now embanked, and some part also of Walland Marsh, still the lands were continually liable to be overflowed by the sea breaking down the walls that had been erected, as may be seen from the following entry in the accompt roll of the Archbishop's Manor of Aldington, about the year 1236: "In expensis Johannis de Watton et Persona de Aldington per tres dies apud Rumenal et Winchelse et Apelder, una cum seneschallo, ad videndam salvationem patriæ et Marisci contra inundationem maris, 41s. 4d.;" that is, "For the expenses of John of Watton and the Parson of Aldington, for three days at Romney, Winchelsea, and Appledore, together with the seneschal, to see to the preservation of the country and of the Marsh against the inundation of the sea, 41s. 4d."

In 1241 A.D. the first Carmelite friars came to England, and settled at Newenden, which was before, as Lambard says, "a woody and solitary place, and therefore (in common opinion) so much the more fit for religious persons to inhabit." The site of this monastery is still to be seen in the midst of an orchard, a little to the south-east of Lossenham House, from which it is still separated by a part of the original moat. On the same estate, also, is a marsh still known by the name of the Friars' Marsh, and on the east side of the spot where the monastery stood is a meadow called the Kitchen Field, each corroborating the truth of the assertion that here formerly stood a religious house.

"This inundation," says Somner, "was the same (I take it) with that mentioned of both the Matthews (Paris and Westminster) in that year." He adds, "the same Matthew Paris, relating the hideous, uncouth, violent rage, and æstuation of the sea in the year 1250, and the inundations consequent, reports thus: 'Apud Winchelsey,' &c. At Winchilsey above 300 houses, with some churches, by the sea's violence were overturned. In an ancient French chronicle, some time belonging to the church of Canterbury, and written by a monk of the place, in Edward the Second's days, which I read thus: 'And the same year, 1286, on the nones of February, the sea in the Isle of Thanet rose or swelled so high, and in the Marsh of Romenal, that it brake all the walls and drowned all the grounds; so that from the great wall of Appledore as far as Winchilsey, towards the south and west, all the land lay under water, lost.' Mr. Camden, I suppose, intends the same inundation when he says, 'That, in the reign of Edward I, the sea raging with the violence of winds, overflowed this tract and made pitiful waste of people, cattle, and houses in every place; as having quite drowned Promhill, a pretty town, well frequented; and that it also made the Rother forsake his old channel, which here beforetime emptied himself into the sea, and stopped his mouth, opening a new and nearer way for him to pass into the sea by Rhie.' To proceed, Mr. Lambard tells us of a strange tempest that threw down many steeples and trees, and above 300 mills and housings in the county of Kent, in the eighth Edward II, in the year 1334."

According to a manuscript quoted by Horsfield, in his 'History of Sussex,' in the year 1250: "The moon being in her prime, the sea passed its accustomed bounds, flowing twice without ebb, and made so horrible a noise that it was heard a great distance inland, not without the astonishment of the oldest man that heard it; besides this, at dark night, the sea seemed to be a light fire and to burn, and the waves to beat with one another. And at Winchelsea, besides cottages for salt, fishermen's huts, bridges, and mills, above three hundred houses, by the violent rising of the waves, were drowned."

Holinshed says: "On the first day of October, 1250, the moon upon her change, appearing exceeding red and swelled, began to show tokens of the great tempest of wind that followed, which was so huge and mighty both by land and sea, that the like had not been lightly known, and seldom (or rather never) heard of by men then alive. The sea, forced contrary to his natural course, flowed twice without ebbing, yielding such a roaring, that the same was heard (not without great wonder) a far distance from the shore. Moreover, the same sea appeared in the dark of the night to burn as it had been on fire, and the waves to strive and fight together after a marvellous sort, so that the mariners could not devise how to save their ships where they lay at anchor, by no cunning or shift which they could devise. At Winchelsey, besides other hurt that was done in bridges, mills, breakes and banks, there were 300 houses and some churches drowned with the high rising of the watercourse."

Jeake, in a note to his 'Charter of the Cinque Ports,' informs us that he found the following memorandum in a book remaining with the records of the town of Rye: "Be it remembered that, in the year of our Lord 1287, in the Even of St. Agath the Virgin, was the town of Winchelsey drowned, and all the lands between Climesden and the Vocher of Hithe."

From the various quotations here given, it must be quite apparent that, during the thirteenth century, this part of the country was visited by very violent storms. We find that, in 1236, great damage had been done to the walls at Romney, at Appledore, and at Winchelsea, showing at the same time that the latter place must have now risen into life, although it has not before come under our notice.

In 1250 a tremendous storm and inundation took place, which made dreadful havoc at Winchelsea, and did such great and serious damage that it is probable the town had not completely recovered from it when the last fatal attack was made upon it by the winds and waves, in the year 1287, by which it was utterly submerged, and has never since appeared above the level of the waters. All that even tradition retains is, that its original site lies on the sands which are never dry, a little to the southwest of Camber, and to the south-east of the present pier-head of the harbour of Rye.

It was this last inundation of 1287, also, that destroyed the town of Promhill; it swept over this unfortunate place as well as over Winchelsea; but, after the subsidence of the waters, Promhill once more became dry land, though it was henceforth denuded of buildings, and almost of inhabitants. All that remains to mark its ancient site is a rude heap of stones, which serves to show the spot on which originally stood the church. I visited this spot on May 10th, 1838, and the following is the result of my observations, viz.: I visited the site of Broomhill, (this is its modern name,) and, where the church is said to have formerly stood I found a few stones, principally boulders. There was one stone, perhaps about three feet long, a kind of sand stone, bearing marks of having been worked into its present shape, and used about a window, or as a coping-stone. On thrusting my stick into an opening among the stones, there appeared a hollow space underneath, whether the remains of a vault or not, I cannot pretend to say. On casting my eyes all around, I could see no indications of a hill—nothing to warrant the supposition that Prome or Broom Hill, was a name given to the place in consequence of its having been built on a hill. I rather incline to the opinion that hill is a corruption of Ile, Ealand, Sax., island. Eal-Ile, Prome-Ile, that is, the Island of Prome.

The more I consider the subject, the more I am convinced that the greater number of the places in the Marsh were originally islands. Prome Hill was an island, Old Winchelsea was an island, as well as many others I have mentioned in the earlier part of this work.

Leaving Broomhill, and passing to the eastward towards Lyd, I came to a place called the Mitherops, or Midrops; it is a spot of some width, containing broad shallow sheets of water, with here and there little spaces of salt marsh, just such as appear at the mouths and sides of all rivers and inlets of salt water; they extend from the back of the full of the beach, in a north-eastern direction, perhaps about a mile. They are about two miles south-west of Lyd, forming at that part the boundary between Lyd and Broomhill. Judging from what I saw, I conceive that, previously to and in the year 1287, the Lymen passed out between Romney and Lyd, and that there was at the same time a wide expanse of water, communicating with the sea, between Lyd and Broomhill, and when the storm of 1287 took place, it effected two opposite evils—it destroyed, by inundation, the towns of Winchelsea and Broomhill, while, by the driving in of beach and sand, it closed the mouth of the Rumanea, or Lymen, between Lyd and Romney, and also that expanse of water which before had communicated with the sea between Broomhill and Lyd. I presume it was the sudden and violent stoppage of these two outlets at one and the same time that forced the waters over Broomhill and Winchelsea, and kept them under until the river found a new mouth near to Rye and to the westward of Broomhill, when the latter place again emerged from the deep, shorn indeed of its former prosperity, but still more fortunate than its neighbour Winchelsea, which lies buried beneath its remorseless waves, even to this day.

Although considerable damage was done at this time to the lands in Romney Marsh, it was Walland Marsh that suffered most in this respect, while the injury was principally felt by Romney, through the immense and (as we shall hereafter see) the irreparable damage done to its harbour; and, being arrived at this part of our subject, it seems to me now to be the proper time to introduce the statutes which were established for the government of Romney Marsh, and which formed the foundation of all the future laws for the guidance of the other marshes in the kingdom.

It was in consequence of these inundations, and the great damage which arose therefrom, that the attention of the king was called to the necessity of framing laws for the future protection of the Marsh.

Dugdale, after speaking of foreign embankments, says: " I shall now proceed to those statutes and ordinances which the care and wisdom of succeeding ages did make for the preservation and defence thereof from being again drowned and destroyed by the violent overflowings of the ocean; albeit we have yet to learn when and by whom they were first framed and composed; it is evident, from the testimony of unquestionable records, that above 400 years since they were called 'antiquas et approbatas consuetudines—ancient and approved customs;' for, in the thirty-fifth Henry III, that is, in the year 1251, the king declares that complaint had been made to him on behalf of the 24 jurats, made choice of for the conservation of the Marsh and Sea Banks of Rumenale."

From this it would appear, I think, that damage must have been done to some of the banks by the great inundation which has been already mentioned as having taken place in the year 1250, as the complaint was made in the following, that is, in 1251.

Seven years after this, namely, in 1258, the same monarch, Henry III, issued his precept to Henry de Bathe (a famous justice itinerant), Nicholas de Hanlon, and Alured de Dene, who sat at Romenhale; and, at the request of the Council of the Commonalty of the said Marsh, made and constituted these following ordinances, viz.:

1st. That twelve lawful men should be made choice of by the commonalty of the said Marsh, viz., six of the Fee of the Archbishop of Canterbury, and six of the Barony who, being sworn, should measure both the old and the new banks, and those others which ought to be new-made; the measure to be by one and the same perch, that is, of 20 feet. And that afterwards the said jurats should likewise, according to the same perch, measure by acres all the lands and tenements which were subject to danger within the said Marsh. And all the said measure being so made, that then twenty-four men, first elected by the commonalty, and sworn, having respect to the quantity of the banks of those lands which lay subject to peril, upon their oaths, to appoint out every man his share and portion of the same banks, which should so belong to him to be made and sustained; so that, according to the proportion of the acres subject to danger, there should be assigned to every man his share of perches, and that the said assignation should be made by certain limits, so that it might be known where and by what places, and how much each man should be obliged to maintain.

2d. And that when necessity should happen, by occasion whereof it might be requisite to withstand or resist the danger and violence of the sea, in repairing of the before-specified banks, that the said twenty-four jurats should meet together and view the places of danger, and consider to whom the defence of the same should be assigned, and within what time repaired.

3d. And that the common bailiff of the said Marsh should give notice to those unto whose defence the said places should be assigned, that they should defend and repair them within the time specified by the said twenty-four jurats, and, if they neglected so to do, that then the said common bailiff should, at his own charge, make good the said repairs by the oversight of the twenty-four jurats; and that afterwards the party so neglecting should be obliged to render to the said bailiff double the charge so laid out by him about those repairs; which double to be reserved for the benefit of the said banks, and the repair of them; and that the party so neglecting should be distrained for the same, by his lands situate within the said Marsh.

4th. Moreover, in case any parcel of land should be held in common by partners, so that a certain place could not be assigned to each partner for his own proportion, viz., a whole or half perch, in respect of the small quantity of the land, that then it should be ordained by the oaths of the twenty-four jurats, and viewed what proportion of the said lands, so held in common, he might be able to defend; and thereupon a certain portion so to be defended by the said partners, in common, to be assigned to them. And if any of the said partners should neglect to defend this portion after admonition given to them by the bailiff, the said portion of the party so neglecting to be assigned to the other partners, who ought to make the like defence, which partners to hold the portion of the party so neglecting in their hands, until he should pay his proportion of the costs laid out about the same defence, by the oversight of the twenty-four jurats, and also double towards the commodities of the said banks and the repair of them, as aforesaid.

5th. And that, if all the partners should happen to be negligent in the premises, then that the common bailiff above mentioned should make good the whole defence, at his own proper costs, and afterwards distrain all those partners in double the charges so by him expended in the said defence, by view of the twenty-four jurats, as aforesaid; saving to the chief lords in the said Marsh the right which they have against their tenants, touching this defence, according to their feoffments.

6th, and lastly. That all the lands in the said Marsh be kept and maintained against the violence of the sea and the floods of the fresh waters, with banks and sewers, by the oath and consideration of twenty-four jurats, at the least, for their preservation, as anciently had been accustomed.

Of these ordinances it may be observed that they apply only to Romney Marsh Proper, that they allude to customs in existence before they were framed, as may be gathered from the concluding expression in the sixth clause, viz., "as anciently had been accustomed." And perhaps it is in consequence of former customs that no mention is here made of the mode of electing or appointing a bailiff, though the common bailiff is mentioned more than once as an officer of some importance. Moreover, I may add that, by clause the first, twelve Jurats are to be elected, whose duty it is to inspect and overlook the banks, and give orders when necessary for their repair; but, in the sixth clause, it says that, for the due execution of the duties there specified, there shall be twenty-four Jurats at the least; thus implying that there must be more than that number, and this discrepancy may probably be referred to the same cause, viz., the existence of former customs, which these ordinances were intended rather to strengthen than to abrogate.

Not only was mischief done to the banks in Romney Marsh, but great injury also to the harbour of Romney, for it appears, according to Dugdale, that about the same time when the ordinances just mentioned were framed, the king, Henry III, had information that his haven of Rumenale was in great danger of destruction, to the no small damage of the public and excessive annoyance of the town of Rumenale, unless the course of the river of Newenden, whereupon this haven was founded, being then diverted by the overflowings of the sea, were reduced to the said port; and that he was informed by an inquisition made by Nicholas de Hanlon, whom he had sent into those parts to provide and ordain in what sort the said stream might be again brought back to the same haven, by its channel, or a new one to be made, that it could not be so reduced, nor the said haven preserved for the common benefit of the said town and port, except certain obstructions which were in the old course of that river were removed; and that a new channel were made near to the same old course, viz., from a certain cross, belonging to the

Hospital of Infirm People at Rumenale (standing by Aghenepend), unto Effetone; and from Effetone to the house of William le Byll, and so to Melepend, and thence descending unto the said port; so that a sluice be made under the town of Apeltre, for reception of the salt water entering into the said river by the inundation of the sea from the parts of Winchelsea, and for retaining thereof in its passage and recourse to the sea, to the intent that the same water might come together with the fresh water of that river by the ancient course, into the before-specified new course, and so by that passage directly to descend and fall into the said haven. And that another sluice should be made at Sneregate, and a third near to the said port, where that water might descend into the sea; for restraint only of the sea-tide on that part, that it enter not into the said course; but reserving the ancient and oblique course from the said cross to the before-specified haven. The king therefore, providently desiring the common profit and safeguard of the said port, by his precept, dated at Oxford, June 21st, 1257, commanded the said Nicholas, that he should repair in his proper person, upon a certain day assigned, unto those parts; together with the shrieve of Kent, unto whom the said king had thereupon sent his writ, and by the oath of twenty-four, as well knights as other free and lawful men of the neighbourhood, by whom the truth might be better known, to make estimation how much of other men's lands would be necessary to be taken for the making of the new channel and sluices, and what those lands were worth by the year, and to make speedy assignation to the tenants of those lands, to the value of the same lands or more, out of the lands or money of the barons or honest men of the same port; as also to remove the obstructions in the same channel, and to make the new channel and sluices, in the lands of whomsoever it should be requisite for the common benefit and advantage of the said port and town of Rumenale, as aforesaid. And the said shrieve of Kent was likewise commanded, that he should diligently assist and attend before the before-specified Nicholas in this business, and to cause the said twenty-four knights and others of the neighbourhood, as aforesaid, to be before the said Nicholas, at the same day and place.

The next thing memorable, touching this Marsh, says Dugdale, is, that King Edward the First, by his letters patent, bearing date at Westminster, Nov. 20th, 1297, granted a commission to John de Lovetot and Henry de Apuldrefeld, to view the banks and ditches upon the sea-coast and parts adjacent, within the county of Kent, in divers places then broken through by the violence of the sea, and to inquire by whose default this damage had happened; and, together with the bailiffs of liberties and others in those parts, to distrain all those which held any lands and tenements there, and had or might have, defence and preservation in any sort by the said banks and ditches, according to the quantity of their said lands and tenements, either by the number of acres or caracutes.

By virtue of the above mandate, the sheriff was required to summon twenty-four jurats of the Marsh of Rumenale, and all the lords of the banks of the same Marsh; as also such and so many honest and lawful men, of all the maritime lands of his bailiwick, by whom the truth in the premises might be the better inquired into and known; and to do further in the premises, as it should be decreed. Who came accordingly, and the said twenty-four jurats of the Marsh, before-named, together with the commonalty of the said Marsh, said, that King Henry, the father of the then king, did, by his charter, grant to them certain liberties in his own lands within the said Marsh, and they therefore required that those then liberties might be preserved; and also that nothing might be attempted or decreed in prejudice of their said liberties; and they produced the same charter of the said King Henry.

They likewise said, that King Henry sent Henry de Bathe, who decreed and ordained for them a certain law and ordinance, by which the Marsh was to that time kept and preserved, and thereupon produced the said ordinance.

John de Lovetot and Henry de Apuldrefeld made the following ordinances:

1st. They confirmed those of Henry de Bathe, adding, nevertheless, that in regard there was no mention made of the election of the king's common bailiff in the same Marsh, how and by whom he ought to be chosen, it was determined for the future, on the decease of the common bailiff or his quitting office, another to be chosen, who should reside and have lands in the Marsh, and that the said election should thenceforth be by the common assent of the lords of the towns lying therein, or by their attornies; and, as the major part should determine, to submit to that election, because till that the usage had been so.

2d. That the double costs, imposed on those who neglected to repair the defaults, should henceforth go to the common profit of the Marsh, and not to that of the bailiff.

3d. And forasmuch as there were divers banks and watergangs in the said Marsh, to the maintenance of which the commonalty thereof did not contribute, except only they whose lands lay contiguous to the same, and that some, through the oppression of the lords of the Marsh, did sometimes pay as much towards their repairs for forty acres, as others did for fifty acres, which was contrary to the ordinance of Henry de Bathe; it was decreed, that henceforth all and singular persons who had lands therein, which were subject to danger from the sea, and had preservation by the said banks and water-gangs, should henceforth be distrained for the reparation and maintenance of them, in proportion to his land.

4th. And because before that time in this Marsh of Romenale, beyond the course of the water of that port, running from Snergate towards Romenale, on the west part of the same port, till it come to the county of Sussex, there had not been any certain law of the Marsh ordained nor used, otherwise than at the will of those that had lands in the same; insomuch as divers dangers and intolerable losses happened by the sea's inundation, to the end thereof that the like perils might for the future be prevented, and the common profit provided for; it was agreed and jointly ordained, that in the said Marsh, beyond the before-specified port towards Sussex, there should be jurats established, chosen by the commonalty, exercising the same powers, &c., as is more fully contained in the ordinance of Henry de Bathe.

5th. That a common bailiff be chosen in the same way as in Romney Marsh.

6th. That the king's common bailiff in the Marsh of Romenale should be the supervisor of the before-mentioned bailiffs and jurats in this Marsh, beyond the course of the water towards Sussex; and that he should summon together to fit places all the jurats chosen on both sides the said course of the water, when need required, to make their ordinances and laws for preservation of the said Marshes; so that always on both parts of that water-course they should abide by the ordinances and considerations of the said jurats, as to the prejudice or more safeguard of any man's land; notwithstanding any custom whatever, saving always the tenour of the king's charter, granted to the commonalty of Romney Marsh and the ordinance of Henry de Bathe, ever to remain in full power and strength.

In 1301 Edward the First sent Henry de Apuldrefield and Bertram de Tancrey to oversee the banks and ditches, which, by reason of the roughness of the sea, were in many places broken; and to inquire through whose fault this had happened. The former ordinances were confirmed, and these ensuing constitutions added, viz.:

That in every hundred and town by the sea-coast, or bordering on the Thames and other waters in the Marsh lands, which are liable to inundation, there be chosen twelve or six lawful men according to their largeness, which men to be assigned keepers of the banks and water-gangs, who shall watch over the same and repair them when necessary, as also shall, in respect of the raging of the sea, raise the said banks, at the least, by four feet higher than they were before, and of proportional thickness.

That all persons shall be assessed in proportion to their lands, protected by the said banks, whether near or afar off.

Edward II confirmed the ordinances of Henry de Bathe.

In 11th of Edward II, A. D. 1318, complaint was made that much loss was occasioned by a certain trench made between Apeldre and Romenale, upon which the king sent Edmund de Passele, John de Ifeld, and William de Cotes, to examine into it; but a dissension having arisen between his barons of the Cinque Ports and the commonalty of Romenal Marsh thereupon, that both sides were preparing to fight it out; the inquisition was stopped, as it would occasion much terror to the people thereabouts, and might also not a little hinder that warlike expedition which the king then intended.

In the same year, 1318, the banks in this Marsh, betwixt Lyd and Dengemareys, were broke; for in the month of June following, I find that the said king issued out his commission to Henry de Shardon, Thomas de Feversham, and William de Robertsbrigge, for the viewing and repairing the same.

Dugdale (to whom I am indebted for my information respecting the ordinances of Romney Marsh) further tells us, that Edward III confirmed the ordinances of Henry de Bathe.

Camden, in his 'Britannia Antiqua,' speaking of Romney, says: "It is seated on a high hill of gravel and sand, and on the west side of it had a pretty large haven, that was guarded against most winds before the sea withdrew itself. But in the reign of Edward I, A. D. 1287, when the sea, driven forward by the violence of the winds, overflowed this tract, and for a great way together destroyed men, cattle, and houses, threw down Promhill, a little populous village, and removed the Rother (which formerly emptied itself into the sea here) out of its channel, stopping up its mouth, and opening for it a nearer passage into the sea by Rhie; then it began by little and little to forsake this town, which has decayed by degrees ever since, and has lost much of its populousness and dignity."

We have already spoken of the storm of 1250; Camden tells us it changed the course of the river, and opened a new and nearer way into the sea at Rye. And though, he adds, every means were used afterwards, by frequent commissions, to view and see to the repairs of these broken walls, yet by future tempests (one in particular in 8th of Edward III, A. D. 1334) all thoughts of the river ever returning to its old channel seem to have been given up, and three years afterwards, that is, A. D. 1337, the king, by his letters patent, granted this old trench or channel leading from an arm of the sea, called Appledore, towards the town of Romene, to the different owners of the soil, with licence for them to obstruct, dam, and stop it up, as it had by reason of the sands and other matter flowing in, been so filled up, that ships could not pass by it; and reciting that there was another trench leading from the same arm to Romene, lately made by force of the sea, by which ships passed to that town, as they had before used to do by the former one, and was more sufficient.

Somner, speaking of the king's grant of this trench, says: "It was become useless and unserviceable, and so having then continued for thirty years past, and upwards. Lay all this, I say, together, and then it will be creditable enough that the old trench was lost and disused upon that inundation about the year 1287, and the new one made and begotten by that other about the year 1334. Here we find that by the sea's impetuosity and rage, the old trench was lost, and a new one made, and succeeded in the room: both the old, when in being, and the new, afterwards, from Appledore to Romney; the time also we have both of the one and the other's beginning. And now, as on the one hand, some violent irruptions of the sea, by the parts of Rye and Winchelsea, had made way for the Rother's mingling her waters with that estuary, and the breaking off its wonted course by Appledore and Romney; wanting the river's wonted help to scour and keep it open, what with that and the working of the sea still casting up and closing it with land and beach, became in time obstructed, and for many ages hath been so quite dammed up, that the sea now lies off at a great distance and remoteness from the town."

Being now come down to the time to which this fourth head of our inquiry is limited, it remains for me to act the part of the judge, to sum up all the evidence that has been adduced, and to leave the public, as the jurors, to decide upon the truth of the conclusion to which I am about to come. From the scanty materials which have come under my notice, respecting the events of these bygone ages, it is difficult perhaps to arrive at the exact truth of the case. But to this conclusion, I think, we may safely come, viz., that in the course of the thirteenth century, and in the beginning of the fourteenth, there were several very violent storms and inundations, which effected great changes in Romney Marsh, and the parts adjacent.

The first of the storms to which I allude, must have taken

place about the year 1236, when it appears that one John of Watton, and the parson of Aldington, were allowed the sum of forty-one shillings and fourpence for their expenses for three days' survey with the seneschal, for the purpose of seeing to the preservation of the country, and of the Marsh, against the inundation of the sea. Now these three days' survey was confined to Romney, Winchelsea, and Appledore, showing the part of the Marsh which was affected by this inundation.

The second storm took place about fourteen years afterwards, that is, in 1250, and is described by the chroniclers of those days as having been of a very violent and extraordinary nature. This also attacked the same part of the coast, for we find that it destroyed at Winchelsea above 300 houses, together with some churches.

In the year 1287 a third storm raged in these parts, the effects of which were, the breaking of the walls and the drowning of the lands, so that, from the great wall of Appledore, as far as Winchelsea, towards the south and west, all the land lay under water, lost. At this time also Promehill was inundated, and the Rother had his course changed, so that it flowed out nearer to Rye.

The year 1334 witnessed a fourth tempest, which destroyed above 300 mills and houses in the county of Kent.

Thus, in the space of a century, this part of the country was visited by four different storms, the effects of which were severely felt, and from which some parts never recovered; such, for example, as Old Winchelsea, which, being finally inundated in 1286, never again emerged from the sea; Promehill, which was also inundated, but which, after the lapse of time, again raised its head above the waters, but was never again a place of any note, not containing, at the present day, more than eighty inhabitants. And, lastly, the port of Romney, which never recovered from the severity of the blow which it then received.

To understand thoroughly the changes which now took place as thus respect the Rother, we must take a retrospective view of the country at that time. We must suppose Romney Marsh to have been then inclosed, with the exception of an influx of the sea at Dymchurch, and a small inlet of water at Snargate. The Rother, after passing the Isle of Oxney, and reaching Appledore, was embanked on both sides, from thence to its mouth at Romney Haven. The wall on the Romney Marsh side of the river was called the Marsh Wall, that on the Walland Marsh side the Ree, or River Wall. The storms of 1236 and 1250 doubtless both affected the river, and consequently the haven of Romney, but more particularly that of 1250; for we find that, in 1251, Henry III had information that his haven of Rumenale was in great danger of destruction, to the no small damage of the public, and excessive annoyance of the town of Rumenale, unless the course of the river of Newenden, whereupon this haven was founded, being then diverted by the overflowings of the sea, were reduced to the said port. From this it would appear that the river had been diverted from its proper channel by the ruption of its banks, and thus, being no longer carried within its old borders and with its usual force, it ceased to operate with power sufficient to keep open the mouth. It was with a view to correct this evil, that Nicholas de Hanlon, whom the king sent down to examine and report on the subject in question, informed his majesty that the river could not be brought back to its former course, nor the haven preserved, except certain obstructions which were in the old course of that river were removed, and that a new channel were made near to the same old course, viz., from a certain cross belonging to the Hospital of Infirm People at Rumenale (standing by Aghenepend), unto Effetone, and from Effetone to the house of William le Byll, and so to Melepend, and thence descending unto the said port, so that a sluice be made under the town of Apeltre, for reception of the salt water entering into the said river by the inundation of the sea from the parts of Winchelsea, and for retaining thereof in its passage and recourse to the sea; to the intent that the same water might come together with the fresh water of that river, by the ancient course, into the said haven. And that another sluice should be made at Sneregate, and a third near to the said port, where that water might descend into the sea, for restraint only of the sea-tide on that part, that it enter not into the said course, but reserving the ancient and oblique course from the said cross to the before-specified haven. In consequence of this information, Henry III, by his precept, dated at Oxford, June 21, 1251, commanded Nicholas de Hanlon, and the sheriff of Kent to see to the execution of the works thus recommended.

Let us next endeavour to trace out the locality of these several works. The channel seems to have been much obstructed, and this was cleaned out from Appledore, (I presume from Appledore, because here a sluice was to be erected,) down to a certain cross, belonging to the Hospital of Infirm People at Rumenale (standing by Aghenepend), unto Effetone, and from Effetone to the house of William le Byll, and so to Melepend, and thence descending to the said port. The cross here alluded to must have stood between Old Romney and Midley, because the Manor of Aghne lies in those two parishes; from this point a new channel was to be made near to the old course, running to Effetone, etc., as above mentioned. In the account of the lands and possessions of the Bishop of Bayon we find the following entry: "In Lamport Hundred, Robert of Romney holds Affetane of the Bishop," etc. It is fair to suppose that Effetone and Affetane are the same; Affetane is said to be in the hundred of Lamport, and Romney is in the same; thus the new channel ran from Old Romney to New, and thence out to sea; whether the present old bed from Old Romney to the sea be what was, in 1251, called the new channel, I will not pretend to say, nor is it very material, as we are told that the new channel was to be made near to the old one, and, consequently, without assuming too much, we may suppose it to be so. And now, to keep this channel open, there were erected three sluices: one at Appledore, one at Snargate, and another near to Romney. But, though all these precautionary measures were taken for the preservation of a channel from Appledore to Romney, still it seems they were all in vain, the port of Romney was doomed to destruction, and no human means seemed capable of averting it; for, whatever good effect the three sluices, erected in 1251, might have had, it was entirely effaced by the succeeding storm of 1286, when the harbour of Romney was so completely dammed up that no future efforts were ever available to restore it to any degree of prosperity. From this time it seems to have lingered on until the final blow was struck in the year 1334, after which the channel from Appledore to Romney was totally abandoned, and in the 11th year of Edward III, that is, in A.D. 1338, the bed of this channel was so dried up that it was granted to the Archbishop of Canterbury, the Prior and Convent of Christ Church, and Margaret de Basings, with liberty to use it as they pleased.

And now, having witnessed the final catastrophe of the Port of Romney, the diversion of the channel of the Rother, and the submersion of Promehill and Winchelsea, we will take a short survey of the state of the country at the period at which we are now arrived.

Since our last summary I find that Ivychurch and Snave were added to Romney Marsh, and finally Snargate, in the reign of Edward I, in the thirty-fourth year of which, A. D. 1305, the manor was held by a family of the name of Allard, one of whom was Gervas Allard, who was Admiral of the western seas at that time. It extends over the Ree Wall, and lies partly in Romney and partly in Walland Marsh. The land is low in this parish, and joins to Appledore Dowels, which is still a swampy spot. In 1251 we have found that a sluice was erected at Snargate, and probably its then low, watery state pointed it out as a fit place for the purpose, forming a natural reservoir for the water; and, as we see that in 1305 Snargate had risen into existence, we may conclude that the erection of the sluice fifty years before, had assisted in collecting the filth and sediment, which eventually brought the land into a cultivable state. I consider it probable that Snargate or Snergate owes its name to a water-gate of some kind, which was erected here for the purpose of draining the low land of this district; for I find that Camden, speaking of the spot, does not call it Sneregate, but "the Sneregate," as though a flood-gate of some kind had been here originally erected, and which was known by the name of the Snere-gate.

Here, too, it may be remarked, that now we meet with the first mention of sluices: but of what description they were, perhaps it is not very easy to say. Thus much, however, I may venture to hazard, that they were not on the large scale they are at the present day. On the old branch of the river, which flowed formerly on the north side of the Isle of Oxney, at a spot nearly opposite to Ebeney chapel, were lately discovered the remains of an erection called the *Shuts*, evidently intended to shut the water back, and which may have been the sluice which is said to have been ordered to be built under the town of Appledore. To corroborate this opinion there was formerly an erection across the Rother, opposite Bodiham Castle, called the shuts, which was built for the purpose of penning back the water, to bring the cannons down from the foundry at Robertsbridge.

Old Winchelsea was destroyed, and never again arose from its watery bed. Promehill was temporarily submerged; Lyd was united to this last place by the influx of beach and sand, and of course ceased to be an island; while the course of the Rother was turned on the west side of Promehill.

The reader will observe that these remarks apply principally to Romney Marsh, and it will now be necessary to bring down our account of other parts of the district, to which our history refers, to the present period A. D. 1334.

Lambard thinks that Rye and Winchelsea might be added to the number of the ports in 1268, because, at that time, he says, he finds by an old record, that Henry III took into his own hands (for the better defence of the realm) Winchelsea and Rye, which belonged before to the Monastery of Fescamp, in Normandy, and gave them in exchange the Manor of Chiltham, in Gloucestershire, and divers other lands in Lincolnshire. This he did, partly to conceal from the Priors Aliens, the intelligence of the secret affairs of his realm, and partly because of a great disobedience and excess committed by Winchelsea against Prince Edward, his eldest son. He thinks, for their own correction, that they were put under the governance of the Five Ports; but not then admitted to their privileges, as that would have been a reward, not a punishment. He adds, that he suspects, when Old Winchelsea was abandoned, and the new town built, the privileges were granted to the towns of Winchelsea and Rye.

Thus it appears that these two towns were united with the Cinque Ports previously to the destruction of Old Winchelsea; for that town was not finally destroyed until 1286, and we see by Lambard's account, that it was placed under the control of the original Ports in 1268, and the new town was founded in the latter part of the reign of Edward I, subsequently of course to the destruction of the old, which took place in 1286.

Some time in the reign of Edward I, a great fleet of Frenchmen showed themselves on the sea-shore at Hythe, having 200 soldiers, and landed their men in the haven; but the townsmen came upon them to the last man, wherewith the residue were so afraid, they hoisted sail, and made no further attempt.

In the fifth year of Edward I, A. D. 1277, in an extent of the Archbishop's Manor of Terring, in Sussex, under the title of Borga de Maghefeud (the borough of Mayfield) is the following entry: "Martinus de Webb tenet quartam partem unius rodæ apud la Limene et debet quad. ad festum S. Mich."—"Martin Webb holds a quarter of a rood on the Limen, and owes a quadrans [that is a farthing] at the feast of St. Michael."

This, I believe, is the last mention of the Rother, under the name of Limen, and this being retained pretty near to its source, serves to show that originally this must have been its name throughout its whole extent.

This reign was fruitful in events relative to our history; for this king, Edward I, built himself a hunting seat at Newenden, and made a liberty of a certain portion of the parish, which still remains, and enables them to choose their own constable, and formerly had their own court; here, too, was a royal fishery.

Thus we find that Newenden has had three remarkable epocha in its little history; it was originally the site of the ancient Anderida, some remains of which are still to be traced (as has been before mentioned) in a small part of the vallum and in the mound, on which formerly stood the castle. Here was founded the first monastery of Carmelite Friars, the traces of which are still visible in the existing part of the old moat, in a meadow adjoining the orchard, in which the monastery stood, and which meadow still bears the name of the Kitchen

Field: and in a Marsh, at this day designated the Friar's Marsh.

And, lastly, Edward I had a hunting seat at this place; and of the truth of this we may be satisfied on finding several remains corroborative of the existence of such a seat; as, for instance, in the map of the estate belonging to the late Samuel Bishop, Esq., there is a Marsh, lying near the Exden river, due north from Newenden Church, called the Drawbridge Marsh, which was probably divided from the residence by a moat, over which the drawbridge was thrown. On the same estate also are found two meadows, lying east of the Drawbridge Marsh, one called Upper Park Field, and the other called Lower Park Field. To the manor of Lossenham is also attached a royal fishery on the river Rother, extending from Udiham Oak, near Bodiam Bridge, to Scot's Float Sluice, being a distance of fifteen miles.

In the reign of Edward I, I find mention is made of Lowden Manor, called also Little Maytham, when it was held by Elwisa de Maytham. Whether the castle was then built I do not know, but I think it not improbable that it was. There are at present no remains of the building itself; but the site of the castle is admirably preserved; it is situated on the high ground on the north side of Exden Bay, opposite to the old castle of Anderida, at the distance of about a mile from it; there is a little inlet from the Bay, which runs up to the very edge of the mound which formerly inclosed the moat of the castle, the land at the east side of which is still flooded in winter. The area of Lowden castle is now a smooth mound of earth, swarded all over with a green turf, and sloping down on three sides into what was formerly the moat, but which is now dry and covered with grass; on the fourth or north-west side are some remains of the moat still containing water. The following are the dimensions and position of the mound: the south-south-west and north-north-east sides are each 52 yards in length; while the south-east-by-east side is 54 yards; the one opposite to it is only 44 yards. The moat is 12 yards wide; it is situated in the parish of Rolvenden.

I visited the site of Lowden Castle on June 9th, 1837, and on the same day also that of Forsham Castle, which lies in the same parish, and on the side of the same hill, at the distance of about two miles to the west of the former. I could learn nothing of the time of its original erection; there are still some traces of a moat which formerly ran round the castle, and which show it to have been of considerable extent. The Marsh runs up within about seventy rods of the moat, so that the castle stood conveniently for the defence of the country against the pirates, who in ancient times probably sailed up the bay, which Exden then was, that is, in the time of Edward I.

I venture to hazard the conjecture, that these two castles of Lowden and Forsham were erected in the reign of Edward I, or at all events in that of the second or third king of this name; and I found my conjecture on the fact, that the first Edward had a hunting seat at Newenden, situated on the opposite bank to that on which Forsham and Lowden Castles were built; and we shall find, as we proceed in our history, that a castle was erected at Iden in the reign of Edward I, and another at Bodiam in the early part of that of Richard II. I consider it very probable that Edward I, residing in this part of the country, became acquainted with its localities, was informed of its necessities, and was thus enabled to apply speedy remedies to such evils as required redress. This part of the country might be infested with pirates, and this might suggest the policy of erecting castles, to protect the inhabitants against their incursions. And to the presence of the king in the neighbourhood, perhaps, may be attributed the speedy redress given to the unfortunate inhabitants of Old Winchelsea by the erection of a new town for their reception so quickly after the destruction of their original place of abode.

Speaking of Winchelsea, Leland tells us, that on the destruction of the old town Edward I (on the suit of the inhabitants thereof) purchased the site of the present town of Sir John Tregose, Knight (chief owner), of one Maurice, and of Battle Abbey. It was at that time a rabbit warren, and contained 150 acres, whereof part is in the Kingmead without the town, and part in the hanging of the hill. Within six or seven years the new town was metely well furnished, and daily after for a few years increased. But or twenty years were expired from the beginning of the building of the new town, it was twice entered by enemies: first by Frenchmen, and secondly by Spaniards, that entered by night at Fareley, about the middle way betwixt Winchelsea and Hastings. At this invasion the town was sore spoiled, and scant since came into the pristine state of wealth; for the common voice is, that at that time there were twenty aldermen in the town, merchants of good substance.

The first mention of the manor of Brookland in public records is in the 19th Edward II, that is, A.D. 1325. The church was appropriated by Pope Clement V, at the request of Ralph Bourne, the abbot of it, in the same reign. This parish takes its name from the several brooks and waterings within its bounds, and lies in Walland Marsh.

Having now registered the birth of Brookland, I find that at this time every place in Romney Marsh had come into existence, with the exception of Dymchurch; and every one in Walland Marsh, excepting East Guldeford.

It may be right here to take a short and retrospective view of some of the places which are situated on the borders of the marshes of whose history we are giving this faint outline. I will accordingly commence with Rotherfield, which stands at the source of the Rother. It was formerly called Ritheramfield, Redrefield, Ritherfield, now Rotherfield, the field or spot in which rises the river Rother. So far back as the eighth century, one Duke Bertoald had an estate and residence here, where he built a church, which he dedicated to St. Denis, near Paris, in return for the relief which he experienced from a heavy sickness by visiting that abbey, and endowed it with all his estate in this place. The charter by which he made the grant was dated A.D. 792. The river now called the Rother is in that charter designated the Salforda.

Mayfield, which is situated on one of the branches of the Rother, was formerly an occasional residence of the Archbishops of Canterbury; and here the celebrated St. Dunstan, who lived in the tenth century, resided, and erected a wooden church. In 43d Henry III, A.D. 1259, the Archbishop obtained a charter for a market and fairs to be held at Mayfield.

In 1332, a provincial synod was held here, when a constitution passed, relating to holidays.

Burwash stands near the Rother. Its ancient name was Burgherst or Burghurst, a burgh in a wood—Burg, Sax., a borough or burgh; Hurst, Sax., a wood. In 26th Edward I, that is, A.D. 1297, Robert de Burghershe, Lord of this Manor, was made Constable of Dover Castle, and the next year Warden of the Cinque Ports. In 1303 he was summoned to Parliament amongst the barons of the realm; and we presume that it is from this place the eldest son of the Earl of Westmoreland to this day takes his title, which is that of Lord Burghersh. In the 3d Edward III, A.D. 1329, John de Brittany, Earl of Richmond, had the King's charter for a market weekly, and two fairs, at his manor of Burghersh.

Etchingham is worthy of note from having given the title of baron to a family, at a very distant period. Simon de Etchingham was Sheriff of Sussex and Kent in the 18th of Henry III, A.D. 1233; and the Barons of Etchingham were hereditary Stewards of the Rape of Hastings. The Barons William and Robert were summoned to Parliament from 5th Edward II, to the 15th of the same reign, that is, from 1311 to 1321. In 1st Edward III, Robert de Etchingham was summoned to Parliament.

Descending the river, Salehurst succeeds Etchingham. It is recognised in Doomsday Book under the name of Salhert, probably a corruption of Salherst; for, in 23d Edward I, William de Etchingham is said to have procured a charter of free warren for his lordship of Salherste or Salehurst. Now may not this name be derived from Sealt, Sax., salt, and Hurst, Sax., a wood—Saltwood, being built on the edge of the forest of Anderida, adjoining the banks of a salt river? There can be no doubt, as we have shown in a former part of this work, that the sea flowed up to this point, and tradition also tells us it reached up to Etchingham. That the water here was salt, and even further up, is proved, we think, by the additional fact, that at Rotherfield, according to the document quoted under our description of that place, the river was in very ancient times called the Salforda, which is literally the Salt-Ford, latinized.

At Robertsbridge, a town in this parish, a Cistercian abbey was founded in 1176, by Alured de St. Martin, as some assert, but by Robert de St. Martin, according to others. We allude to these two names, Alured and Robert, by way of giving some idea of the origin of the name of this place. Many people are of opinion that the proper name is Rotherbridge, and not Robertsbridge. We differ from these, inclining to Robertsbridge in preference to Rotherbridge, and for the following reasons. The Chronicle of the Church of Rochester has this record: " Anno milessimo centesimo septuagesimo sexto, Robertus de Sancto Martino, regnante Henrico Rege Secundo, eique familiaris, condidit super flumen Rothori, abbatiam de Ponte Roberti"—" In the year 1176, Robert de St. Martin, in the reign of Henry II (he being friendly to it), founded, on the river Rother, the abbey of Robert's Bridge." Salehurst and Robertsbridge are on opposite sides of the river, the latter on the south and the former on the north. This spot, in very ancient times, as was the case with all rivers, was in all probability a ford. Few greater benefits in those early days could be bestowed on the inhabitants of such a locality than the erection of a bridge; and this benefit, we imagine, was bestowed by Robert de St. Martin, with a view to connect the abbey with the *town* of Salehurst; and hence the bridge was called by his name, and the abbey, from its contiguity to the bridge, assumed the same appellation. It is said to have been built on the river Rother, and called Robert's Bridge. In 1197, the abbot's name was William de Ponte Roberti—William of Robert's Bridge. The name of Rotherbridge does not appear, as we are aware, in any public document.

Alice, wife of Alured de St. Martin, gave to the monks of this priory all her lands in Snargate.

Simon de Etchingham gave to the monks at Robertsbridge, a certain watercourse, between Saleham and Ocham.

The Abbot of Robertsbridge, in the year 1192, was sent into Germany with the Abbot of Boxley, to find out the king (Richard I), who had been taken prisoner on his return from the Holy Land They discovered him, and were present at the peace and agreement concluded between the emperor and the king.

That Robertsbridge, not Rotherbridge, was and is the proper name, is further confirmed by reference to the impression of the seal of the abbey, on the red wax appended to the instrument of surrender, when it was given into the hands of Henry VIII, bearing date April 16th, 1537. The inscription on the seal is, "S. Coe. Abbatis et Conventus de Ponte Robti"—"The Convent Seal of the Abbot and Monks of Robert's Bridge." Thus we find that its name, both at its foundation in 1176, and on its suppression in 1537—at a distance of 361 years from each other, was decidedly Robertsbridge.

Of Bodiam we shall not here stop to say much, as the castle was not erected until a period subsequent to the one of which we are now speaking. We shall merely observe here, that the manor is mentioned in Doomsday Book.

On the opposite side of the river to Bodiam, lies Ewhurst, the manor of which is in Doomsday Book called Werste, and is stated to have been held by the Earl of Eu; and hence probably its name, Eu-hurst—the Wood of the Earl of Eu. It is also recognised in the reign of Edward the Confessor. Stephen of Burgherst, or Burwash, held the manor in the reign of Edward II.

In Doomsday Book, Northiam is mentioned under the name of the manor of Hiham, and was held by the Earl of Eu, having been previously the property of Earl Godwin. In ancient writings it is called Nordhamme, North-ham—North Village. Here was pannage for two hogs.

Beckley had not at this time risen into being, unless this is the place which Alfred, by his will, gave to his kinsman Osforth, under the name of Villa de Beecaule. Some suppose it to be Beckley in Surrey, to which I should rather incline, as there seems no mention of this Beckley in Sussex in Doomsday Book.

The first mention we find of Peasmarsh is in the 3d Edward II, A.D. 1309, when Stephen Burghersh had free warren in Pesemershe. And a free warren signifies a franchise or place

Edwardu[s]
Omnib[us]
q[uo]d de gra[tia]

dilecto et fideli nostro E
de petra et castr[o] firmare
suis i[m]p[er]petuu[m] sine oc[casione]
alio[rum] ballio[rum] seu a[liorum]
patentes. Teste me i[ps]o

privileged by prescription or grant from the king, for the keeping of beasts and fowls of the warren, which seem to be only hares and rabbits, partridges and pheasants.

The manor of Iden existed in the time of Edward the Confessor, when it was held by Ednod, a freeman. In Doomsday Book, it is said to contain one villein and seven cottages, two ploughs, two ploughlands of arable, and six acres of meadow.

In the reign of Edward I, there was a mansion in the parish of Iden, belonging to Edmund de Passeleye, and he obtained permission from the king to fortify and embattle it. The king's grant, beautifully written on parchment, is still in existence; and, by the kindness of Thomas Pix, Esq., of Woodside, in the parish of Peasmarsh, we are enabled to place a copy of it before our readers, which, to every true lover of antiquity, cannot fail of proving a rich treat. The accompanying is an exact copy of the grant, in the old chancery hand, in which it was originally written.

For the convenience of those who may not be well acquainted with this old hand, we shall now insert a copy in the modern characters; and lastly, to aid those who are ignorant of the Latin language, shall give an English translation.

LATIN COPY.

"Edvardus, Dei gratiâ, Rex Angliæ, Dominus Hiberniæ, et Dominus Aquitaine: Omnibus balliuis et fidelibus suis ad quos presentes litteræ pervenirint, salutem: Sciatis quod de gratiâ nostra speciali concessimus et licentiam dedimus pro nobis et heredibus nostris, dilecto et fideli nostro Edmundo de Passeleye, quod ipse mansum suum de la mote in comitatu Sussex muro de petra et calce firmare et kernellare, et mansum illud, sic firmatum et kernellatum tenere possit sibi et heredibus suis in perpetuum sine occasione vel impedimento nostri vel heredum nostrorum, justiciariorum, vicecomitum, aut aliorum balliuorum seu ministrorum nostrorum quorumcunque. In cujus rei testimonium has litteras nostras fieri fecimus patentes. Teste me ipso apud Ebor, decimo die Decembri, anno regni nostri duodecimo. SIBTHORP."

"*Per ipsum Regem.*"

ENGLISH TRANSLATION.

"Edward, by the grace of God, King of England, Lord of Ireland, and Lord of Aquitaine. To all bailiffs, and to his faithful subjects, to whom these present letters may come, greeting; Know ye that, by our special grace, we have granted and given licence for ourselves and our heirs, to our beloved and faithful Edmund de Passeleye, that he may strengthen his mansion of mote, in the county of Sussex, with a wall of stone and mortar, and fortify it with battlements; and having so strengthened and embattled that mansion, to hold it to himself and his heirs for ever, without let or impediment of us, or of our heirs, our justiciaries, sheriffs, or other bailiffs, or of any of our officers whomsoever. In testimony of which grant, we have caused these our letters to be made patent. Witness ourself at York, this tenth day of December, in the twelfth year of our reign. SIBTHORP."

"*By the King himself.*"

This document (as I have before said) is beautifully written, and is in high preservation; to it is appended a very large seal of green wax, fastened by means of some green and pink silk braided together. The seal is round, being four inches in diameter. On the obverse is the king on horseback, clad in a complete suit of armour, with his sword drawn. His shield and his horse-armour are ornamented with Lions courants. The outer edge of the seal is broken away, so that the only letters visible on it are "rdus Dei," the probable remains of Edwardus Dei Gratiâ, &c. On the reverse is the king seated, with a crown on his head, the sceptre in his right hand, and the ball in his left. Behind him appears a large building, which is probably intended to represent Westminster Abbey. The letters on this side are too much effaced to be legible.

It may be well to observe here, that in these days subjects were not allowed to fortify their houses without permission from the king, lest if great numbers were indiscriminately permitted to do so, they might become too powerful for the monarch, and set his authority at defiance. It would imply also, that the party to whom the grant was made, was a man of substance and importance, and one in whose loyalty the king could place confidence.

This mansion of mote afterwards passed into the family of Iden, one of whom, Alexander Iden, who was sheriff of Sussex and Kent, in the reign of Henry VI, in 1450, slew the rebel Jack Cade, at Cade Street in the parish of Heathfield, in Sussex. I have been informed that this Alexander of Iden was buried in Iden Church, and that some years ago, a brass plate was taken away, bearing the effigies of a man in armour, and which is supposed to have belonged to his tomb.

I shall close this account of Iden with stating that the site of the mansion of mote is still visible, though no building is now remaining on it. The walls of the castle on the north and south sides, were respectively 150 feet in length, and those on the east and west 140 feet. Between the walls and the inner edge of the mote, all round was a space of ground 120 feet in width. The mote was 360 feet square, and 45 feet wide. There is no keep at present to be seen. This was the state of the place in the year 1836, when I visited it.

Playden is mentioned in Doomsday Book, and is there called Pleidenam. One Siulf held it of King Edward the Confessor.

Udimore is recognised in Doomsday Book under the name of Dodimer, as Horsfield says, in his 'History of Sussex;' but we will not pretend to say whether he is right or not in this conjecture. In 23d Edward I, William, Lord Etchingham, procured a charter of free warren for his lordship of Odymere. He held it till the reign of Henry VI.

The name is said to be derived from Eau-de-Mer—Water of the Sea, the sea having formerly flowed up on both sides of it; and tradition does say, that in the reign of King John a fleet sailed up there.

Brede, which follows Udimore, was early endowed with important privileges, having a court of its own, which is a branch of that at Battle.

Seddlescombe Manor was held by Earl Godwin in the time of Edward the Confessor, and Harold was seized of that of Whatlington at the same time.

We next come to Battle, a place of great note, as being the spot on which the memorable contest took place between Harold, King of England, and William, Duke of Normandy, for the crown of this country; from this great contest the place afterwards assumed, and has to this day retained the significant and appropriate name of Battle, *the battle* having been here fought. Previous to this time, its name appears to have been Hetheland.—Heath-land, from the nature of the soil around, which is very congenial to the growth of heath. In commemoration of this battle, the Conqueror erected here an abbey, which he richly endowed. Succeeding monarchs made additional endowments, and it retained more or less of its splendour until its final suppression in the 30th of Henry VIII.

Much of the original building still remains, forming the chief ornament and attraction of the town of Battle, while part is yet inhabited by Lady Webster and her family.

The manor of Westfield was held by one Wenestan in the reign of Edward the Confessor. In Doomsday it is called Westwelle.

According to Doomsday, Geoffrey de Floc held Gestelings (Guestling) of the Earl of Eu. Ulbald held it of King Edward.

Icklesham owes its name to a union of Latin and Saxon— Ecclesiæ, Lat., of the church, Ham, Sax., village. The village of the church, designating the part of the parish in which the church stood and distinguishing it, at the same time, from the spot on which Winchelsea was afterwards built, and which was then known by the name of Petit Iham. Petit, French, little; Heath, Saxon, high; Ham, Sax., hamlet. The little high hamlet; being called little, compared to the part where the church stood, and high, from its situation on a hill. It is not recognised in Doomsday under the name of Icklesham; whether by any other, I will not pretend to say. The name first occurs in the 11th Henry III, A.D., 1226.

Of the foundation of the present town of Winchelsea we have already spoken, and therefore shall pass on to Pett and Fairlight, which two places complete our survey of the adjacents to the Marshes of which we are treating.

The manor of Pett is recorded in Doomsday Book, and is said to have contained one plough in the demesne, and a villein and three cottages, with two ploughs.

Fairlight is not to be found in Doomsday under its present name. It is recognised under this name in the reign of Henry III, when it was held by William de St. Levdegaria, who then obtained a charter of free warren for it.

In this hasty outline we do not profess to give anything approaching to a history of the various places at which we have merely glanced; our object has been to show what was the state of the country around the marshes at the early period to which this present head of our work alludes. We find that manors were existing in all these places, with very few exceptions, at the time of the Conquest, and even in that of Edward the Confessor; it may therefore be desirable to ascertain what was the nature of a manor in these early days: "The word manor (according to Jacob, in his 'Law Dictionary') is derived from manoir, Fr., habitation, Lat., or rather from manendo, Lat., abiding, because the lord did usually reside there. Touching the original of manors, it seems that, in the beginning, there was a circuit of ground granted by the king to some baron, or man of worth, for him and his heirs to dwell upon, and to exercise some jurisdiction, more or less, within that compass, as he thought good to grant; performing such services, and paying such yearly rent for the same as he, by his grant, required; and that afterwards this great man parcelled out his land to other meaner men, enjoining such rents and services as he thought good; and so, as he became tenant to the king, the inferiors became tenants to him." Thus when we read of any place being a manor, we may conclude that here was a mansion and a residence for a man of wealth and influence; but, to render the subject more intelligible, let us take the example of some one parish, described here, and endeavour to analyse all the component parts herein described. The following is the description of Iden in Doomsday Book: "The manor of Iden contains 1 villein and 7 cottages, 2 ploughs, 2 ploughlands of arable and 6 acres of meadow."

Thus Iden contained a baron's or gentleman's residence, as implied in the word manor; one villein—a villein in tenure, that is, one who held lands under the lord, subject to the performance of certain services in return; he was a sort of copyhold tenant. Seven cottages, that is, houses without any land attached to them, and occupied by the lowest class of workmen, men who were probably villeins by blood—*adscripti glebæ*—slaves. Here were two ploughs, which were kept, of course, to till the two ploughlands, which quantity of land was as much as the two ploughs could cultivate in the course of the year. Now, as to the contents of a ploughland, there is much difficulty in deciding; some say it was as much as would support a family, and others that it was 100 acres, and even 120 acres. But I can by no means think the ploughland could contain so much as 100 acres; half the quantity seems to me much nearer the mark, this being as much as a single plough-team could cultivate in the present day; and, although cultivation is now carried to a state of improvement far beyond anything that could be contemplated in those days, and the implements used in agriculture are equally improved, yet it must be remembered that much more work in ploughing, harrowing, rolling, etc., is now bestowed on the land than in the eleventh century; and therefore, if we allow the improved implements to enable the farmer to do the extra work, the same expense will have been incurred by both parties (that is allowing the prices of all things to be the same at both periods), and the advantage gained by the farmer of the present day will arise from his increased produce, arising out of his superior skill; and, lastly, there were six acres of meadow, that is, so much taken from the waste or common, and improved and manured for the purpose of producing hay for the cattle in the winter.

To place this picture before us at one view, we must suppose Iden to possess one large rude mansion, built of wood, occupied by the lord of the manor, one smaller, under dwelling, which was a species of farm-house, inhabited by the villein, who was the farmer of the day; six cottages of very inferior construction, without windows, save of lattice-work, and with no chimneys; suitable dwellings for the slaves that inhabited them. In the parish were only two ploughs, and the extent of arable land was 100 acres, while that of meadow was confined to six acres.

Let us next see the present state of the parish of Iden. There is one handsome mansion, the rectory; five substantial farmhouses, besides several smaller ones, and numerous very comfortable cottages; there are upwards of 500 inhabitants, and 2863 acres of land, of which only 188 acres are wood; 1280 acres are marsh, gained from the water since the Conquest, and 1395 acres are upland arable and pasture; thus showing that 1289 acres have been reclaimed from the forest in the midst of which this parish was then situated.

In some manors mentioned in Doomsday Book, we find there was pannage for hogs, as was the case in Northiam, and here it will be well to inquire what pannage was: Pannage, or pawnage, in Latin pannazium, French pasnage, signifies the mast of beech or acorns, on which hogs were allowed to feed at the proper season, and of course the grant of pannage implies the existence of woods in the place where it was made. Having now introduced this subject of pannage, I feel this will be a proper place to make some remarks on the fact which Doomsday Book records of pannage having been granted at that time in the parish of Medley, in Walland Marsh. The words are these: "There is a church and 10 acres meadow; wood for the pannage of 10 hogs."

This extract clearly shows that wood must at this period have existed in the Marsh; and this is further corroborated by what Hasted says of Appledore Dowles, which place he describes as a large swamp, about a mile south-eastward of Appledore, which there are reasons to believe were once wood; among which reasons are the fact that the Dean and Chapter of Canterbury have a parcel of land in the western part of the Dowles, which in the records of that church are said to lie in Appledore Wood; and that, at the depth of from three to six feet there have been found, in different parts of this tract of land, oak leaves, acorns, birch, and willow, and the stalks of brakes, &c., in high preservation; and likewise large trees of various kinds and sizes, lying in different directions, and sometimes across one another; and (what is worth observation) they appear to have been cut down with an axe, or sharp instrument, and not with a saw—strong proofs that these Dowles were once part of the forest, and covered with trees and wood.

In the wet level, which lies on the north side of the present channel of the Rother, in the parish of Wittersham, many large trees have been discovered, the limbs of some of which were evidently (as I have been informed) severed by an axe.

In the bed of the Rother, which has been dug out for the purpose of deepening it, within these few years from Scot's float sluice to Bodiam Bridge, Mr. James Elliott (under whose excellent management the work was conducted) informs me that many large oak trees were discovered, and many stems so situated as to leave no doubt of their having borne trees upon them in the same spot; these same stems standing upright, and bearing evident marks of having had the trunks severed from them where they then stood.

In digging the military canal from Hythe to the foot of Fairlight Cliff, leaves and branches of trees were found in all parts of it; more particularly hazel-boughs, and nut-shells in great abundance.

About twenty years ago a gentleman of my acquaintance, in attempting to embank a piece of ground from the sea in the western part of Sussex, had occasion to take the mud and soil from the harbour, where the work was going on, to a considerable depth, when he discovered many remains of trees, and particularly of hazle; together with great quantities of nut-shells.

In conclusion, allow me to add that Dugdale, when speaking of the fens in Lincolnshire, states that at the depth of several feet below the surface were found trees, and many other things indicating that such lower part was once dry land, and that this is confirmed by the discovery of a ladder at the same depth.

All these instances here adduced, would seem to imply that, at some very distant period, dry land must have existed at a much lower level in many parts than it does at present. In the course of ages, we are well aware that great changes have taken place on the face of the globe, and that still silently, though not always visibly, change is continually going on. Let us instance a few of the changes which have taken place, in order to show that our opinion is not a mere idle conjecture. The vast and barren plains of Tartary, extending from the borders of China to the sea of Azof, are supposed once to have been an immense sea, but the waters, from some cause, burst the barriers which had heretofore confined them, and forced their way into the lower level of the sea of Azof, and thence through the Euxine, the Bosphorus, the sea of Marmora, the Dardanelles, and the Mediterranean, into the Atlantic, thus converting sea into land, and land into sea.

The author of 'Germany and the Germans,' says: "The Baltic is tideless, and this, combined with the many rivers that flow into it, is the cause of its being so frequently frozen over, and as these rivers descend from the mountains, and take their course through a country whose soil is principally sand, they carry with them large quantities, which, in process of time, has accumulated, and continues accumulating, near their mouths in vast masses; so that future ages may witness the verification of the prophecy of the famous witch of Rugen, who predicted that the day would come when travellers should pass on dry land from Germany to Sweden and Denmark."

This same author also, speaking of the vast plain which extends from the Ural Mountains to the Baltic, says: "It seems as if this immense expanse had been the last resting place of the waters of the deluge; for it extends from the German ocean along the base of the Harz, Erz, and Riesengebirge mountains, to the Baltic, and from thence (including a great part of Poland and Russia) it reaches the foot of the Ural Mountains in Siberia. The soil throughout is an alternation of sand and morass, and certainly gives no contradiction to the hypothesis that the whole of this region was, at one time, covered by the waters of the Baltic. It is moreover asserted by German writers, that marine plants, remnants of ships, implements of labour, and human skeletons have been found some eight or ten feet below the surface, which corroborate the opinion.

Lord Teignmouth, in his 'Islands and Highlands of Scotland,' says: "In 1097 (according to Boethius) many villages, castles, towns, and extensive woods, both in England and Scotland, were subverted by an exundation of the German Ocean, by the weight of which tempest the lands of Goodwin, near the mouth of the Thames, were overwhelmed with sand, which, in the present day, are called the Goodwin Sands. At the very same time, likewise the lands of Moray in Scotland were desolated by the sea, castles subverted from their foundations, some villages destroyed, and the culture of man defeated by a discharge of sand from the sea; monstrous thunderings came on, roaring so loudly terrible, in such tremendous crashing, that many men in the fields were struck, some cattle were killed, and by their shock also, even towns were prostrated."

Lyon, in his 'History of Dover,' says: "The fruitful valley, in which we now find the villages of Littlebourne, Beakesbourne, Patricksbourne, and Bridge, at the time of Julius Cæsar's expedition was a considerable branch of the large estuary, leading through the central vale from Rutupiæ (Sandwich) to Ashford. In the reign of Edward III, this branch had a sufficient depth of water to float one of their ships of war. He granted the privileges of the Cinque Ports to Beakesbourne, by a special writ for providing him a ship. Richard de Beches held lands, by grand sergeantry, for furnishing Henry III with a ship every time he crossed the seas. When the sea covered

Romney Marsh; there is nothing improbable in its having flowed up near Ashford, and (if it did) it entirely insulated the maritime states, as related by Cæsar."

The 'Encyclopædia Londinensis,' under the head of Holland, has the following remarks: "The estuaries of the Meuse and the Scheldt have also been opened to great inroads from the ocean; and the latter in particular, which anciently formed a mere delta, with four or five small branches, now presents the islands of Zealand and the most southern of those of Holland, divided by wide creeks of the sea. This remarkable irruption is supposed to have happened at the time that the Goodwin Sands arose, by the diffusion and consequent shallowness of the water. These great changes may be conceived to have made a slow and gradual progress; and none of them seem so ancient as the time of Charlemagne."

We have thus laid before our readers an account of some few changes which have taken place on the face of the globe, and shall now offer some remarks by way of elucidation; and first as relates to Medley. We have seen in the early part of this work that Medley rose into existence as early as the eighth century, soon after emerging from the water; I suppose timber must have grown upon it, so that in the latter part of the eleventh century, when Doomsday Book was written, there must have been sufficient to constitute the pannage for ten hogs, as therein specified. But how this timber was eventually destroyed I am unable to conjecture, unless the great inundation, which swept over Broomhill in the thirteenth century, also spread its devastating waves over the isle of Medley.

With regard to the trees found in Appledore Dowles, in the West Level, in the Military Canal, in the west of Sussex, and in the fens of Lincolnshire, one remark will apply to them all, which is this of Dugdale's: that at some very early period these spots were productive of vegetation, though they might not all be cultivated, at a much lower level than at present; that afterwards they were subjected to an inundation of the sea, and, after a lapse of time, were subsequently again rescued from the water and brought into cultivation. This double metamorphosis seems also to have taken place in the vast plain extending from the Ural Mountains to the Baltic and to the German Ocean. Previously to the flood which overwhelmed this plain, it must have been inhabited, or how otherwise could human skeletons and implements of labour have been found there? These were swept away by the flood; the flood abated, and dry land is again found on the same spot. This same flood probably forced its way into the German Ocean, through dry land, which is now the

Baltic Sea, and in the course of a few centuries this sea may once more become a cultivable spot of earth.

Then the great deserts of Tartary were a vast ocean; the Black Sea and the Mediterranean were solid earth; the bursting of the waters through those former barriers reversed the scene, and (as I have before observed) land became sea, and sea became dry land.

In remote ages, that is, previously to the eighth century, the spot known by the name of the Goodwin Sands was part of the ocean; shortly after this time, owing to an irruption of the sea upon some of the lands in Holland, the water was withdrawn from the former spot, and the Goodwin Sands began to appear above the waters, when they were, in all probability, embanked by Earl Goodwin, who gave his name to them; and they remained in this preserved state until the year 1097, when, we have seen (according to Boethius), they were again immersed, and have from that day to this formed once more a part of the great deep. And thus, as history bears us out in the assertion that such changes have actually taken place, we cannot be considered as drawing too largely on the faith of our readers, if we presume to conclude that Romney Marsh has really undergone the changes we have mentioned.

It now remains to add what little information has reached us respecting the marshes not strictly included in that of Romney; and here we find that in 17th Edward I, A.D. 1288, William Barry, of Rolvyndenne, complained that whereas one William de Potone, in respect of his lands lying within the Marsh of Newbrok and Rolvyndenne, near to the sea-coast, betwixt Smalhede and Mayhamme, ought to repair and maintain certain banks, &c., against the violence and rage of the sea, when the king constituted Henry de Appeltrefeld, Robert de Savaunz, and Henry de Ledes, his commissioners, to inquire into the truth of the complaint.

In 18th Edward I, A.D. 1289, on complaint of Osbert de Forsham, Hugh de Herindenne, and Eustace de Casinghamme, that whereas John Malemeins, by reason of his lands in Rolvyndenne aforesaid, lying near the sea-coast, between Mayhamme and Newindenne, ought to repair and maintain certain banks, &c. for the defence of the said lands, and the lands of others, against the force of the sea; the king appointed Henry de Apletrefeld and Bertram de Tancre to inquire into it. William de Barry of Rolvyndenne also made complaint against the said John Malemeins, who, by reason of his lands in Westbroke, ought to have repaired certain banks and ditches there, and neglected to do so, when the said Henry and Bertram were directed to examine into it.

In 20th Edward I, A. D. 1291, the king being informed that Richard Ferynge, parson of the church of Lymene, having, by reason of his lands and tenements belonging to his said church, at his own proper costs, repaired (and was still ready to do so) a certain bank at West Hythe, situate near the sea-coast, as often as need required, and that therefore he ought not to contribute to the repair of any other banks, forasmuch as neither he nor his predecessors, parsons of that church, had ever been accustomed to do; and that, nevertheless, John de Chert, bailiff of Romenhale Marsh, and the twenty-four jurats, had newly distrained him for the repair of the banks and ditches near the sea-coast at Appledore. Stephen de Pencestre and William de Echingham were made commissioners to see into it.

In 2d Edward II, A. D. 1308, Waresio de Valeyns, John de Malmeynes, and Henry de Worhope, were assigned to make inquiry of the banks, ditches, &c., in the Marshes of Mayhamme and Gatesdenne, upon the sea-coast betwixt Smallyde and Mayhamme, then wanting repair through the default of Raphe de Therdonne, Scoland de Forshamme, Thomas Fitz-Hubert of Hechyndenne, and Walter de Marcleshamme, who held lands in these Marshes.

In the year 1314, William de Basinges, William de Swantone, and William de Leteriche were constituted commissioners to oversee the banks, &c., in the Marshes of Romenale and Oxene.

In 1318, Edmund de Passele, William de Dene, and John de Ifeld, were assigned to take the like view near Newendene and Rolvyndene.

In 20th Edward II, the Prior of Belsyntone represented to the king, that whereas John Maunsell, the founder of the monastery, had given to their house the Manor of Over-Bilsyngtone, with its appurtenances, whereunto a certain salt marsh, situate in Lyde, near Romenale, containing 60 acres, did belong, which, both at the time of the said grant and since, had been always drowned by the flowings of the sea, humbly petitioned to be allowed to drain it, and defend it with banks, according to the marsh law. Whereupon the king issued forth a writ of *Ad quod damnum* to his escheator of the county, commanding him to inquire into it; upon which inquiry the jury certified upon their oaths that it might be done; and that the said marsh contained 240 perch in length, and 40 in breadth, and that it was of no value before the draining and banking; but that, being so banked and drained, it might be yearly worth thirty shillings, every acre prized at sixpence.

From the information here given we may gather that the sea

still flowed up as far as Newenden, or at all events between this place and Mayhamme, now called Maytham, the distance between which is very trifling. The embankments, I should suppose, commenced at the foot of the high grounds, and were carried out by little and little as the water receded, until the land was all inclosed, as we now see it, up to the very bank of the river. Maytham Hall, the property and residence of a branch of the Moneypenny family, is situated in the parish of Rolvenden, and no doubt derived its name from the same origin as that part of the marsh, which is thus designated at this day.

Among the commissioners appointed to inquire into the truth of the complaints made respecting the state of the banks, we find the names of Edmund de Passele and Osbert de Forshamme, the former the owner of the mansion of Mote, of which mention has already been made,—and the other of Forsham, to whose name I allude principally for the purpose of corroborating the opinion I have before hazarded, that Forsham Castle was built in the reign of Edward I, and that this Osbert was then the possessor of it. The two names further serve to show that the commissions were formed of men of rank and importance.

I shall now make some allusion to the sixty acres of land belonging to the Priory of Bilsyngtone which were banked and drained, and thus from a state of no value whatever were rendered worth thirty shillings a year, or sixpence per acre, a sum in our days scarcely worthy of notice, but, according to the different value of money at the two periods, may be considered equal to five shillings per acre, or fifteen pounds per annum.

By way of showing what part of the marshes was now inclosed, I shall give some account of the various commissions issued for their preservation.

In 1st Edward II, A.D. 1307, John Malemeyns, Lucas atte Gate, and Robert Paulyn were appointed to overlook the banks, &c., in the Marshes of Mayhamme and Losenhamme. This Lucas atte Gate I suppose to have been the possessor of the estate now in the hands of the executors of the late Francis Tress, Esq., of Northiam, and which is now known by the name of Gate Court.

In 1313, A.D., a commission was granted to John Malemeyns, of Stoke, Robert de Echynghamme, and Matthew de Knelle, for the banks on both sides of the river of Newendene, betwixt Maytham and Bodihamme Bridge.

In the name of Matthew de Knelle we recognise the existence of the Knell Estate, in the parish of Beckley, the property of Mrs. Curteis, of Windmill Hill.

In 10th Edward II, Robert de Bardelby, and Edmund de

Passcleye were commissioned to overlook the banks between Ridehulle, and the town of Roberts-brigge, on each side of the river Lymene.

In 14th Edward II, John de Ifeld, John de Malemeyns of Hoo, and Richard de Echinham were appointed to inspect the Marshes between the towns of Apuldre and Robertsbrigge, on each side of the said river of Lymene.

Here we find that, as late as the year 1320, the river was still known by the name of the Lymene.

In 17th Edward II, two more commissions were issued to view the same Marshes.

The commissions hitherto mentioned, have reference either to the Marshes in Kent alone, or to those adjoining in Kent and Sussex. I shall now call the reader's attention to some relating to Sussex alone.

In 31st Edward I A. D., 1302, the king being informed that the banks and ditches which had been made in Winchelsea, for the defence of his lands there, and the preservation of the adjacent parts, were then so broken by the overflowing of the sea, that the said lands were in danger of being drowned and lost, and that his tenants of those lands, by reason of a certain ancient composition made betwixt them and the tenants of other lands in that Marsh, which was, that the said king's lands should be defended in such reparations by the other landholders there, refused to contribute to the repair of those banks and ditches; and being also informed that the tenants of the other lands were unable to undergo these repairs, by reason of the great expense which would be requisite thereto. Taking care therefore of his own indemnity, and the preservation of those Marshes, he directed his precept to Thomas Alard, guardian of his lands of that Marsh, commanding him that he should, for the present occasion, cause an equal distribution to be made out of those his lands, according to a just and proportionable tax with the said other landholders, lest, for want thereof, a greater loss might afterwards happen, for which he, the said Thomas Alard, was to receive allowance out of the exchequer.

In the following year, on a view, it was found that the said Marsh of Winchelsea could not be defended by the old wall situate towards the east, and that if it ought to be defended, it would be necessary to have a certain new bank there of the length of 350 perches, and that the said new bank could not be made by those who, according to the ancient composition before mentioned, had wont to repair that old bank; forasmuch as they, who were in that sort liable to the repair of the said old bank, were not able, in regard of the diminution of their lands, to bear the whole charge thereof themselves, he therefore directed another precept to Thomas Alard, requiring him to take care that such contribution should be made thereto, out of his own lands, and the lands of others, as is above expressed; and hereupon the said king issued out a commission to Robert de Septem Vannis, William de Hastings, and Robert Paulyn, who had taken the view, to see that the contribution, which the said king's bailiff was to make therein, should be well and also faithfully assessed.

In 6th Edward III, A.D. 1332, Thomas de Faversham, Richard de Groshest, and Robert de Bataile were commissioned to view the banks in North Marsh, near Rye, and Spadelond Marsh, between Winchelsea and Danise Wall.

This North Marsh, I should suppose, was the first piece inclosed on the north side of the town of Rye, lying between Leesham Wall and the road leading from the land gate to the foot of Rye hill.

Being now arrived at the conclusion of our fourth head, we must pause awhile to take a retrospective view of the state of the country as it then was. Romney Marsh was now inclosed (with the exception of Dymchurch), and contained the parishes of Old Romney, New Romney, Hope, Ivychurch, Snave, Snargate, Brenzett, St. Mary's, Newchurch, Burmarsh, Orgerswyck, Eastbridge, Blackmanstone, and West Hythe. The Lymen ceased to flow under the Kentish hills. Since our last summary under the third head of our work, it assumed the name of Rumenea, on passing out to sea at New Romney, and its course was now diverted from this town, its mouth being more to the westward, and consequently nearer to the town of Rye. The course of the river being thus changed, Lyd ceased to be an island. Promhill had risen from the deep, and again been buried beneath it. Old Winchelsea had also experienced an ephemeral existence; but soon sank to rise no more.

Brookland and Fairfield had now made their appearance in Walland Marsh.

Considerable embankments had been made in what are now called the Upper Levels, that is to say, between the isle of Oxney and Robertsbridge, on either side of the river; some lands had also been inclosed near Rye and Winchelsea.

There was still a great pressure from the sea, the banks, as we have seen, requiring continual inspection; but still the work of embankment had made great progress, and from the point to which it had now attained there was no retrogression; but, on the contrary, a steady, though perhaps a slow, advance towards the completion of the vast work which we, in our days, have seen accomplished.

SECT. V.

The Changes which took place from the year 1334 to 1600; being a period of 266 years.

Having arrived at this stage of our journey, we have fewer difficulties to contend with; a greater light of information now breaking in upon us, and more numerous and more safe guides appearing to lead us on our way. In the conclusion of our last head we observed that the banks required continual inspection, and this observation will still apply to the onward progress of our work; in confirmation of which we shall proceed to lay before our readers some account of the many commissions which were issued for the purpose of surveying the various embankments with a view to their protection, and for which we are greatly indebted to Dugdale in his 'History of Imbanking and Draining.' But to begin: we find that in the 13th Edward III, A. D. 1339, in the month of April, a commission issued to Thomas de Brockhill, William de Oralston, Robert de Sharden, and Geffrey de Basham, for those banks on the sea-coast in the Marsh of Lyd near Romenhale, and in October (the first commission having taken place in April) of the same year, to the same parties touching those which lay betwixt the town of Romne and a certain place called Longerake, and betwixt the church of Lyde and the sea, within the town of Lyde.

In 18th Edward III, June 1344, Thomas de Brokhill, John de Erde, Thomas de Rethelin, and William Allen of Brokeland were commissioned to inspect the banks in Romenhale Marsh.

In 33d Edward III, A. D. 1359, grievous complaints were made of the daily liability of the Marsh of Romene being overflowed, in consequence of their lawful bailiff, one John atte Lose, being terrified by one Matthew at More, and others, who had chosen another bailiff, and hindered by them in his duty.

In 35th Edward III, A. D. 1361, Thomas de Lodelowe, Robert Belknap, and Thomas Colepeper were appointed to oversee the banks, and to make such new laws as were necessary, which, with the consent of the lords of the towns, the bailiff, 24 jurats, and commonalty of the said Marsh, they did as follows, viz.:

1st. That the common bailiff, who has lands and residence therein, should be elected by the public consent of the lords of the towns of the same Marsh, or their special attornies, which election to be made at Demecherche or Newcherche, or some other fit place within the compass of the said Marsh, on the fifteenth of St. Michael yearly, on summons of the before-specified bailiff, except, on necessity and reasonable cause, the said bailiff ought to be removed within that year, and another put in his place.

2d. And if the person elected refuse to act, to be fined forty shillings, and then a new bailiff to be chosen who will undergo the office, and he then to receive for his fee the double of all the money assessed upon any whatsoever for their negligence. And if the bailiff is hindered, the parties so hindering him to be severally punished by the said electors, in such sort as the said bailiff would have been if he had refused to take his oath and bear the same office.

3d. If the person chosen bailiff be absent, his goods and chattels to be distrained by the preceding bailiff, and impounded until he shall repair to the Archbishop of Canterbury, the Abbot of St. Augustine's, and the Prior of Christ Church, or to one of them, and take his oath of office.

4th. That the collectors and expenditors do make account of their receipts, and that any jurat being absent, without reasonable excuse, be fined twelve pence.

5th. Vacancies to be supplied within the year, of any jurat, collector, or expenditor.

6th. Jurats elected and not acting, to be fined twenty shillings.

7th. Every jurat refusing to come when summoned to the common or several Last, so that a sufficient number are not present, to be fined six pence, the bailiff to account for the same at the principal Last.

8th. Jurats to be sworn to act justly.

9th. Collectors and expenditors the same.

10th. The bailiff the same.

11th. No man henceforth to make any dams, or fords, or other impediments in any water-gangs, &c., whereby the right course may be hindered.

12th. Proclamation to be made in certain places, of any tax to be assessed, and when.

13th. That any land, wanted for banks, ditches, water-gangs, &c., be bought at forty shillings per acre, and no workman to be taken away, while any of these works are going on, under a penalty of ten shillings.

14th. That the water shall not be diverted from its regular channel to the damage of any man, but upon penalty of the value thereof.

15th. The bailiff and jurats to have their expenses paid in

going to other places, in consequence of all the maritime lands, from the Isle of Thanet unto Pevense, as well in Kent as Sussex, being under the customs of Romene Marsh.

16th. If any man rescue a distress, he shall be fined forty shillings.

In 43d Edward III, A. D. 1369, Thomas de Lodelowe, Robert Belknap, John Woodhall, Roger Dygge, William Topclive, and William Horne were constituted commissioners to overlook the banks and ditches.

In 48th Edward III, A. D. 1374, William Latymer (Constable of Dover Castle and Warden of the Cinque Ports), Thomas Reynes (his Lieutenant), Roger Dygge, and some others, were assigned by the king to view the banks, water-courses, &c., lying betwixt the towns of Hethe and Newenden; by which commission they had power to impress as many carpenters and other labourers as they should deem necessary for the accomplishment of the work in hand, wheresoever they could be found within the county of Kent.

In the same year Robert Belknappe, Roger Dygge, William Horne, and others, were appointed commissioners for the Marshes in Romene, Promhelle, and Newendene.

In 49th Edward III, A.D. 1375, Robert Belknappe, Thomas Reynes (Lieutenant of Dover Castle and Warden of the Cinque Ports), with Roger Dygge, and others, were appointed for those banks extending from the town of Hethe to Romeney, and thence to Promhull and Apuldre.

In the same year Sir John de Cobham, knt., John de Sudbury, William Toppeclive, and others, for the banks, &c., in the Marsh called Court Broke, in the Isle of Oxene.

We have now brought down to the end of the reign of Edward III all the commissions issued for Kent alone, and shall now add those which combine marshes in Kent and Sussex, and those relating to Sussex alone, but previously thereto shall insert the particulars of the grant of the old bed of the Rother, from Appledore to Romney, which was made to certain parties therein specified.

In 11th Edward III, A.D. 1337, upon a writ of *ad quod damnum*, the jury asserted that it would not be prejudicial to the king or any other, if licence were given to John Archbishop of Canterbury, and the Prior of Christ Church, Canterbury, to suffer an ancient trench leading from an arm of the sea, called Apuldre, towards the town of Romeney, which passed through the proper soil of the said Archbishop and Prior, and which was then newly so obstructed by the sea-sands, that ships could not pass thereby to the said town of Romeney as they had used to do, to be wholly stopped up and filled, so that they might make their benefit thereof, as they thought fit, in regard that there then was a certain other trench leading from the said arm unto Romeney, lately made by the force of the sea, by which boats and ships might pass without impediment to the town, as they had wont to do by the other, before it was filled up. And they said, moreover, that the said ancient trench was the proper soil of the Archbishop, Prior, and Margaret de Basinges, and that it had been obstructed in such a sort by the space of thirty years and more, then last past, by silt and sea-sand, as that ships could not conveniently pass that way, and that the new trench was more proper and sufficient while it was open than the said old one for the passage of ships to Romeney above mentioned, and did so remain at that time; and, moreover, that the same new trench was the soil of the said Archbishop, Prior, and Covent, Margaret de Basynges, and the Abbot of Robertsbridge. And, lastly, that the said old trench contained in length 700 perches, and in breadth 10 perches; and the new one 500 perches in length and 20 in breadth.

We now proceed to the examination of the commissions above alluded to, where we learn that, about the beginning of Edward III, it being found, by an inquisition taken before William Trussel, the king's escheator on this side Trent, that the channel of a certain river running betwixt the lands of Geffrey de Knelle and Isabell Aucher, between a certain place called Knellesflete, in the confines of these counties, and the town of Robertsbrigge, was so much enlarged by the flowing of the sea-tides into it, that 650 acres, part belonging to the said Geffry and part to others, were thereby totally drowned and consumed. And that a certain causey, which is the common highway between the land of John de la Gate, in Sussex, and the bridge of Newenden, as also the said bridge, were broken and demolished by those tides; and, moreover, that divers lands in the said parts would, in a short time, be drowned and destroyed, except a speedy remedy were had; and likewise that it would not be to the damage or prejudice of the said king, or any other, if he did grant licence to the said Geffry and Isabel, and to other persons having lands contiguous to those places, to exclude the said tides, and to raise a bank at Knelle-flete aforesaid, between the lands of the said Geffry and Isabel, in that place, to resist the tides, for the preservation of the lands, way, and bridge, to the end that the ancient course of that river be preserved by sufficient gutters, placed in that bank; and that unless it were by such an exclusion of the tides, by making such bank, that the said lands, &c. could not be in safeguard. The king, therefore, being careful in all respects to provide for the defence of this his realm, as was fit, granted licence to the said Geffry and Isabel, as also to all those who were likely to have benefit by that exclusion, that they should raise a certain bank at Knellesflete, before mentioned, for that purpose, and to make sufficient gutters therein for the issuing out of the said fresh water, and to repair the same banks and sluices, being so made, when and as often as need should require.

Edward the Third, in the tenth year of his reign, A.D. 1336, constituted William of Orlauston, Thomas de Gillingham, Stephen de Padiham, and John de Betenham to take view of the above bank and sluices, which had been erected under the superintendence of Roger de Bavent, Roger de Hegham, Thomas de Lincoln, and William de Northo, but were then in decay.

In 10th Edward III, A.D. 1336, William de Robertsbrigge, William de Recolvere, Joceline de Gatele, and Robert Bataille were appointed to oversee the making of certain sluices, banks, and gutters (for the safeguard of lands) in the towns of Wightresham, Idene and Pesemershe, and to assess all such as had lands in those parts, which were to take benefit therefrom.

In 22d Edward III, A.D. 1348, there being a petition presented to the king, on behalf of James de Echingham, importing that those lands, that is, of Geffrey de Knelle and Isabell Aucher, might have been preserved by the repair of the old banks on the verge of that river, and that the bank made by virtue of the said king's letters patent (which thwarted the stream) was raised, as well to the damage of the king as of him, the said James, forasmuch as thereby such ships and boats, which had used to pass with victual and other things from divers places in these counties of Kent and Sussex, unto his manor of Echingham through this channel, were then hindered; as also the destruction of his market town of Salehurst, situate upon the said river, and of his market there, which, by the course of that water, had been supported; and out of which he and his ancestors had used to receive tolls and commodities. The king, therefore, taking the same into consideration, and that the said James was no party to the above-specified inquisition, nor at all called at the taking thereof, did revoke his said letters patent, and command that the said bank should be demolished; and desiring to be certified whether the said lands might be preserved by the repair of those old walls on the verge of the stream or not; and whether the said bank, so raised, although that stream were to his damage, or that of any other person, did by his letters patent, dated April 8th, 1348, assign John de Strode, John de Ore, Robert de Sharndene, and Philip en la Wyke, to inquire and certify the truth thereof.

In 24th Edward III, A.D. 1350, Thomas de Passele, Thomas de Pympe, Stephen Scappe, William de Haldene, and William de Wystresham were appointed to take a view of the same.

In 25th Edward III, A.D. 1351, Stephen Scappe, William de Wightresham, William de Pageham, and Stephen Donet, for the repairs of banks, &c. in Promhill Marsh, between Long Shotteswall and Westhevedes Wall, Newlandeswall and Scallotes Walls, in the confines of these counties, (that is, of Kent and Sussex.)

In 27th Edward III, A.D. 1353, William de Clinton, Earl of Huntingdon, William Fifhide, Reginald del Dik, John de Ore, Stephen Scappe, and John de Hodlegh, between Apuldre and Robertsbrigge.

In 28th Edward III, A.D. 1354, Stephen de Valoignes, William Waver, John Brode, Stephen Scappe, and William de Wightresham, for Promhill Marsh.

In 30th Edward III, A.D. 1356, complaints were made that sums of money had been collected for the repairs of banks, &c. between Hethe, near Saltwood, in Kent, and Lewes in Sussex, and had been kept by the collectors themselves, so that the banks, &c. were out of repair; letters patent were granted to Geffrey de Scey, Raphe de Frenyngham, William de Fifhide, and others, to inquire into the same.

In 37th Edward III, A.D. 1363, a commission was granted to Robert Belknap; William Haldene, William Topclive, Henry Gosebourne, and John Lyvet, for Promhill Marsh.

In 38th Edward III, A.D. 1364, to Sir Andrew Sakevill, knt., William Haldene, and William Batesford, between Hastings and Newenden.

In 40th Edward III, A.D. 1366, Robert Bealknap, William Haldene, William Horne, Robert de Ore, and John Lyvet, for Wightresham, Ebbene, Stone in Oxene, and Idenne.

In 42d Edward III, A.D. 1368, to Thomas de Lodelowe, Robert Bealknap, William Batesford, and others, for Promhill.

In 44th Edward III, A.D. 1370, to Thomas de Lodelowe, Robert Bealknap, John Colepeper, William Horne, Roger Ashburnham, Robert Echyngham, John Edward, and John Broke.

The following commissions relate to Rye and Winchelsea principally.

In 8th Edward III, A.D. 1334, William de Robertsbrigge, Robert de Shardenne, and Robert de Bataille were appointed commissioners to view the banks and water-gangs in North

Mershe, near Rye, and in the Marsh called Spadelond, between Wynchelse and Danise Wall, and in other marshes adjoining; and they found that there were 128 acres of land in the said Marsh, belonging to the king's manor of Ihamme, and that his bondsmen held of him 30 acres, called Spadelond, in the said Marsh; also that the said king's lands, and the lands of others, could not be preserved, except a contribution were made out of them for necessary charges tending to their safeguard. The king, therefore, consented his lands should be assessed.

In 16th Edward III, A.D. 1342, a precept was issued to John Clynde, the bailiff of the king's manor of Ihamme, to repair the banks in North Mersh and Spadelond, as they were for the most part very ruinous.

In 19th Edward III, A.D. 1345, a fresh precept was issued to Stephen Padiham (bailiff of Ihamme), to repair the last-mentioned banks.

In 25th Edward III, A.D. 1351, John de Ore, Stephen de Horsham, Robert Arnald, and William de Pageham were appointed commissioners to view the banks, &c., between Wynchelse and Danneswalle, and between Pyhammyl and Treeherie, which, through the force of great tempests, were broken and decayed, so that the town of Wynchelse and the parts adjoining were likely to be 'depauperated.'

In 40th Edward III, A.D. 1366, Raph Spigurnell, Robert Bealknapp, Andrew de Guldeford, and others, were assigned to view and repair those marshes within the liberty of the town of Rye, towards the east, unto the king's highway, which leadeth from Pladen to Rye, and towards the south, to the said town of Rye, and towards the west, to the sea-bank called Melflet, and towards the north, to the lands which are called Bernardeshille, from Kyngeswyst.

In 44th Edward III, A.D. 1370, Godfrey Folejaumbe, Robert Belknapp, Roger Ashburnham, and others, were appointed to view and repair the banks between the towns of Borne and Rye.

In the same year 1370, the king being informed that the burghers of Wynchelse had, for the advantage of that town, and advantage of the whole country, built a certain bridge at Pypewell, over a water called the channel of Wynchelse, on the said king's soil, on both sides of the water, for the passage of people and all carriages, which was not done at little charge. And that, by the violence of the tides and floods of fresh water passing to the sea, the said bridge and banks on each side of the said water, between the said town of Wynchelse and the towns of Odymere and Rye, were so broken down and ruined, and all the highways about the said town of Wynchelse so overflowed, that scarce any one could come in or out thereof; he granted commission to the Abbot of Bataille, Thomas de Reyns (Lieutenant to the Constable of Dover Castle), William Batesford, Roger de Ashburnham, and others, to view the said bridge and banks, and to take order for the repairing of them.

Having now recorded the numerous commissions issued, previous to and during the reign of Edward III, we conceive this to be a proper time at which to offer some remarks on the various records we have made.

The first commission which we find on record, is the one issued to Henry de Bathe, Nicholas de Hanlon, and Alured de Dene, who made the celebrated ordinances by which Romney Marsh was then to be governed, and by which in after times all the other Marshes of the kingdom were and are regulated to this day. Though this commission was issued in the 42d Henry III, A.D. 1257, the commissioners allude even at that time to customs much more ancient by which the Marsh of Romney had been previously governed; but these customs not having the full sanction of law, the king appointed this commission for the purpose of giving this sanction, and accordingly these ordinances, thus framed, have indisputably ruled the Marsh from that time to this.

From this time to the end of the reign of Edward III, being a period of 110 years, numerous commissions, as we have seen, were issued, serving to show that the Marshes, being only partially inclosed, were much exposed to the violence of the sea, and, consequently, continually requiring supervision. At this early period the Marshes were not placed under regular commissions as they are at present, and therefore, when the banks and ditches required repairs, complaints, I suppose, were made on the part of those owners or occupiers who felt themselves aggrieved, through the king's officers to the king himself, who, as he considered necessary, appointed a commission to view and repair the parts which were suffering from the neglect of the parties whose business it was to keep them in good order; but who, either from unwillingness or from inability, refused to do so.

There seems some difficulty in thoroughly understanding the exact power which was possessed by the persons who were appointed to carry the ordinances of Henry de Bathe into effect; for though a certain method seems laid down in them for the superintendence and the keeping in repair of the banks, ditches, and water-gangs, still we find that commissions were continually issued by the sovereign, for the time being, to repair to the Marsh to survey the banks, &c., and to order the necessary works to be done. There do not seem, down to this period at least, to have been regularly appointed commissioners, who, officiating as they now do by virtue of an Act of Parliament, are always on the spot, holding regular meetings, and thus always prepared to act as any emergency may require.

As regards the changes which had now taken place by the recession of the sea, we may observe that the old bed of the Rother, from Appledore to Romney, was now entirely abandoned, and the soil granted to the Archbishop of Canterbury, the Prior of the Covent of Christ Church, in the same city, to Margaret de Basynges, and the Abbot of Robertsbridge.

The next thing worthy of observation is, that it appears certain lands had, previously to the time of which we are now treating, been preserved from the sea between the spot which was then known by the name of Knellesflete, and now by that of Knell-Dam, and the road leading from Northiam to Newenden Bridge, which had then been raised, and was known by the name of a causey. It also further appears that the sea, at the beginning of the reign of Edward III, broke into these lands, and that the king was requested, in order to secure their subsequent safety, to allow a sluice to be placed across the river Rother, near to Knellesflete, with which request the king complied, and thus more than 500 years ago was the first sluice erected on the Rother, and the first foundation laid of the many disputes which have since arisen on the question of the legality of such erections, and which question has caused the expenditure of so many thousands of pounds.

In the 10th year of this king's reign, we already find the sluice was fallen into decay, and in the 22d, that James de Echingham complained that, by thus stopping the navigation of the river, he was seriously injured, inasmuch as vessels could no longer pass up it to the town of Salehurst, wherein he held a market, from which he received tolls and commodities. In consequence of this remonstrance, the sluice was demolished, and we thus further learn that vessels at this period still navigated the river as high up as Robertsbridge.

In the preceding account we recognise the names of Geffrey de Knelle and John de la Gate, the remembrance of which is still retained in the two estates of Knell and Gate Court, adjoining each other, the former in the parish of Beckley, and the latter in that of Northiam.

In the year 1332, I find mention is made of North Mersh, near Rye, and of a Marsh called Spadelond, between Wynchelse and Danise Wall; and again in 1342, as requiring repairs to their walls; but where the exact position of Spadelond was, I am unable to say; though the North Marsh (as I have before stated) was the first of those inclosed at the back of the town of Rye.

In 1366, the Marshes at the back of the town of Rye, commonly known by the name of the Corporation Marshes, had been inclosed; by the boundaries then set forth, it appears that a highway led from Playden to the town, through what is now called Landgate; this road was liable then, and for many years afterwards, to be overflowed by the sea, but was at this period, in all probability, improved from its original state; as it was in the reign of Edward III that the town was walled in, and this road formed the principal entrance, leading from the high land to the beautiful gateway which was then erected, and which still constitutes the greatest ornament of the place. The town then, as now, formed the southern boundary: where Melflet the western boundary stood, I do not know, unless the present wall, which still preserves them from the overflowing of the river on the west, be it; and this I think is by no means improbable, making due allowance for such changes as the lapse of years never fails to bring upon all the works of man, however durable. The northern boundary was doubtless then what it is now, the hills facing Rye in that direction, then known by the name of Bernardeshill. But the description concludes with the expression from Kingeswyst; and the question arises, where was Kingeswyst, and what is the meaning of the concluding words, Bernardeshill from Kingeswyst? The only answer which seems to me applicable is this: adjoining the southwest corner of the marshes of which we are now treating is a spot, without the walls of the town, called the Wish, and this part was formerly called the Wish Ward. Further, I find by Jacob, in his Law Dictionary, that the word Wista signified among the Saxons a measure of land, containing half a hide. This part being, at the time we are speaking of, most probably uninclosed, might be considered as the property of the king, and be called Kingeswyst, that is, the King's Wista; while the change from Wista to Wish is sufficiently probable to connect the spot, known in 1366 by the name of Kingeswyst, with the spot now known in 1838 by that of the Wish.

The last point on which I wish to observe here, is the case of the Winchelsea road, which happened in the year 1370. From this we learn that the communication between Rye and Winchelsea at that time was by means of a bridge over the river, then known by the name of the channel of Winchelsea, and now by that of the Brede river. This is the same bridge which is still in existence, called the Ferry-bridge; the road over it leads to Udimore, and thence to Rye; and this was the only one at that period; for the sea then, and for some centuries afterwards, flowed up between the towns of Winchelsea and Rye, preventing all communication by land in this quarter.

Perhaps it may not be altogether uninteresting to notice the names of the various persons who, at different times, filled the office of commissioners up to this period; for, as the commissions seem to have been composed of the leading men of the adjoining counties of Kent and Sussex, it may hence be seen what were the then leading families, and whether any of their descendants remain to this day.

We shall arrange them alphabetically, under the respective kings in whose reigns their names appear, and of course shall begin with

HENRY III.

Bathe, Henry de.
Dene, Alured de.
Hanlon, Nicholas de.

Henry de Bathe was a celebrated justice itinerant, who was appointed by Henry III to frame that code of laws which has from that time to this governed Romney Marsh, and which has since become the basis of the laws, by which all the other marshes of the kingdom have been regulated.

In the "Roll of Battle Abbey," which contains a list of the names of the Norman gentry who came into England with William the Conqueror, we find that of Dine; but, whether Alured de Dene, which is but a slight corruption in the spelling, and which gives the true French pronunciation, was one of this family, we will not take upon ourselves to say. We will only observe, that Horsfield, in his 'History of Sussex,' mentions a family of the name of Dyne, who, at the commencement of the seventeenth century, were possessors of the manor of Longhurst, in the parish of Westfield, and which is now held by Musgrave Brisco, Esq., into whose family it came by the marriage of his father with one of the Dynes. The manor of Buckhurst, in Withyham, was held by Ralph de Dene when Doomsday Book was made.

EDWARD I.

Apuldrefield, Henry de.
Etchingham, William de.
Ledes, Henry de.
Lovetot, John de.
Pencestre, Stephen de.
Savauuz, Robert de.

Henry de Apuldrefield doubtless took his name from his residence at Apuldrefield, the present Appledore.

The family to which William de Etchingham belonged was one of great note. Simon de Etchingham was Sheriff of Kent and Sussex in the 18th Henry III. His successors, William and Robert, were summoned to parliament from the 5th to the 15th of Edward II; and the William de Etchingham, of whom we are speaking, was, we presume, the same person who was called to parliament by Edward II, and thus assumed the title of baron.

Henry de Ledes may have been the proprietor of Leeds Castle in Kent.

Of John de Lovetot and Robert de Savauuz I can say nothing.

Stephen de Pencestre was the owner of the present Penshurst, near Tunbridge, and which was formerly called Penchester, as well as Penshurst. Peneshurste Place, in the reign of Edward I, was possessed by Sir Stephen de Peneshurste (Constable of Dover Castle).

EDWARD II.

Basinges, William de.
Bardelby, Robert de.
Bataille, Robert de.
Cotes, William de.
Cobham, Stephen de.
Dene, William de.
Echingham, Richard de.
Echingham, William de.
Echingham, Robert de.
Feversham, Thomas de.
Filoll, John.
Gate, Lucas atte.
Ifeld, John de.
Knelle, Matthew de.
Leteriche, William de.
Malmeyns, John de.
Passele, Edmond de.
Paulyn, Robert de.
Robertsbrigge, William de.
Shardon, Henry de.
Swantone, William de.
Tancrey, Bertram de.
Valeyns, Waresio de.
Worhope, Henry de.

William de Basinges was of a family of some note, as we find in the year 1337, that Margaret de Basinges was considered one of the parties who was entitled to a share of the old channel-bed leading from Appledore to Romney, the other two parties entitled being the Archbishop of Canterbury and the Prior of Christ-Church, in the same city.

Robert de Bataille was, I suppose, a resident and proprietor of the town of Battle, from which he took his name.

Stephen de Cobham was the proprietor of Cobham, near Rochester, in which parish is situated Cobham Hall, the seat of the Earl of Darnley.

William de Dene was of the same family as Alured de Dene, before mentioned.

The Echinghams still continued to be an influential family, as we find three of them named in this reign.

Thomas de Feversham, to judge from his name, must have lived at Feversham in Kent.

John Filoll—is it conjecturing too much that he was of a family that came into England with William the Conqueror—as we find in the Battle Abbey list the name of Filioll?

Lucas atte Gate was the proprietor of Gate Court in the parish of Northiam, and of which mention has been before made; but of this name I wish to say a few words before I dismiss it. It will not have escaped the observant reader that the affix to the other names is *de*, whereas to this one it is *atte*. This latter word is Saxon, signifying at, that is, Lucas at Gate; while de is French and means of, as Thomas de Bataille—Thomas of Battle. Now this Lucas, prefixing atte instead of de to his place of residence, would seem to imply one of two things—either that the family of this Lucas was Saxon, and had retained their old name, or that the Saxon names had again begun to revive after a lapse of more than 200 years.

John de Ifeld was the possessor of Ifeld, the modern Isfield near Lewes, in Sussex.

Matthew de Knelle possessed the estate of Knell in the parish of Beckley, Sussex, now the property of Mr. Curteis of Windmill Hill.

William de Leteriche.

John de Malmeynes was of a family which came in with the Conqueror, and afterwards possessed property in Rolvenden, as appears from a complaint made against a John de Malmeynes in the year 1289.

Edmond de Passele was the same man to whom Edward I granted the privilege of embattling his mansion of Mote in the parish of Iden, A.D. 1283.

Of Robert de Paulyn I can say nothing.
William de Robertsbrigge was resident at Robertsbridge.
Henry de Shardon.
Swantone, William de.
Bertram de Tancrey.
Waresio de Valeyns was probably of the family called, in the Roll of Battle Abbey, Valence.
Henry de Worhope.

EDWARD III.

Allen, William, of Brookland.
Arnald, Robert.
Ashburnham, Roger.
Basham, Geffrey de.
Bataille, Abbot of.
Bataille, Robert.
Batesford, William.
Belknap, Robert.
Betenham, John de.
Brockhill, Thomas de.
Brode, John.
Colepeper, Thomas.
Cobham, Sir John de, Knt.
Clinton, William de, Earl of Huntingdon.
Colepeper, John.
Dygge, Roger.
Donet, Stephen.
Dik, Reginald del.
Erde, John de.
Fifhide, William.
Freningham, Raphe de.
Faversham, Thomas de.
Folejaumbe, Godfrey.
Groshest, Richard de.
Gosebourne, Henry.
Guldeford, Andrew de.
Gatele, Jocelyn de.
Gillingham, Thomas de.
Horne, William.
Haldene, William de.
Hodlegh, John de.
Horsham, Stephen de.
Lyvet, John.

Latymere, William (Constable of Dover Castle, and Warden of the Cinque Ports).
Lodelowe, Thomas de.
Orlauston, William de.
Ore, John de.
Pageham, William de.
Passele, Thomas de
Pympe, Thomas de.
Padiham, Stephen de.
Rethelin, Thomas de.
Reynes, Thomas, (Lieut. to the Constable of Dover Castle.)
Recolvere, William de.
Shardon, Robert de.
Sudbury, John de.
Strode, John de.
Scappe, Stephen.
Say, Geffrey de.
Sackville, Sir Andrew, Bart.
Spigurnell, Raph.
Topclive, William.
Valoignes, Stephen de
Woodhall, John.
Wyke, Philip en la.
Wystresham, William de.
Waver, William.

William Allen of Brookland, Robert Arnald, and several other names in this last list, thus simply written without the De affixed to the Christian name, serve to show, either that a change was now taking place in the way of writing persons' names, and thus that an approximation was making towards the modern fashion; or else, that persons of smaller note were already admitted into the commissions appointed for the management of the affairs of the Marshes.

Roger Ashburnham was an ancestor of the present family of this name, one of whom was Sheriff of Kent, Sussex, and Surrey, and Constable of Dover Castle, which he stoutly defended on the landing of William the Conqueror.

Geffrey de Basham, we suppose, resided at Bosham, near Chichester; and the old mode of spelling it (Basham) seems to strengthen the story, that it was originally presented to an ecclesiastic for a kiss, which, in the Norman language then used, is Baiser; whence comes Basham—the village of the kiss, —now converted into Bosham.

Robert Belknap was of a family which came in with the Conqueror, and they formerly possessed the estate of Knell, in the parish of Beckley.

John de Betenham, Thomas de Brockhill.

John Brode was probably of Brede, as I think I have somewhere seen this place spelt Brode in ancient times.

Thomas Colepeper. This family was of great note for many generations in the county of Sussex, having possessed property in Salehurst, Folkington, and Ardingly.

The Cobhams we have before noticed

William de Clinton, Earl of Huntingdon. The family of Clinton is descended from William, Chamberlain of Normandy, whose three sons came over to England with William the Conqueror; they took their name from the lordship of Climpton, now Glimpton, in Oxfordshire. This William, who served Edward III in his wars in Scotland and France, was, by that Prince, constituted Lord High Admiral of England, July 16th, 1333, and was created Earl of Huntingdon, March 16th, 1337. This family is now merged in that of Clinton, Duke of Newcastle.

Thomas de Gillingham was most probably from Gillingham, near Strood, in Kent.

Andrew de Guldeford was of a family of great property and influence for some centuries after this time, in this part of the country, having resided in the parish of Rolvenden, in Kent, in one of the windows of the church of which are the effigies of Sir John Guldeford; and having, in all probability, given their name to the parish of East Guldeford, where they held a large tract of land.

William de Haldene was of Halden Place, near Tenterden, in the parish of Rolvenden; and the Haldens and Guldefords intermarried with each other.

John de Hodlegh was of Hadlow, Kent.

Stephen de Horsham, of Horsham, Sussex.

William Latymere (Constable of Dover Castle and Warden of the Cinque Ports). The Latymers were a family of great note, and it is to them that "Latimers," the seat of the Hon. Charles Compton Cavendish, M.P. for East Sussex, owes its name. The name of Latomere appears in the Battle Roll.

In the parish of Selmeston, about seven miles from Lewes, is the manor of Ludlay; but whether Thomas de Lodelowe took his name from thence, we will not take upon ourselves decidedly to say, leaving it to others to form their own opinion on the matter.

William de Orlaustone was from the modern Orlestone, in Kent.

John de Ore, from Ore, near Hastings, Sussex.

William de Recolvere, of Reculvers, near Margate, in Kent.

John de Strode was of Strood, Kent.

Geffrey de Say. The family of Say came in with the Conqueror. Geffrey (this very man) fought with Edward I, in his Scotch wars, and was summoned to parliament in the first year of the reign of Edward III.

Sir Andrew Sackville, Bart. The Sackvilles descended from the Norman chief, Bertrand de Sachavilla, who came over with William the Conqueror, and who resided for six centuries at Buckhurst House, in the parish of Withyham, in the county of Sussex.

Ralph Spigurnell. The name of this family is given by Stowe, in his list of noblemen and gentlemen who came over with the Conqueror.

Stephen de Valoignes may be the same as Valeyns, mentioned in the last reign,

Philip en la Wyke.

William de Wytresham came from the present Wittersham, in Kent.

On reference to the commission issued in 48th Edward III, we find that power was given to impress so many carpenters and other labourers as should be considered necessary for the accomplishment of the works ordered to be done. In ancient times, it appears that the king had power, not only to impress seamen, but also men for the land service, and likewise for the king's own pleasure, and to attend on his person. It was under this power, that these carpenters and other workmen were impressed,—a power which happily now no longer exists.

It was in the reign of Edward III, (if I rightly understand Lambard), that a beacon was first erected on the Ness Point. His words are these: "Before this neshe lieth a flat into the sea, threatening great danger to unadvised sailors. In the reign of Edward III it was first ordered that beacons in this country should have their pitch-pots, and that they should no longer be made of wood-stacks or piles, as they be yet in Wiltshire and elsewhere." This must imply that either a beacon was now first erected on the Ness Point, or that there had previously been one composed of wood, and for which a pitch pot was now introduced as being considered preferable. In either case it militates against the assertion of Jeake, that Dengeness Light was first projected by Mr. Allen, a goldsmith, of Rye, in the reign of James I. I should be extremely happy, for the sake of my adopted town, that Jeake should have been correct; but I fear such is not exactly the case, unless he means to say that Allen first projected the modern lighthouse; but this cannot be the case, because this was only erected in 1792, previous to which time it was an open light consisting of a raised platform on which were nightly burned a heap of coals, which gave a very uncertain light, as when stirred they emitted a bright blaze, and then sunk almost into utter darkness until again roused by the attendants, whose business it was to attend the fire. We have seen that originally the light was composed of wood stacks, then pitch pots were introduced, to these succeeded coals on an open platform (and this probably was the light to which Jeake referred, for his work was written in 1678, and he died shortly after.) And lastly came the modern lighthouse.

It is during the reign of Edward III that we first meet with the name of Dymchurch. In the commission granted to Thomas Lodelow and others bearing date A. D. 1359, being the 33d of that king's reign, it is ordered that the assemblies shall be held at Demecherch or Newcherch. How long previous to this time Dymchurch was rescued from the sea it may not be easy exactly to decide, but from the information I have obtained from a source to be depended on, we may conclude that the church was built at the commencement of the twelfth century, and if so, the wall known by the name of Dymchurch Wall, and which protects the greater part of Romney Marsh from inundation must have been erected at a period even anterior to that, inasmuch as the church stands on a spot of ground which (were it not for the wall) must have been under water at spring tides.

We here close the reign of Edward III, which extends to the year 1377, and proceed to that of Richard II, in the first year of which I find that Richard de Horne, Stephen Bettenham, John Fraunceys, and Hamon Wodeman were put in commission to supervise the banks from Hethe all along the sea-coast to Apuldre, as also in other marshes within this county from the haven of Romney to Promhill Church, and thence by the sea-coast to Apuldre, they being at that time in decay in sundry places thereof.

In the same year, William Horne, Stephen Bettenham, and John Fraunceys, for Ebbenesbrok and Sharlee.

In 3d Richard II, A. D. 1379, Robert Belknap, John Barry,

William Horne, William Makenade, Stephen Bettenham, Stephen Pestenden, and John Brode, were commissioned for the parishes of Stone, Witresham, Appuldore, and Snergate, in Kent, and of Idenne in Sussex.

In this same year, 1379, Richard II, upon complaint made to him by the commonalty of the town of Wynchelse, showing that there was a common way (called Copgreys) then lately leading from the said town to Battaile, as also a certain marsh, called Dynsdale, lying between the towns of Wynchelse and Hastings, which way and marsh, through the neglect of some persons who of right ought to repair and maintain them, were destroyed and overflowed by the sea, by the assent of his prelates, barons, &c., then sitting in parliament, assigned the Abbot of Battaile, Robert de Belknappe, and William de Batesford, to make view of the said way and marsh, and to inquire by the oaths of honest and lawful men, through whose default these damages had happened, and who had used and ought to repair them; and to compel them thereto in such sort as in Romeney Marsh in the like case had been accustomed. And, moreover, to do and perform all things therein, according to the laws and customs of Romeney Marsh aforesaid.

In 6th Richard II, A. D. 1382, the king directed his precepts to Adam de Limbergh, guardian of his manor of Iden, commanding him that out of the farm of the said manor he should cause the banks and ditches belonging thereto to be repaired, where need was, according to the judgment of honest and lawful men of those parts.

In 7th of Richard II a commission was granted to Robert de Ashton (Constable of Dover Castle), Robert Bealknapp, Sir Edward Dalingrugge, Knt., William de Horne, Peter Rede, and William Battlesford, for those banks, &c., in the towns of Idenne, Rye, Odymer, Brode, Farlegh, Pette, Wynchelse, Iclesham, Gestling, and Westfield.

In the same year, to Robert Bealknap, William de Halden, William de Horne, William Makenade, William Batesford and others, between Newenden and Etchingham. Also to Robert Belknap, William Horne, William Batesford, Stephen Betenham, William Makenade, William Brenchesle, and John Frauceys, between Robertsbrigge and Smallyde.

In 9th Richard II, A. D. 1385, William Horne, William Makenade, Stephen Betenham, and John Lyvet, were commissioned to view those banks between Fairfield and Apuldre, with power to take so many carpenters, with other artificers and labourers, as should be needful, at competent wages.

In 13th Richard II, John Wadham, William Horne and

others, betwixt Fairfield, Apuldre, and Snargate, then broken with the violence of the tide.

In the same year, John Devereux (Constable of Dover Castle, and Warden of the Cinque Ports), Thomas de Hungerford, William Rikhill, William de Horne and others, between Bourne in Sussex, and Apuldre in Kent.

In 14th Richard II, Sir Thomas Colepepper, Knt., William Rikhill, Roger Ashburnham, Stephen Bettenham, and John Edwards, for those banks between Kentbrigge and Newenden, then much broken by the violence of the sea.

In 17th Richard II, William Rikhill, William Brenchesle, Vincent Fynche, Robert Oxenbrigge, and John Lynot, for Farlegh, Pette, Gestlyng, Brede, Westfield, and Odymere.

In 22d Richard II, A. D. 1398, Stephen Betenham, Robert Oxenbrigge, William Berton, and Thomas Ikham, between the town of Ebbene in Oxene, and the town of Brensete.

Richard II confirmed the ordinances of Henry de Bathe, and also, at the request of the inhabitants of the marsh, granted to the twenty-four jurats, and bailiff, and their successors, exemption from serving at any assizes or juries, inquisitions, or recognitions, as well within the County of Kent as out of it, (excepting in what should relate to the said king and his heirs,) from being shrieve, escheator, bailiff, collector of tenths or fifteenths, or of any other subsidy, charge, tax, or tollage, to be granted to him or his heirs. And the reason assigned for this privilege was, that by their absence the whole marsh (as he had been informed) might be overflowed in a very short time, and so utterly lost and destroyed, to the infinite peril and damage of all his liege people in those parts.

I shall now draw my reader's attention to some of the circumstances connected with the reign of Richard II, which ended in the year 1399; and the first thing to attract our notice is the name of Sharlee (now called Shirley) Moor, which now appears for the first time. This marsh lies at the back of Appledore, being in the several parishes of Appledore, Ebony, and Tenterden; it contains 1245 acres, and is about three miles in length and two in breadth.

The next thing is the destruction of the road leading from Winchelsea to Battle by the overflowing of the tide; this road, I apprehend, was the present one by the way of Icklesham; and the marsh called Dynsdale lay without the New Gate, near the road leading hence to Hastings; for there is still a marsh known by the name of the Dimsell, through which the military canal was cut. This matter seems to have been considered of some moment, as the king, on issuing his orders for the necessary repairs, took the advice of his parliament upon it.

Lastly, we find power was still given to take such workmen as were requisite for the performance of the repairs.

To the former names of commissioners already recorded I will now add the following, viz.:

>Ashton, Robert de, (Constable of Dover Castle.)
>Barry, John.
>Battlesford, William.
>Brenchesle, William.
>Berton, William.
>Dalingrugge, Sir Edward, Knt.
>Devereux, John, (Constable of Dover Castle and Warden of the Cinque Ports.)
>Edwards, John.
>Fraunceys, John.
>Fynche, Vincent.
>Hungerford, Thomas de.
>Ikham, Thomas.
>Lynot, John.
>Makenade, William.
>Oxenbrigge, Robert.
>Pestenden, Stephen.
>Rede, Peter.
>Rikhill, William.
>Wadham, John.
>Wodeman, Hamon.

Of these names there are not many of which I find anything to say.

Ashton, Robert de, having been Constable of Dover Castle, we may see that men of some note were still placed in the commissions.

Brenchesle, William, was probably of the modern Brenchley, not far from Tunbridge, in Kent.

Dalingrugge, Sir Edward, Knt., was of an illustrious family that then owned Bodiam Castle, which was built by them, and of whom I shall have more to say hereafter.

Fynche, Vincent. The family of Finch is descended from Henry Fitzherbert, Lord Chamberlain of the household to Henry I, and of this family is Finch, Earl of Winchelsea. This Fynche may or may not be of this family; but seeing that the family seat has for a very long time been in Kent, and that the title is that of Winchelsea, it is not improbable that they then possessed property, and, consequently, influence in the neighbourhood, which would lead to an appointment of this kind.

Oxenbrigge, Robert. The Oxenbrigges are a very old family who possessed Brede place and extensive lands in this parish at the time of which we are now speaking.

The erection of Bodiam Castle having taken place in the reign of Richard II, I shall proceed to mention a few particulars respecting it. It was built in the year 1386, by Sir Edward Dalingrugge, Knt., who is described as a valiant captain, having fought under Edward III.

In the public records of Richard II, bearing the date of 1386, is the following entry: " Quod Edwardus. Dalingrugge, Miles, possit divertere et tenere quendam cursum aquæ currentis de Dalyngrigstay in Villa de Salehurst usque ad molendinum suum de Bodyham;" which in English is—" That Edward Dalingrugge, Knight, may divert and retain a certain stream of water, running from Dalingrigstay in the Vill of Salehurst, close to his mill at Bodyham."

Just below the mound which incloses the moat of water on the south side, is at this time a piece of low pasture surrounded by four banks, and which is still called the Pond; this, probably, is the spot into which the proprietor, Sir Edward Dalingrugge was allowed to divert and there retain the stream of water mentioned in the grant above cited, and which then constituted the millpond wherein the water was collected for the purpose of turning the mill.

The sea had now, I presume, begun to partially leave the level above, and, at low water, the course of the Rother was here already traced out.

We have already seen that about a hundred years previous to the foundation of Bodiam Castle, that is to say in the year 1283, the mansion of Mote was embattled and fortified, we now find, in 1386, that the former was erected.

Bodiam has experienced a better fate than Mote, being still a fine and magnificent ruin. Grose describes the moat in his time as being overgrown with rushes and duckweed; it is now clear of these nuisances, and the whole building has undergone such valuable repairs as are necessary to its preservation, without deteriorating the silent grandeur of its antiquity, to which it owes its principal beauty. Every lover of the antique, every man who has a wish to see those characteristic features of English scenery, so strongly marked by the numerous mossy ruins, which point with silent hand to days that are long since passed—every man, I say, who wishes to see these preserved, will willingly join with the author in thus publicly recording his gratitude and thanks to the present owner of Bodiam Castle, (Augustus Fuller, Esq., of Rose Hill,) who has taken such pains and bestowed so much money in the preservation of this fine old pile, which has withstood the buffets of time for nearly five hundred years.

"The figure of the castle is nearly square, having a round tower on each angle, gates on the north and south fronts, and a square tower in the centre of the east and west sides. The grand entrance is on the north side, over a kind of causeway defended by an advanced gate, the remains of which are still standing. The great gate is extremely grand, flanked by two square machicolated towers. The east and west walls, from centre to centre of the towers, measure one hundred and sixty-five feet; those facing the north and south only one hundred and fifty."

This is the description of the castle, as given by Grose, towards the end of the last century, and its present state testifies its accuracy.

I shall here record one other circumstance as connected with the reign of Richard II, and which should have preceded the previous one, when I shall proceed to that of Henry IV.

The circumstance here alluded to is the destruction of Appledore Castle, which was built by the Danes about the time of Alfred the Great, and was destroyed by the French in the year 1380, who at the same time burnt the town, and tradition adds that the present church was erected on the spot where formerly stood the castle. In the latter part of this reign 200 houses at West Hythe were consumed by fire in one day. Master Twyne says that Old Hythe, alias West Hythe, was the town burned along the shore, where the ruins of the church then stood. From this it appears that as the sea receded from West Hythe, houses were erected to follow the water until they reached to the spot on which the present town now stands, and thus the two towns were connected in the same way as Old and New Romney were, but this fire produced a separation which has ever since remained. The new town increased and the old one perished.

Henry IV commenced his reign in 1399, and he confirmed all the former charters relating to Romney Marsh.

In 1st Henry IV, William Makenade, Stephen Betenham, William Bertom, William Bertyn, and Henry Horne, were commissioned to view the walls on the sea-coast between the towns of Smallhyde and Promhelle, when it was then and there found that 628 acres of marsh, lying in a place called the Becard, which had long lain in danger of the sea, and at that time were often overflowed, ought to be preserved and defended by a certain bank, beginning at Fayrefield's Hole in the said place, called Becard, and so extending itself by the sea-side unto the bank of the prior and convent of Christchurch, Canterbury, towards the north, which bank ought to be made on that sea-coast at the common charge of all persons receiving advantage and benefit thereby, and that the abbot and convent of Robertsbrigge were then possessed of 271½ acres of the said marsh, for which they ought to contribute to the said charge of making that bank, and that Thomas, Archbishop of Canterbury, with the said prior and convent of Christchurch, and certain other persons, were possessors of the residue thereof, for the which every one of them, according to the proportion of what he so held, was to contribute.

Upon which verdict there grew a dispute between the said prior and the Abbot of Robertsbrigge, the abbot and his convent alleging that their proportion of the said marsh, so to be defended, was much greater; for they said that Henry, sometime Earl of Augi, by a certain grant of his, gave to the Abbot of Robertsbrigge (predecessor of the present abbot) and the convent of that house, 700 acres of marsh in the town of Snergate, as well within the bank as without, of which the marsh, then to be taken in, was parcel; and, to make good this claim, did exhibit the charter of the said Earl, made time out of mind; as also the letters patent of Richard I and Henry III, kings ratifying the same. Whereunto the Prior of Canterbury answered, that, upon the making that charter by the said Earl of Augi, there arose a controversy between Alan, then Prior of Christ-Church, and his convent, as lords of the manor of Apuldre, within the precinct whereof the said marsh lay situate, and Dionyse, then Abbot of Robertsbrigge, and the convent of that monastery for the title of that whole marsh, and that, upon an amicable agreement made between them, the said abbot and convent did quit all their title thereto unto the before-specified Prior and Convent of Christ-Church. But the said prior, out of a pious regard to the wants of the said abbot and convent, did, by their special favour, then grant them and their successors 100 acres of those 700 acres, viz. 100 acres lying next to the bank of the said abbot and convent near unto the land of Adam de Cherringe, which, at that time, they had inclosed about the Newewodrove, and that this agreement was, by the before-mentioned Earl, then ratified and confirmed as the instrument testifying the same, then exhibited, did fully manifest; so that the said abbot and convent ought not to challenge anything more in that marsh, other than those 100 acres so given to them, as aforesaid.

In consideration therefore of all the premises and circumstances thereof, and especially of the antiquity of the evidences produced on each part; as also of the obscurity of the bounds and limits of the said towns of Snergate and Apuldre, the perfect knowledge whereof, by reason of the great and continual inundation of the sea, could not (nor was ever likely to be) well discovered; all parties, therefore, more desiring peace than strife and contention, did unanimously agree that the said Prior and Convent of Christ-Church should release unto the Abbot and Convent of Robertsbrigge, and their successors, all their title to that parcel of land called the Newewoderove, and in twenty-eight acres of land, then newly inclosed in the Becarde towards Apuldre, and in the 271½ acres then to be inclosed in the Becarde, adjoining to the said parcel of land, called the Newewoderove, lying in length under the bank dividing the said land of the Newewoderove, and the said Marsh so to be inclosed in the Becarde, so that the said Prior and Convent of Christ-Church, nor their successors, should have power to claim any right therein after that time. And in like manner the said Abbot and convent of Robertsbrigge did release unto the said Thomas, Archbishop of Canterbury, and to the Prior and Convent of Christ-Church, and their successors, all their right and title to the residue of that marsh, lying next to the church of Fayrefelde towards the east, and the course of the sea, passing from Rye to Apuldre, towards the west and the bounds, dividing the counties of Kent and Sussex towards the south, so that they should challenge no title therein from thenceforth.

Which agreement was made by the said instrument under their public seals, and bears date at Canterbury, March 20th, 1399.

In 2d Henry IV, A. D. 1400, Thomas Erpyngham (Constable of Dover Castle), William Brenchesle, Robert Oxenbrigge, William Marchant, and others were commissioned to survey the banks between Farlegh in Sussex, and Apuldre in Kent.

In 3d Henry IV, William Rikhill, William Makenade, Stephen Betenham, William Bertyn, Henry Horne, and John Proude, to inspect the Marshes of Lyde, Promhill, Middele, and Old Romney.

In 8th Henry IV, A. D 1406, a commission was issued to Sir John Dalingrugge, Knt., George Ballard, Stephen Bettenhamme, William Snaythe, Henry Horne, and others, for the view and repairs of the banks on the sea-coast from Blacknose in Kent, unto Rye in Sussex, and the coasts of the water, called Apoldreflete, from the sea to Bodihamme, on both sides the said water, which, at that time, were much broken with the tides.

In 10th Henry IV, A. D. 1408, George Ballard, Stephen Betenham, Robert Oxenbrigge, Vincent Fynche, Thomas Oxenbrigge, William Marchant, John May, and John Lonsford, were commissioned to view the banks between the towns of Romney and Promhill.

We find in this reign, which ended in the year 1413, that another large inclosure took place, amounting to 628 acres, lying between Fairfield and Appledore. We see also that the sea still flowed up to Bodiam, and that the course of the Rother was much farther to the eastward than it is at present, as we find the boundaries of the Becard, now inclosed, to have been the marsh, lying next to Fairfield Church on the east, and the sea on the west, which is described as flowing this way from Appledore to Rye.

The only name which I shall add to our former lists of commissioners is that of Thomas Erpyngham (Constable of Dover Castle), serving to show that men of consequence still continued to be appointed for the purpose.

In 2d Henry V, A. D. 1414, upon an inquisition taken before Thomas Erpingham (Constable of Dover Castle), William Brenchesle, Robert Oxenbrigge, and others, for the view and repairs of the banks between Farleghe, in Sussex, and Apuldre, in Kent, the jurors presented, on their oaths, that there was a certain small marsh, near unto the town of Rye, within the liberty of the Cinque Ports, called St. Mary Croft, containing, by estimation, forty-eight acres of land, which could not be well defended against the force of the tides, except an old gutter therein were stopped up: and they said, it would be necessary and profitable for the preservation and clearing of the said marsh that there were a new gutter and sewer made beyond the bank of the said marsh, and the land of John Chitecroft, in a certain marsh called Corboyle's Marsh, containing about a quarter of an acre, and so to pass into the water-course coming from Levesham's Wall unto the sluice at Melflet. And they further said, that John Chitecroft should receive forty shillings per acre for his land, which was afterwards confirmed, the mayor and bailiff of Rye having summoned John Chitecroft and the landholders of the marsh called St. Mary Croft to appear before the lieutenant of Dover Castle at Rye, on Wednesday next before the Feast of the Nativity of the Blessed Virgin.

In 3d Henry V, A. D. 1415, a commission was granted to Sir John Pelham, Knt., Richard Wakeherst, Robert Oxenbrigge, Vincent Fynche, Adam Iwode, and William Marchaunt, to view and repair the banks between the towns of Pesemarsh, Rye, Farlegh, and Pette.

In the 3d Henry V, A. D. 1415, John Darelle, Roger Rye, Thomas Elys, Henry Horne, and William Marchaunt, were commissioned to inspect the walls between Smallhede and Romney.

In 9th Henry V, A. D. 1421, Robert Oxenbrigge, Henry Horne, John Hall, jun., William Cheyne, and Adam Iwode, were appointed to inspect the banks between Ashewalle and the course of the sea-water running from the town of Rye to Appuldre and Bodyham, in the towns of Wytresham and Stone, in Kent, and to Idenne, Pesemershe, and Bekkele, in Sussex.

The names which I have thought fit to add to those of former reigns are—

   Iwode, Adam.
   Pelham, Sir John, Knt.
   Wakeherst, Richard.

In the parish of Warbleton, in the county of Sussex, is a manor called Iwood, where probably this Adam Iwode might have resided, and whence he might have his name, which some years previous to this might have been Adam de Iwood, or Iwode; but now we find the *de* is dropped, and it is simply Adam Iwode.

The Pelhams are a very old family in Sussex, to which belongs the present Earl of Chichester. John de Pelham was one of the esquires of John of Gaunt, Duke of Lancaster, and attending him in his wars, had the honour of knighthood conferred upon him before the 43d Edward III, A.D. 1369. Sir John had certain lands and houses in Winchelsea in marriage with Joan, daughter to Vincent Herbert, alias Finch, ancestor to the present Earl of Winchelsea. Thus it appears that a Sir John Pelham possessed property in and about Winchelsea; but whether the distance of time between his knighthood, previously to 1369, and the appointment of the commission in 1415, may be thought to render it improbable, I will leave to others to judge, merely observing that it is not impossible.

Wakehurst is the name of an ancient seat in the parish of Ardingly, in Sussex. In the year 1430, Richard Wakehurst was assigned by the king's writ to have the custody of the peace for the county of Sussex, and it is by no means improbable that this was the very man we have now before us.

I find mention made in this reign of a marsh near Rye called St. Mary Croft, but which is the identical spot I cannot say; however, it is certain it must have been within the bounds of the corporation, as it is described as being within the liberty of the Cinque Ports, which it would not be had it been without those bounds. We have another clue to guide us in the circumstance already recorded in the year 1366, respecting the boundaries of the marshes at the back of the town where Melflet is described as the western, and which I have assumed to be the spot where stands the present Leesam Wall. Melflet, I presume, then, to have been the name of the stream which then, as now, flowed under Leesam Hill, but which is now called the Tillingham river: and therefore St. Mary Croft must have lain on the east side of the river, within the bounds of the corporation on that side. We further gather from this account also, that there must have been a sluice on this river at this time, but of what description it may not now be easy to determine. On inquiry, since writing the above, I find the four marshes adjoining the Rope-walk, being the most eastern of those lying at the back of the town, are called St. Mary's Marshes.

Henry VI confirmed the former charters.

In 6th Henry VI, A.D. 1427, the king, by advice and assent of his lords, spiritual and temporal, and at the special instance of the commons of the realm, then assembled at Westminster, having considered the great damage and losses which had often happened by the excessive rising of waters in divers parts of the realm, and that much greater were likely to ensue (if remedy were not hastily provided), issued several commissions of sewers in the ten ensuing years, giving, among other things, special power and direction by that Act, "to make and ordain necessary and conveniable statutes and ordinances for the salvation and conservation of the sea-banks and marshes, and the parts adjoining, according to the laws of Romney Marsh."

In the year 1439, 18th Henry VI, an Act of Parliament was passed to continue the commissions as heretofore had been customary; and in 1444, another.

In 10th Henry VI, A.D. 1431, Humfrey, Duke of Gloucester, Sir Thomas Echyngham, Knt., John Halle, William Fynche, and others, were appointed to view the banks between Farlegh, Sussex, and Derlande's Knokke, Kent.

In 18th Henry VI, A.D. 1439, Richard Wakeherst, William Bertyne, Thomas Betenham, Thomas Hordene, Walter Colepepper, and John Derham, to view between Smallhithe and a place called the Pendynge, and between Farnehill and a bank leading from Mayteham to Pendynge, in Tenterden and Rolvenden, with power to make statutes and ordinances for the preservation of those places; as also to take diggers and labourers.

In 28th Henry VI, 1449, William Kene, Esq., John Bamburgh, Stephen Slegge, and others, to view between the town of

Redyng and Redehill, thence to Huntebornbrigge, thence to the upland of Bregge, and thence to Redyng, in Tenterden, Apuldre, and Woodchurch; and to make statutes and ordinances.

In 34th Henry VI, A. D. 1455, Sir Richard Ferrys, Knt., Thomas Echyngham, Richard Dalyngregge, and John Passele, Esquires, Bartholomew Bolney, and Martin Oxenbrigge, for the banks between Sedlescombe Bregge, in the parish of Sedlescombe, on the west part of Snaylham, and the place called the Pyke in Brede, and Guestling on the east, on both sides the common water-course, betwixt the said town of Sedlescombe and Wynchelse.

In 37th Henry VI, A. D. 1458, Sir John Pelham, Knt., Thomas Echyngham, Henry Hall, Robert Oxenbrigge, and John Copeldyke, Esquires, Bartholomew Bolney, and Martin Oxenbrigge, between a place called Fodyr and the town of Wynchelse.

I find no particular name in this reign which I think it necessary to insert here; but one observation seems requisite, in consequence of the title of Esquire being now for the first time found adjoined to the names of some of the parties appointed to the different commissions. Previous to this time no title has been appended, except to a peer or a knight; therefore one might be led to conclude that now it was that this title of Esquire was first introduced.

The reader can scarcely have failed to remark that all the commissions, issued for many years previous to this time, were for the view of the banks, &c., out of Romney Marsh, properly so called. In 35th Edward III, A. D. 1361, on complaint made to the King, Thomas de Lodelowe, Robert Belknapp, and Thomas Colepeper were appointed to make such new laws as were necessary, which (with the consent of the lords of the towns, the bailiff, twenty-four jurats, and the commonalty of the said Marsh) they did. Although regular laws had been framed for the government of Romney Marsh, as long back as the reign of Henry III, still it appears that various commissions were afterwards issued at different times up to the period when Thomas de Lodelowe and his fellows made the new laws in 1361, since which, I think, we may say that the affairs of Romney Marsh have been managed by the regular commissioners appointed for this purpose; for although I find that in 1375 a commission was issued to certain persons therein mentioned, to survey the banks extending from the town of Hethe to Romeney, and thence to Promhull and Apuldre, and another in 1377, from Hethe all along the sea-coast to Apuldre, as also in other marshes within the county, from the haven of Romney to Promhill Church, and thence by the sea-coast to Apuldre; yet these commissions are confined to the outer boundary wall, and do not relate to any of the interior parts; and, after this time, they cease altogether. We find, moreover, that in the 6th Henry VI, A.D. 1427, when many parts of the realm were likely to suffer from inundations, and new laws were necessary to be made for their preservation, orders were given that they should be framed on the model of those by which Romney Marsh was governed. Thus these laws were fully and satisfactorily recognised, and by these, and these only, have Romney Marsh been ever since regulated.

We here see that the sea had been excluded from the lands lying in what is now called Brede Level, as far down as Winchelsea, on either side of the Brede river.

Edward IV, in that notable charter (says Dugdale) bearing date at Westminster, Feb. 23, 1461, incorporated the bailiff and jurats of Romney Marsh, and, in the preamble, states that many towns and places, situate near the sea, had been laid waste by the spoils and burnings of the enemy, and through the affrights of the inhabitants, who thereupon forsook them, were left uninhabitable and desolate; thinking it therefore most necessary to repair the said towns and places, or to new build others near them, and being so built, to endow and arm them with privileges and liberties, that, being so fortified, they may, by the people's recourse to them, be made more powerful and strong for the better safeguard of the whole country. And considering, that in this Marsh of Romney in Kent, which is situate near the sea, there was not at that time such a plenty of people and inhabitants as were wont to be; but, were it better defended, there would be a much greater confluence resort thereto and dwell therein, for the more safeguard of the whole country, as he, the said king, had been informed from the credible relation of the inhabitants of the said Marsh and other parts adjacent. Taking therefore the premises into consideration, at the instant request of all the commonalty and inhabitants within the said Marsh, as also for the preservation thereof, he gave and granted to the same inhabitants, residing within the limits and bounds thereof, that they should be one body in substance and name, and one commonalty perpetually incorporate of one bailiff and twenty-four jurats, and the commonalty of the said Romney Marsh. That they should have a continual succession, and they and their successors for ever called, termed, and named by the name of the bailiff, jurats, and commonalty of Romney Marsh, in the county of Kent, and that they shall have a common seal for their affairs and businesses relating to them: the said bailiff, jurats, and commonalty, and their successors, shall plead and be impleaded, answer and be answered, by the name of bailiff, jurats, and commonalty; which said bailiff and jurats to be elected in like manner and form; as also exercise their offices and be displaced from them, as heretofore it was wont and accustomed to be in the said Marsh. And, moreover, the said bailiff, &c., shall have a certain court at some convenient place within the same Marsh, to be held from three weeks to three weeks for ever; and have full power and authority to hear and determine in the same court by bills of complaint therein, all and singular pleas of debts, accompts, covenants, contracts, trespasses by force and arms, or otherwise, in contempt of the said king or his heirs, with many other liberties and privileges, of which for brevity I omit the rehearsal, referring my reader to the record itself, if he desire to be further informed therein.

And the said king granted them that they should, from time to time, have power to make reasonable ordinances and constitutions of good credit for the common good of the same Marsh.

And that the said bailiff, &c., for the necessities and profits of the said Marsh, shall, among themselves, assess and levy taxes, and lay impositions on the goods, lands, tenements, and merchandises of the inhabitants and residents being within the bounds and limits of the said Marsh. And, moreover, granted to the said bailiff, &c., that none of them should be put or impanelled in any assizes, juries, recognitions, attaints, or any other inquisitions whatever, out of the bounds and limits of the said Marsh; nor that any of them be made an assessor, taxer, or collector of tenths, fifteenths, or any parcel thereof, or of any other charge, subsidy, or tallage whatsoever.

In 14th Edward IV, A.D. 1474, the king having received advertisement that the banks, ditches, &c. lying on the seacoast, and marshes between Robertsbrigge in Sussex, and the town of Romney in Kent, were, by the raging of the sea and violence of the tides, much broken and decayed, to the great damage of those parts, and being therefore desirous that some speedy remedy should be used therein, did by his letters patent, dated at Westminster, constitute Sir John Fogge, Sir William Haute, and Sir John Gilford, Knts., and John Elryngton, John Brumston, Henry Auger, William Belknap, and Robert Oxenbrigge, Esquires, as also Bartholomew Bolney, Roger Brent, John Fyneux, Vincent Fynche, John Nethersole, and John Hert, his commissioners to take view of the said banks, and make all necessary inquiries into the business, as to the owners, &c., and to make statutes and ordinances according to the custom of Romney Marsh; and at the same time to take workmen and labourers for the execution of the works.

Whereupon afterwards, on April 10, 1478, these justices were informed that all the lands and fresh marshes lying between Cowelese Marsh towards the north, the lands in the Ree leading from the said Marsh to Lynkehoke, near Romney towards the east, the way leading from Lynkehoke by the inside of the bank at Lyde, and through the midst of the High Street of that town, to Pigwell and a place, called the Holmestone, lying without the bank, called the Wikewall, the land of Promhill, situate without the banks, called Simonde's Wall and Kent Wall, and the gulf of salt water, running from the Camer to the said Marsh, called Cowelese, towards the west, except the Kete, Denecourt, and Bourghser's Marshes, and other marshes lately taken in by John Elryngton and Richard Gilford, Esquires, with the banks belonging to them, were daily subject to the danger of inundation by default of repairs in East Marsh and Beccard, and divers others lying within the limits above specified.

Sir John Fogge and his fellow justices, finding the walls as represented, made the following ordinances, viz.:

1st. That within the lands and marshes aforesaid, there should henceforth be two bailiffs, twenty-four jurats, two collectors, and two expenditors; ten or eight of the jurats, at least, to govern, keep, defend, and preserve from the peril of the sea and inundation of the fresh waters by banks, water-courses, &c.

2d. That Symonde's Wall and Kent Wall, and the banks in Eastmersh and Becard, were defective, and that they should be sufficiently repaired, and be kept and continually maintained for the safeguard and defence of the said lands and marshes within the limits aforesaid.

3d. That for the immediate reparation of Symonde's Wall and Kent Wall (on certain reasonable considerations) every person having land within Symonde's Wall and Kent Wall, and the bank called Gore's Wall, and every one having land in the Marsh called Ockholt, should pay 2*d.* per acre extra; but afterwards the same to contribute equally with all others.

4th. Workmen, when engaged in repairs, to have liberty to go over the inner and outer foreland of every bank.

5th. That twice every year a principal and general Last should be held within the said land and marsh by the said twenty-four jurats, or ten, or eight at least, once within the 15me of Easter, and again within the 15me of St. Michael the Archangel, at Brokland, or in another place within the precinct of those lands and marshes, and that other several lasts should be here held, when and as often as there might be occasion by the summons of the bailiffs.

6th to 17th. These clauses relate to the mode of electing the bailiffs, and to their various duties.

18th. That no one henceforth should be allowed to make dams or any other impediments in any lands, land-eas, watergangs, &c., whereby the common course of the waters might be impeded; and if any such things were done, and the same witnessed by the bailiffs and six of the twenty-four jurats, the party delinquent be amerced, and the amerciament levied by the said bailiffs to the common profit, and if any private person receive prejudice therein, he should make satisfaction to the party wronged, at the discretion of the said bailiffs and six jurats.

19th. That all taxes be publicly proclaimed in certain places within the district, and the place and day of payment fixed.

20th. That all land required for banks, ditches, &c, be bought at 40 shillings per acre, and measured by a rod of twenty feet.

21st. That all the sewers be kept open, so that the water might not run out of its proper course to the injury of any one.

22d. That the jurats, &c., should have the same powers as those of Romney Marsh, and that the lords of the fee, with the jurats, might decree to have fewer jurats, bailiffs, collectors, &c.

23d. That if any person should make rescue or give resistance to any officer making a distress, or in the execution of their duty, he be fined 10s., to be levied on his goods and chattels, for the common profit.

24th. That no sheriff or king's officer make replevin of any distress taken by the bailiffs; nor any of the said king's officers to arrest any one within those limits being then in the public work.

25th. And, lastly, it was decreed, that if any tax, properly assessed and proclaimed, should not be paid at the proper time and place, then the bailiffs should lay out of their own proper monies, so much as the part, so being in arrear, called warrys, might amount unto, for the common profit. And the said bailiffs, as well for the said parcel, so in arrear, called warrys, as for the double thereof, to distrain in all the lands and tenements of him or them who ought to pay the same, by all their goods and chattels, and the distresses, so taken, to be kept three days or more; and, if the arrears be not paid in three days, then the goods and chattels, by two or one of the jurats, to be sold within the said limits, and the said part, so in arrear, called warrys, together with the double thereof, out of the money arising of the said goods and chattels, so sold, to be delivered to the same bailiffs to their own use.

In 17th Edward IV, A.D. 1477, upon an inquisition taken at a place called Dencourt's Marsh, the Friday next after the Feast of the Nativity of St. John the Baptist, before Sir Thomas Echyngham, knt., Henry Aucher, Gervase Horne, Robert Oxenbrigge, William Belknap, Henry Belknap, John Bradford, John Copeldyke, John Wody, and Thomas Oxenbrigge, commissioners to view and repair the banks between the river of Apeldoure to Rye on the west part, and thence to the wall called Fresh Wall, on the east part; and the wall of the Monks of Christ-Church, Canterbury, called New Wall, as far as the lands belonging to the Abbey of St. Augustine did reach, on the south part; the jurors did then and there present, upon their oaths, that it would be very necessary and profitable, for the safeguard, amendment, and clearing of the said Marsh, and the prevention of drowning to that part of the country adjoining thereto, that there were a new bank made from the said wall, called New Wall, by the channel leading from Apeldoure to Rye, and to the said water called Moreflete, and thence to the said place called Fresh Wall, as far as the lands then belonging to the Abbey of St. Augustine did extend. And that the said bank should be in length from the said wall, called New Wall, unto Moreflete aforesaid, and thence to the place called Fresh Wall, upon the flat marsh 1280½ rods; and in creeks and flats 69 rods. And they say that every rod of the said bank upon the plain marsh might be made for 2s. 4d., and every rod in the creeks for 11s. And they further say that, within the same Marsh, by the making of that bank, there might be saved from the overflowing of the tide 1412 acres of good marsh, 1082 acres of which are in Kent, and 330 acres in Sussex; and that all the said acres in both counties did lie together and contiguous to the bounds of those counties, and adjacent to the said Marsh, and that no one acre could be conveniently taxed to the making of the said bank without the other, the assessment having been so time out of mind; and because, before that time, there was no certain law of that Marsh constituted nor used; and that the said Marsh, being drowned, lay to the sea, therefore the said commissioners, by virtue of their commission, by the assent of bailiff, jurats, and commonalty of the said Marsh, did ordain that, for the future, the bailiff for the time being should have one principal last in the said Marsh yearly at the least, within the octaves of St. Michael the Archangel, in such place, where he, the said bailiff, should think most convenient.

It appears that Sir John Elryngton was the first bailiff on this Dencourt's Marsh.

In 19th Edward IV, A. D. 1479, the king, by his letters patent, directed to Thomas, Archbishop of Canterbury, Cardinal of England; William, Prior of Christ-Church, Canterbury; Richard, Prior of Hortone; Robert, Prior of Bylsingtone; William, Master of God's House, Dover; Sir John Fogge, Sir William Haute, Sir John Scotte, knts.; William Cheyne, John Broomston, Henry Hoorne, Gervase Hoorne, John Fyneux, Vincent Fynche, Roger Brent, William Brent, and John Nethersole, constituted them commissioners for the view and repair of the banks, etc. from Appuldoure to Cawmbury, and from Cawmbury to Fulstone, then ruinous by the violence of the sea; and to make laws and ordinances for the same, according to the laws and customs of Romney Marsh. And, lastly, to take so many diggers and other labourers to be employed therein, upon competent salaries, as should be thought requisite, in respect of the urgent and instant necessity of the work.

The charter of Edward IV seems to be the last charter that was granted, and this was confirmed by Henry VII, in the year 1485, which was the first of his reign.

Henry VIII likewise, in this first year of his reign, A. D. 1509, confirmed the charter of Edward IV.

It appears that, so late as the year 1509, the tide flowed up to Small Hythe, on the north side of the Island of Oxney, and to this place the river Rother, at that time, appears to have been navigable, and, as a confirmation of the fact, a licence was, in 1509, granted by Archbishop Wareham for the inhabitants to repair and establish a chapel in that ville, in which power is given for the burial, in the chapel yard, of the bodies of such as should be cast by shipwreck on the shore, "infra oppidum de Small Hyth," that is, "under the town of Small Hythe."

In this reign Hasted tells us that the haven of West Hythe seems to have been in great measure destroyed by the sands and beach cast up on this shore by the desertion of the sea, for Leland describes it as being, at that time, only a small channel or gut left, which ran within shore for more than a mile eastward from Hythe towards Folkstone, where small vessels could come up with safety.

In the year 1547 Edward VI confirmed the charter of Edward IV, and in 1558 Queen Elizabeth did the same.

In this latter reign, the small channel leading from the sea to

West Hythe, as described by Leland, was 'swawed up' and lost, and thus the harbour, which had its original existence in the fifth century (in the time of the Romans), was finally dammed up in the sixteenth, after a lapse of 1100 years. Thus perished the harbour and river of Limen from the locality were they were originally recognised, and though the river in all probability still exists in the Rother, the name of the Limen is for ever erased from all modern maps.

We have taken occasion in the foregoing part of this work to mention the first appearance of the several parishes in the Marsh, as they came to our knowledge, and, having thus recorded the names of all except that of Guldeford, the time now seems to have arrived when we can introduce this to our reader's notice. It is scarcely necessary to mention, at this time of day, that many places have taken their names from the original proprietors of the soil on which such places stand; but, were proof wanted, I might mention one connected with this history, viz., Blackmanstone—Blackman's Town, Blackman having been the original proprietor. And thus the parish of Guldeford, as it is now written, took its name from the Gilfords, who were a very ancient family in these parts, having resided at Rolvenden as far back as the reign of Edward III. In the year 1478 I first meet with the name as possessing land in this part of the Marsh, when allusion is made to certain marshes lately taken in by Richard Gilford, Esq.; after this time, I presume, some one of the family continued to inclose the marsh, as the sea receded until about the year 1534, in the reign of Henry VIII, when the embankment had secured the spot on which the church was then built, after which it is probable the inclosed lands assumed the rank of a parish under the name of Guldeford, or East Guldeford, to distinguish it from Guilford in Surrey, which every one knows lies to the westward of it.

It appears from the Burrell MSS., as quoted by Horsfield, in his 'History of Sussex,' that soon after this time complaint was made of the two havens of Rye and Camber having fallen into decay, in consequence of which an inquisition was taken at the ancient town of Rye on the 25th of May, 1562, before Edward Lord Clinton, Lord High Admiral of England, and others, by virtue of the Queen's commission to them directed, to inquire into the decay and ruin of the said havens by a jury. In answer to which the jurors present and say: First (of the haven of Camber) that the inning of marshes is the cause of the decay of the said haven, and hath been begun since 1532. Item— they present Sir John Guldeford, Knt., hath inned, since 1542,

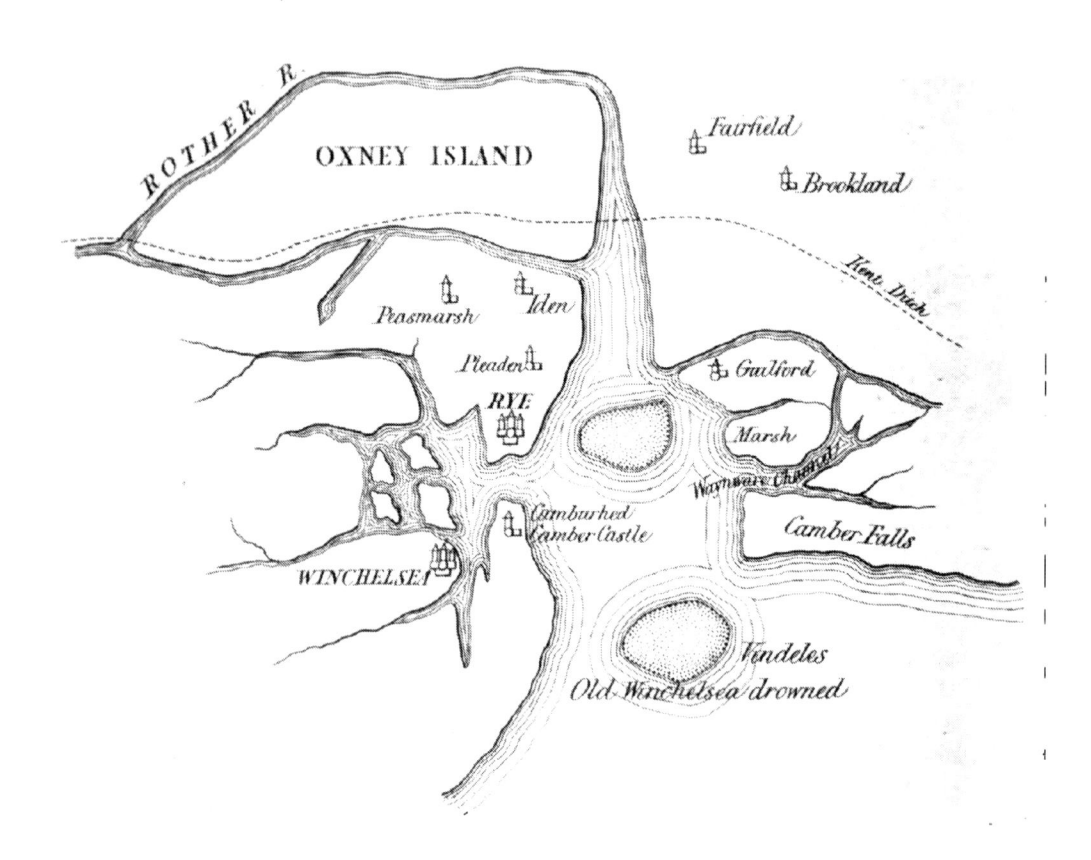

A PLAN
OF
RYE HARBOUR
and its
VICINITY.
FROM
CAMDEN'S BRITANNIA. 1586

in Guldeford Marsh, in his second inning, three great and huge creeks, which have been and are an utter decay of the haven of Camber. Item—they present the said Sir John Guldeford's late inned new marsh hath hurt and been the decay of the said haven; for, being two feet lower than the salts, it holdeth a great quantity of water, which is now stopped and letted of its course. Touching the amendment of the Camber, the jurors present first, that the said creeks may be opened, that the salt water may have its course into the same; this would amend the haven in a short time. Item—that the said new marsh of Sir John Guldeford, lately inned, may be laid open again; this would not only hold a great quantity of water, but also, by reason of the lowness, would not depart till the ebb be well spent, and then it would scour, in going off, and amend the said haven.

Speaking of the Camber, it may be well here to mention what I conceive to be the origin of the name, and also to mention Camber Castle, which was erected some years previous to this time. Whence the Camber had derived its name I was for a long time much at a loss to discover, until looking into Camden's 'Britannia Antiqua,' in the description of Portsmouth, I met with the following note: " Through the growth of naval action in England, it is now reckoned among the principal chambers of the kingdom for the laying up of the royal navy." Thus I consider Camber to be a corruption of chamber, and chamber signified a harbour or place in which ships might lie in safety. At Portsmouth, within the harbour, there is still a spot known by the name of the Camber, and the Camber we are now speaking of was originally a chamber or place of safety for ships to lie in, when they wished to escape either the violence of the sea or of the enemy. And it was with a view to protect this chamber from the attacks of the latter, that Henry VIII, about the year 1539 or 1540, erected the castle, which goes, even to this day, by the name of Camber Castle. When first built, it was very eligibly situated close to the sea, on a point of land which commanded the entrance into the chamber, which constituted at that time the harbours of Rye and Winchelsea. But the real situation of it will be much better comprehended by an inspection of the accompanying sketch, which is taken from Camden's map of Sussex, published in 1695.

Tradition tells us that ships could formerly sail so close to the castle, that a man on board might throw a biscuit into it; the beach has since increased in front of it to the south so much, that it is now full a mile and a quarter from the sea at high water. From the time of the first erection of the castle the

Fulls of Beach (as the different ranges of it are here called) have each gradually formed to the westward, under Fairlight Cliff in the first instance, and then travelled eastward, until it met the run of the Rother, which prevented its further progress, when a new one commenced to the westward, still ending in the same way. The last one is now almost close to the mouth of Rye harbour.

In 5th Queen Elizabeth, A.D. 1562, the old bed of the river, running from Appledore to New Romney, was granted to the corporation of the latter place, as may be seen by the following extract from the charter of New Romney, a copy of which was very obligingly lent to me by William Stringer, Esq., the town clerk of this Cinque Port: "Know ye that we of our especial grace and of our certain knowledge and mere motion for certain considerations us especially moving, have given, and by these presents granted, to the said mayor, jurats, and commonalty of the town and port of New Romney, in the county of Kent, and to their successors, all and singular those sandy pastures, marsh-lands, as well fresh as salt, now or heretofore called or known by the name of the Helmes, and the sand hills lying and being partly on the east of the said town of New Romney, to the land of Lawrence Ashburnham, in right of his wife, or late Adams, called Jeston, towards the east and north-east, to the land of John Estdeey, Thomas Jowle, Arthur Blechenden, and John Tadlow towards the north, to the deep sea and to the marsh called the Common Marsh towards the south, and to the same marsh called the Common Marsh towards the west, and all and singular that marshy ground, as well fresh as salt, called the Common Marsh, lying to the said sandy ground called Helmes, towards the east, and to the salt marsh called the Common Salts of the town of New Romney, and to lands of the cathedral church and metropolitan of Canterbury, called Sextry's Land, towards the south, and to land called Belgar Land towards the south-west, and to land called Lynkhooke towards the west, and to the cemetery called St. Nicholas Churchyard of Romney Post Limina, called the backsides of divers messuages of several inhabitants of the town of New Romney aforesaid, and to the said sandy ground called the Helmes towards the north, and all and singular the marsh grounds called the Salts of the town of New Romney, lying to the said fresh marsh called the Common Marsh, towards the north, and the said sandy ground called the Helmes towards the north-east, and to the Land dior., Decain, and Capitli, called the Sextrye Salts, towards the west, and to the deep sea towards the south-east. And also all and singular those lands called the Land between the Walls, extended in longitude to the said fresh marsh, called the Common Marsh, directly towards a certain place called Redhill, between two walls or walles, one of which is called Romney Marsh Wall, and the other Walland Wall, which said land lying between the said two walls instar cresesivie aquagii are fact., Anglice, in manner of a creek or waterway swawed or dried up. To have and to hold all and singular the said lands, marshes, and other the premises and their appurtenances, to the aforesaid mayor, jurats, and commonalty, and their successors for ever, to the only and proper use of the said mayor, jurats, and commonalty, and their successors for ever, in free socage as of our ancient barony of our Cinque Ports, to wit, per servitium navigii. And yielding therefore yearly to us, our heirs, and successors, forty shillings of lawful money of England, at the receipt of the Exchequer of us, our heirs, and successors, at the Feasts of St. Michael the Archangel and the Annunciation of the Blessed Virgin Mary, by equal portions yearly, to be paid for all rents, services, executions, and demands whatsoever. In testimony whereof, &c., witness the Queen at Northawe, the fourth day of August, 1562.

By Writ of Privy Seal."

From the foregoing document we may learn that New Romney had now entirely ceased to be a port. That sandy space of land which lies to the eastward of the town, and is known by the name of the Warren, had then been left by the sea; and on this spot, in the year 1833, the remains of a large vessel were dug up, and which probably was one of the old war ships of the port. This spot was then called the Helmes, which I suppose is a corruption of Holmes, signifying a fenny ground or land lately left by the sea. We find, also, that other marshes had been formed on the south, south-west, and west sides of the town, as may be seen by tracing on the map the situation of Belgar on the south-west, and Lynkhooke on the west. The old bed of the Rother, here conveyed, extends from the marsh called the Common Marsh, and which lay to the south-east of the town, to a place called Redhill.

In this charter, also, the name of the western wall is altered from its former designation of Ree Wall to that of Walland Wall. The bed of the river is still in the possession of the corporation of New Romney.

By far the greater part of the marshes was now inclosed, and some little idea of their value may be acquired from the following report of the record in the 13th year of Queen Elizabeth, A.D. 1570, as to the sums of money levied in the name of a tenth and fifteenth on each town and place, viz.:

The Lathe of Shepway, Hundred of St. Martin.

	£	s.	d.
The town of Newchurch	1	0	3
" St. Mary's	2	9	0
" Hope	12	7	10½
" Ivychurch	3	8	1
" Medley		4	2
	19	9	4½

Lathe of Shepway, Hundred of Langport.

	£	s.	d.
The town of Nicholas*		16	0
" Lydd	9	2	4
" Romney		13	4
" Hope	1	9	0
	12	0	8

Lathe of Shepway, Hundred of Alowsbrege.

	£	s.	d.
The town of Snargate	2	17	11
" Brenset	4	0	2
" Brookland	3	17	0
" Fairfield	2	4	9
" Snave	1	12	6½
" Ivychurch	1	11	4
" Newchurch		7	1½
	16	10	10

Lathe of Shepway, Hundred of Newchurch.

	£	s.	d.
The town of Newchurch	1	13	2
" Snave		8	4
" St. Mary	1	14	4
	3	15	10

Lathe of Shepway, Hundred of Oxney.

	£	s.	d.
The town of Wyttresham	2	16	1
" Stone	3	18	4
" Ebbene		12	6
	7	6	11

Lathe of Shepway, Hundred of Hame.

	s.	d.
The town of Snave	10	2

* This, I suppose, was a parish in New Romney.

Lathe of Shepway, Hundred of Worthe.

	£	s.	d.
The town of Dymchurch	3	1	10
" Burmarsh	4	8	4
" Newchurch		6	2½
" Eastbridge	2	0	1
" Blackmanstone		12	0
" West Hythe	1	3	2¼
" Aldingweke & Orgerswick	1	2	5
	12	14	0¾

Lathe of Scray or Sherwinhope, Hundred of Tenterden.

	£	s.	d.
The town of Ebbene	1	17	10

Lathe of Scray or Sherwinhope, Hundred of Blackborne.

	£	s.	d.
The town of Appledore	2	5	5¼

Lathe of Scray or Sherwinhope, Hundred of Selbrittenden.

	£	s.	d.
The town of Newenden		8	0

Lathe of Scray or Sherwinhope, Hundred of Marden.

	£	s.	d.
The town of Newenden	1	4	11½
	1	12	11½

The tax, called a tenth in this report, was the tenth part of the annual value of every spiritual benefice, according to the valuation in the king's books; being that yearly portion or tribute which all ecclesiastical livings formerly paid to the king. They were anciently claimed by the Pope; but they had often been granted to the king by him upon divers occasions, sometimes for one year, and sometimes for more, and were annexed perpetually to the crown by the statutes of the 26th Henry VIII, cap. 3, and 1st Elizabeth, cap. 4.

The fifteenth was a tribute or imposition of money anciently laid generally on cities, boroughs, &c., through the whole realm, so called because it amounted to a fifteenth part of that which each city or town was valued at, or a fifteenth of every man's personal estate, according to a reasonable valuation.

In this report, unfortunately, the tenth and fifteenth are mixed up together, so that, unless we had the value of each benefice before us, we cannot say how much goes to the tenth and how much to the fifteenth.

Since writing the above I have been favoured with an extract from a work entitled 'Liber Regis vel Thesaurus rerum Ecclesiasticarum,' by John Bacon, Esq., Receiver of the First Fruits, dated 1786, and which is compiled from the survey made in 26th Henry VIII, A.D. 1534. This work gives the value of the livings in Romney Marsh, with the amount of the tenths, with a few exceptions hereafter to be mentioned, but unfortunately will not elucidate the matter so fully as I could have wished; however, so far as it does go, it shall now be laid before the reader.

The following is extracted from a work entitled, 'Liber Regis vel Thesaurus rerum Ecclesiasticarum, by John Bacon, Esq., Receiver of the First Fruits;' date of work, 1786. The work is compiled from instructions for a survey, directed by King Henry VIII, to certain commissioners for that purpose, and the date of the commission is "vicesimo sexto regni:"

KING'S BOOKS.		YEARLY TENTHS.
£ s. d.		£ s. d.
6 16 3	NEW RUMNEY, V.—(St. Nicholas) with the chapels of St. Marten's and St. Lawrence. Exempt from the Archdeacon. All Souls' College, Oxford, Propr. and Patr. Ordinatio Vicar. dat. 22 Oct. 1402. Reg. Arund. MSS. Lambeth. Endow. in 7 acr. terr. gleb. 14s. in decim. prædial et personal. oblat. et spiritual. profic. per ann. £18 12s. 4d. Red. solut. Archiep. Cant. 7d. duob. Capellan, £13 6s. 8d. Marsh. Scot. 2s. 11d.	0 13 7½
15 19 2	OLD RUMNEY, R.—(St. Clement) Redd. et Mar. Scot. 10s. Archbishop of Canterbury. In 25 acr. terr. gleb. Prox. 7s. 6d.	1 11 11
55 12 1	LYDDE, V.—(All Saints.) Exempt from the Archdeacon. Abb. Tinterne Prop. in comitatu Monmouth. Archbishop of Canterbury. Endow. in 22 acr. terr. gleb. et quiet. red. £6. In decim. prædial. personal. oblat. et al. spiritual. profic. per ann. £50. Prox. 8s. Orig. endow. dat. 10 Maii, 1321. Reg. Reyn. MSS. Lambeth.	5 11 2¼
30 0 0	MIDLEY, R., alias MEDLEY.—(The church demolished.) John Unwin, esquire, two turns; Charles Eve, esquire, one turn; John Unwin, 1782. This is charged with 20s. per annum for tenths payable to the Crown Receiver; and the remaining 40s. is payable to the Archbishop.	3 0 0
17 6 8	SNARGATE, R.—(St. Dunstan.) Marsh. Scots. 6s. Archbishop of Canterbury. Prox. et Sinod., 34s. 8d.	1 14 8

KING'S BOOKS.				YEARLY TENTHS.		
£	s.	d.		£	s.	d.
17	12	8½	BROOKLAND, V., alias BROKELAND—(St. Augustine). Mon. Sti. Augustini Cantuar. Propr. Dean and Chapter of Canterbury. Endow. in terr. gleb. per annum 10s. 4d. In decim. predial. personal. oblat. et al. spiritual. profic. per ann. £17 10s. Prox. 7s. 6d. Orig. Endow. dat. 15 Aug. 1360. Reg. Islip MSS. Lambeth and Brit. Mus. Faustina, A. 1.	1	15	3¼
23	3	9	ST. MARY'S, in RUMNEY MARSH, R.—Archbishop of Canterbury. Prox. 16s.	2	6	4½
7	18	11½	BRENSET, V., alias BRENSETT—(St. Eauswith). Redd. Prior. Christchurch, 6d. Marshland, Scots. 12d. Colleg. loye Propr. Ralph Drake Brockman, clerk, 1770. £71 6s. 0¼d. certified value. Endow. in mans. and 2 acr. marisc. 10s. in decim. predial. personal. oblat. et al. spiritual. profic. per ann. £7 18s. 1d. Prox. 7s. 6d.	0	15	10¾
19	7	11	SNAVE, R.—(St. Augustine). Marsh. Scots. 5s. 9d. Archbishop of Canterbury. Vide X Script. Col. 2113. In 9 acr. terr. gleb. Prox. 7s.	1	18	9½
44	16	8	IVECHURCH, R.—(St. George). Marsh. Scots. 4s. 8d. Exempt from the Archdeacon. Archbishop of Canterbury. In 11 acr. terr. gleb. Red. solut. Archiep. Cantuar. 2s. 2d. Prox. 20s.	4	9	8
10	1	0½	HOPE, R.—(All Saints). Marsh. Scots. 3s. 4d. The King £80. In mans. and terr. gleb. ad val. 20s. Prox. 11s.	1	0	1¼
4	0	0	BLACKMANSTON, R.—Destructa. Archbishop of Canterbury.	0	8	0
8	4	2	NEWCHURCH, R.—(St. Peter and St. Paul). Exempt from the Archdeacon. Archbishop of Canterbury. 2 acr. terr. gleb.	0	16	5
19	16	0½	NEWCHURCH, V.—(St. Peter and St. Paul). Exempt from the Archdeacon. Archbishop of Canterbury. Endow. in 4½ acr. terr. gleb. per ann. 9s. 4d. in decim. predial. personal. oblat. et al. spiritual. profic. per ann. £19 6s. 8d. Ordinatio dat. 3 Jan. 1297. Reg. Winch. MSS. Lambeth.	1	19	7¼
7	2	8½	DYMCHURCH, R.—(St. Peter and St. Paul). The King £80. In £80. 7 acr. marisc. gleb. Mars. Scot. 4s. 8d. Prox. et Sinod. 10s. 10d.	0	14	3¼
3	0	0	ORGARSWICK, R.—Ecclesia destructa. Dean and Chapter of Canterbury. In un. acr. terr. gleb. ad val. 2s.	0	6	0
5	6	8	EASTBRIDGE, R.—(The church demolished). St. Thomas Hospital. Archbishop of Canterbury.	0	10	8
8	14	4½	WESTHETH, V., alias WESTHYTH—(St. Mary). Archdeacon of Canterbury, Propr. and Patr. Endow. in mans. and dimid. acr. terr. per ann.	0	17	5¼

HISTORY OF ROMNEY MARSH.

KING'S BOOKS.		YEARLY TENTHS.
£ s. d.		£ s. d.

	1s. 8d. In decim. predial. personal. oblat. et spiritual. profic. per ann. £9 0s. 4d. Prox. 7s. 6d.	
20 10 10	BURMERSH, R.—(All Saints). Marsh. Scots. 1s. 3d.	2 1 1
150 0 0	The King. In mans. and 3 acr. terr. gleb. per ann. 10s. Prox. 5s. 7d.	
	EAST GUILDFORD, alias EAST GUILDEFORD, R.—(St. Mary). Terr. gleb. ad valor. 4s. 6d., &c. Sir George Choute, bart. 1699; Edward Symes, gent. 1706; Robert Margerison, clerk, 1753.	
	Clear yearly value . . . £41 4 0	
8 4 7	King's Books 8 4 7	0 8 5½
	Living discharged.	
	BROOMHILL, Curacy.—Not certified. Eccl. destructa. It stood in Sussex.	
	FAIRFIELD, C.—(St. Thomas Becket). £50 certified value. Exempt from the Archdeacon. Earl of Guildford, Patr. and Propr.	

From this list I exclude the parishes of Fairfield, Booomhill, and East Guldeford, as they are not complete. The whole amount of tenths and fifteenths is £62 16s. 2¼d. in the above parishes, and that of tenths is £32 11s., which, being deducted from the whole, leaves £30 5s. 1¼d. as the amount of the fifteenths; but when we come to analyse the several parishes, as is done below, we find a different result.

Tenths and Fifteenths.	PARISH.	Tenths.	Fifteenths.
£ s. d.		£ s. d.	£ s. d.
0 16 0	New Romney	0 13 7½	0 2 4½
0 13 4	Old Romney	1 11 11	—
9 2 4	Lydd	5 11 2½	3 11 1½
0 4 2	Midley	3 0 0	—
2 17 11	Snargate	1 14 8	1 3 3
3 17 0	Brookland	1 15 3¼	2 1 8¾
4 3 4	St. Mary's	2 6 4½	1 16 11½
4 0 2	Brensett	0 15 10¾	3 4 3¼
2 11 0½	Snave	1 18 9½	0 12 3
4 19 5	Ivechurch	4 9 8	0 9 9
13 16 10½	Hope	1 0 1¼	12 16 9¼
0 12 0	Blackmanstone	0 8 0	0 4 0
3 6 9	Newchurch	2 16 0¼	0 10 8¾
3 1 10	Dymchurch	0 14 3¼	2 7 6¾
1 2 5	Orgarswick	0 6 0	0 16 5
2 0 1	Eastbridge	0 10 8	1 9 5
1 3 2¼	West Hythe	0 17 5¼	0 5 9
4 8 4	Burmarsh	2 1 1	2 7 3
£62 16 2¼		£32 11 0	£33 19 7¼

In examining this account, we find some curious results. We might have expected that, as the tenths amount to £32 1s., the fifteenths should be £30 5s. 1¼d., but instead of this the fifteenths amount to £33 19s. 7¼d.; while in two cases, those of Old Romney and Midley, the tenths in the King's books exceed the tenths and fifteenths combined, according to the Record of Queen Elizabeth. The tenths and fifteenths in this last account exceed those of the Record by the sum of £3 14s. 5d., which is the difference between the tenths alone of the parishes of Old Romney and Midley, and the tenths and fifteenths combined in the Record.

Another thing which cannot fail to strike the reader is the very great difference between the amount of fifteenths paid by different parishes; as, for instance, Hope paid £12 16s. 9½d., while New Romney paid only 2s. 4½d., the former being a parish with very few inhabitants, and the latter a considerable town. If the fifteenths were laid on cities and towns alone, I am unable to account for this incongruity; because here we find the principal town of the district almost exempt. If I might be allowed to hazard a conjecture, I would say that perhaps the fifteenths and tenths mentioned in Queen Elizabeth's Record only ran over the land in the several parishes, and that the towns and villages were taxed separately to the fifteenths; so that the small sum of 2s. 4½d., set down as the fifteenth paid by the town of Romney, did in fact arise from some few houses without the boundaries of the town, and thus Midley, being then without a church, and probably with few or no inhabitants, was not liable to pay any fifteenths. I do not insist on this being the case, but again repeat that I know of no other solution of the difficulty, and must leave it to others, more versed in these matters than myself, to clear it up.

Since our last summary we see that Guldeford Church had been erected, and thus the whole of the parishes in Walland, as well as in Romney, Marsh had come into existence, though there were still some lands in this parish as yet uninclosed, but of which mention will be made in our next chapter.

SECT. VI.

The Changes which took place from A.D. 1600 to 1838; being a period of 237 years.

JAMES I, in the first year of his reign, A. D. 1603, confirmed the charter of Romney Marsh.

It appears that on Dec. 17th, 1591, Robert Carpenter, mayor, and the jurats, had written to Lord Treasurer Burghley to recommend an Italian emigrant for repairing the harbour. The following is a copy of the address: "Our dutyes to your honour most humbly remembered, so it is, if it please your honour that the bearer hereof, an Italyan, now of late having examined our haven and harbour of Rye, and all yndraughte, sea markes, and water-sprynge near to the same, he hath faithfully promysed that within few years he will make the said haven and harbour of Rye (the Camber only excepted) more serviceable than it hath been at any tyme heretofore, which worke he wolde be content to begynne in the springe of this next yere, yf it may stande with the good pleasure of your honour and of the rest of the lords of her Majesty's most honorable Privye Councell, wherein we most humblye desire your honorable furtherance to her Majesty towerde such a werke as your honour shall find the same to be profytable and commodious for the moste parte of the realme useing the seas, and also to harbour her Majesty's shipps when cause requireth, and to maintane the provysion of fysche, wherewith her Majesty and divers of great honour have been from hence well served. Towarde the advancement of which werke your honour shall finde us most reddye to the uttermost of our abilities. But herein the Italian desireth her Majesty's priviledge, that during his lyffe none to attempt to preserve or amende any havens or creeks in England by that means that he shall do this worke by (the same not being putt in use by any other heretofore). And thus referrynge ourselves and the estate of this our town and countrye adjoyninge to your honorable consideration, we most humblie take our leave, at Rye, this 17th Dec. 1591. Your honour's most bounden, the maior and jurats of Rye.

ROBT. CARPENTER, Maior.	THO. COLBRAND.
ROBT. BITT.	WILLYAM TOLKYER.
WILLYAM RADCLYFF.	WM. DIDSBURY.
HEN. GAYMER.	

" To the Right Hon. and our very good Lord Burghley,
    Lord High Treasurer of England."

The name of this Italian was John Baptist de Trento, to judge from two letters annexed to the petition. He boasts of great knowledge of foreign coasts, more particularly of China, and alludes to his acquaintance with Mr. Loch, Factor-general of the Muscovy Commission, to whom he had spoken of his experience in havens; also of being known to Lord Cobham, and Mr. Rodolphus Warcopp (secretary to Lord Walsingham); and of having lived two years and a half in the house of Mr. George Smythe, brother of Sir Thomas S——, whom he styles "grande secrettario" (doubtless the same Sir Thomas who was chairman of the East India and Muscovy Companies, and afterwards ambassador to Russia). The Signor's brother is described as a talented physician of the court; and the Signor as no needy adventurer, having, three years prior to writing the second letter, brought with him 2000 crowns from Italy, of which sum 350 only were remaining. He then hints about coming over to the Protestant church, vows he takes the sacrament every month, and wishes he may suffer all the pains of hell if he ever had (notwithstanding the council had decided against him) any sinister intention relative to her Majesty or the crown. The Signor concludes by alluding to some grand plan for the benefit of England, which he will communicate by word of mouth only, and is to be found at the "White Horse, Lymptrit (Lyme street?), and ready to serve my lord, and pray for his eternal peace and welfare." As far as Rye harbour was concerned, De Trento was an ignis fatuus.

In 1618 the following petition was presented to the Lord Warden of the Cinque Ports, showing that the scheme of the Italian, if ever put in practice, had no good effect.

"Right Honorable: Our most humble duty be remembered. The experience of your honorable disposition, care, and desire of good towards this our poor decayed town, hath moved us yet once again to make known to your good lordship our wants and miserable poor estate, as unto our only stay and refuge, next under God and his Majesty. And whereas, we have heretofore been, by reason of a harbour, in some trade and commerce by sea, enabled to bear about the charge and maintenance of this town; but now (although we have long sued for help in this case) is our harbour so decayed, that all trade hath forsaken us; and besides the importable charge in defending the rage of the sea from eating up our ways to the town, and maintaining the jetties and places of refuge for our few fisher-boats yet remaining, with the extreme poverty of our fishermen, who, by reason of the great spoil of fish and fishing-places so decayed, that thousands of them are ready to beg and starve for want;

and many of them forsaking the town, have left their wives and children to be parish charge; and those of trades, as God knoweth, there are very few, and them so burdened and surcharged by continual sesses and taxes, we having no revenues or other means to maintain the town, are most of them determined rather to seek other dwellings than here, by such extraordinary impositions and taxes, to decay and impoverish themselves; whereby it is likely that in short time this town, that hath been not long since of good respect and importance, is now in possibility (if some gracious aspect shine not upon it) to be quite depopulate and abandoned.

"Your honour's most humbly at commandment,

"THE MAYOR AND JURATS OF RYE.

" From Rye,
March 3d, 1618."

About this time, or at least before 1623, the Wet Level was made a reservoir for the drainage of the levels below Knell; at or about which spot was a wall, called the Bush Wall, which prevented the waters above from running into this reservoir. In consequence of this, the levels above were flooded, and the people from Ewhurst came down and cut the wall, letting their waters into the Wet level.

In 1627, being the 3d of Charles I, the following brief was granted by the king for the benefit of Rye harbour:

"Charles, by the grace of God, King of England, Scotland, France, and Ireland, Defender of the Faith, &c. To all and singular archbishops, bishops, archdeacons, deanes, and their officials, parsons, vicars, curates, and to all spiritual persons: and also to all justices of the peace, maiors, sherifs, bayliffs, constables, churchwardens, and headboroughs: and to all officers of cities, boroughs, and townes corporate: and to all other our officers, ministers, and subjects, whatsoever they be, as well within liberties as without, to whom these presents shall come, greeting.

Whereas, we are credibly given to understand, as well by the humble supplication and petition of the maior, jurates, and inhabitants of the towne and port of Rie, in our county of Sussex, as also by a certificate made at the second sessions of the peace, holden for our said countie, the tenth day January last past, under the hands of our trusty and wellbeloved subjects Sir Thos. Pelham, Bart., Sir Thos. Sackvill, Sir John Thurley, and Sir Thos. Parker, Knts., Richard Amherst, sergeant-at-law, Richard Lewkenor, Robt. Foster, and Anthony Fowle, Esquires, justices of the peace within our foresaid county, That the said towne, being an ancient port towne within the Cinque Ports, and the most convenientest passage between England and France, and the chiefest sea towne for provision of fish for our house, and heretofore flourished in wealth and prosperity by their great trade and trafficke by sea, their harbour being then able to receive two hundred good ships, which bred up great store of mariners for our service, is now very much impoverished, by reason of the wharfes, sea-wall, sluices, and jetties made for preservation of the said haven are greatly decayed and ruined by extraordinarie storms and violence of the sea, which hath occasioned the decay of trade and trafficke of the said towne, whereby the inhabitants are become unable either to repair the said haven, or amend the decayed breaches of the said walls, and to erect new keys, jetties, and sluices, or to defend the said towne and dwellings from utter inundations, if some speedy relief be not afforded them to prevent the same. And inasmuch also as ships and barkes have no other safe harbor upon all that south coast to avoyde the pursuing enemies or stormes at sea, the same being also of great importance to the *confining* parts of this county for exportation and importation of vendable commodities, and hath beene and still is replenished with very many inhabitants: and by decay of the said harbor many ships are like to perish; and by overflowe of the said towne the inhabitants inforced to abandon the same, to the prejudice of the county, and that part of the kingdome next towards the sea. The said inhabitants, being willing to save the said towne from utter losse, and the country from damage by the losse thereof, are ready to extend themselves to the utmost of their abilities to repair the said harbor, and to expresse their forwardnesse therein, they have caused the same to be surveyed by men of the best skill and experience they could get, in whose judgments lesse than three thousand pounds will not defray the necessary charges of the timber and other worke to be employed upon the same; which said summe the inhabitants are in no wayes able to disburse. And therefore they have most humbly besought us, that out of our princely care to workes of this nature, we would be graciously pleased to afford unto them such reliefe as to others in the like cases hath been granted, by way of a collection of the charity of good people, within certaine counties and places hereafter mentioned, unto whose request, tending to the publicke good of this our realme, we have most willingly condiscended; not doubting but that all good Christians and our loving subjects, well weighing the premises, will be ready and willing to extend their most free and liberall contributions towards the furtherance of so good and needful a worke.

"Know ye, therefore, that of our especiall grace and princely compassion, we have given and graunted, and by these our letters patents doe give and graunt, unto our true and loyall subjects, the maior and jurats of the port and towne of Rye aforesaid, on behalf of the rest of the inhabitants, and to their deputie and deputies, the bearer or bearers hereof, full power, licence, and authority to aske, gather, receive, and take the almes and charitable benevolence of all our loving subjects whatsoever inhabiting within our cities of London and Westminster, with the suburbes and liberties thereof, and in our counties of Sussex, Surrey, Kent, Southampton, Dorset, Essex, Suffolke, Norfolke, Lincolne, Middlesex, Hartford, Buckingham, Devon, Cornwall, Somerset, and Wilts; with our city of Chichester, our borough of Southwarke, our citties of Canterbury, Rochester, and the Cinque Ports; our citty of Winchester, our towne of Southampton, and our Isle of Wight; our towne and county of Poole, and in our citties of Norwich, Lincolne, Exeter, Bristoll, Bath, Wells, and Salisbury; and in all other citties, townes corporate, priviledged places, parishes, villages, and in all other places whatsoever within our said counties, and not elsewhere, for and towards the repairing of the said harbour.

"Therefore we will and command you and every of you, that at such time and times as the said maior or jurats, or their deputie or deputies, the bearer or bearers hereof, shall come and repaire to any your churches, chappels, or other places, to aske and receive the gratuities and charitable benevolences of our said subjects, quietly to permit and suffer them so to doe, without any manner your lets or contradictions. And you the said parsons, vicars, and curates, for the better stirring up of a charitable devotion, deliberately to publish and declare the tenor of these our letters patents, or the copy or briefe thereof, unto our said subjects upon some Sabbath day, when as the same shall be tendred unto you, and exhorting and perswading them to extend their liberall contributions in so good and needful a worke. And you the churchwardens of every parish where such collection is to be made (as aforesaid) to collect and gather from seate to seate, the almes and charitable benevolence of all our loving subjects, as well strangers as others. And what shall be by you so gathered, to be by the minister and yourselves endorsed on the backside of these our letters patents, or the copy of briefe thereof, in words at length, and not in figures. And the summe and summes of money so gathered and endorsed, to deliver to the bearer or bearers of these our letters patents, and to no other person, when as thereunto you shall be required, they showing unto you upon their demand these our letters patents, together with a deputation under the hands and seales of two of the justices aforesaid and the maior of the said towne, as a true warrant for them and no other to receive the same. And our will and pleasure further is, that all such monyes as shall be collected upon these our letters patents, be delivered into the hands and charge of John Sharpe, maior of the said towne, and Richard Cockram, one of the jurats there, to see the same laid out and disposed of according to the true intent and meaning of these our letters patents: and perfect accounts from time to time to be kept thereof by them: any statute, law, ordinance, or provision heretofore made to the contrary, in anywise notwithstanding.

" In witness whereof we have caused these our letters to be made patents, for the space of one whole yeere next after the date hereof to endure. Witness ourselfe at Westminster, the seventh day of February, in the third year of our raign.

" STEWARD.

" God save the King.

(Dated) " Feb. 7th, 1627."

This brief was read at Stone, as appears from the following indorsement on it, viz.:

" Oxney, Stone, Janua 25
1628.

" Gathered for this briefe } Tho. Martin, vic.
" Three shillings.

" Henry Austen } Churchwardens."
" William Austen

In consequence of the civil wars which commenced in the reign of Charles I, and the disturbed state of affairs arising therefrom, we meet with no records particularly relating to Romney Marsh; the time of the Protectorate was equally barren, and it is not until the second year of Charles II that anything took place worthy of notice here, when a grant was made to Edward Guldeford, Esq., the nature of which will be best understood by a perusal of it; for which purpose I here subjoin a copy, for which I am indebted to William Lucas Shadwell, Esq., of Hastings.

Copy of grant to Edward Guldeford, Esq., of the Manor of Higham, in the County of Sussex. Dated Jan. 8th, 1661.

"Charles II, by the Grace of God, of England, Scotland, France, and Ireland, King; Defender of the Faith. To all to whom these present letters shall come, greeting: Know ye, that we, for divers good causes and considerations, as hereunto especially moving of our special grace, and of our certain knowledge and mere motion, have given, granted, and confirmed, and by these presents for us, our heirs and successors, do give, grant, and confirm to our beloved and faithful subject, Edward Guldeford, Esquire, his heirs and assigns, all that the lordship or manor of Higham, otherwise Iham, in our county of Sussex, with all and singular its rights, members, and appurtenances; and also the increase and decrease of the sea there; and all the lands, tenements, rents, reversions, and services, meadows, feedings and pastures, marshes, woods, underwoods, rivers, pools, knights' fees, wards, marriages, reliefs, escheats, advowsons, donations, presentations, free dispositions, patronage, and right of patronage of churches, chapels, and chantries, wreck of the sea, courts, franchises, and liberties whatsoever to the said lordship or manor, in any wise howsoever belonging or appertaining. And also all that the office of bailiff of our town of New Winchelsea; of which town the ground and area were anciently parcel of the aforesaid lordship and manor of Higham, otherwise Iham aforesaid, and the rents of assize of all and singular free tenants and bondmen, residents and non-residents, and all the lands, tenements, waste grounds, places, and herbages, as well within the town aforesaid as without, on the descent of the hills on which the said town is situated, or surrounding the said town; and with the custom of ships and fishing-boats, called shares; and with the custom of divers merchandizes, as well arriving by water as brought by land; and also the custom of wood for tanning, corn, barley, malt, peas, and other grains, beer, sea-salt, pitch, cheese; and of feather-beds, and also lastage, stallage, terrage, ancorage and wharfage, bubrage, tronage, presage, passage, and perquisites of courts and leets, as well of pleas internal and foreign; and also fines, forfeitures, and amerciaments of bakers, maltsters, and other victuallers whatsoever: and for trespasses against the peace of us, our heirs and successors, done and to be done; and with the chattels of felons, fugitives, persons outlawed and attainted, fines for the effusion of the blood of foreigners and inhabitants, waifs, strays, infangthefe and outfangthefe; and also all and all manner of other fees, profits, commodities, authorities, liberties, privileges, jurisdictions, advantages and emoluments whatsoever, to the said office of bailiff of the town aforesaid antiently due, accustomed, and belonging; and which such bailiffs in the same office, to the use and profit of us and our progenitors, have had and received, or have been accustomed to have, receive, and levy. Also we give, and by these presents for us, our heirs and successors, for the consideration aforesaid, grant to the aforesaid Edward Guldeford, his heirs and assigns, all that creek called the Camber, otherwise Wenway; and all those marshes, fresh and salt, and lands, stony, sandy, clayey, and covered with water, called the Camber Marsh and the Camber Salts, and the Camber Beach, and the Camber and Wenway Sands, lying and being in the parish of St. Thomas and St. Giles, within the liberty of the town of Winchelsea, and in the parish of Ecclesham, in Bromehill, or either of them; and all that creek called the Puddle, lying and being in the parish of St. Thomas and St. Giles aforesaid, within the liberty of the town of Winchelsea aforesaid, and either of them; and also the advowsons and free dispositions of the churches of St. Thomas and St. Giles aforesaid, and of every of them; and which creek called the Camber, or otherwise Wenway, and the Puddle, and Marsh and lands aforesaid, called Camber Marsh, Camber Salts, Camber Beach, and Camber and Wenway Sands, and the aforesaid advowson of the aforesaid churches of St. Thomas and St. Giles, appertain or belong to the aforesaid lordship or manor, and to the office of bailiff aforesaid, or either of them, or to the aforesaid lordship or manor, and to the office of bailiff aforesaid, or either of them, are known, had, or reputed to belong or appertain. And also all and singular messuages, mills, houses, edifices, buildings, barns, stables, dove-houses, yards, orchards, gardens, lands, tenements, meadows, feedings, pastures, commons, demesne lands, lands overflowed, lands recovered from the sea, lands concealed, subtracted, or unjustly detained, lands left by the sea, glebe lands, wastes, furze, heaths, moors, banks, walls, ditches, shores, grounds, waste places, marshes, as well fresh as salt; marsh lands and lands subject to inundations of the sea between the flux and reflux of the sea; lands clayey, stoney, sandy, and lands covered with fresh or salt water, creeks, fisheries, whales, sturgeons, the increase and decrease of the sea, waters, watercourses, wears, rivers, passages beyond or over waters, fisheries, fishings, rents, revenues, and services, courts leet, views of frank-pledge, perquisites and profits of courts and leets, and all things which to court leet and view of frank-pledge appertain; chattels of felons and fugitives, felons of themselves and of persons put in exigent, goods and chattels of persons outlawed, or in anywise howsoever condemned, deodands, bondmen, bondwomen, and villeins, with the sequels, estovers, and common of estover, fairs, markets, tolls, tributes, rents, reversions and services, rents charge, rents seck, and rents and services, as well of free as customary tenants, reserved upon any demises or grants whatsoever; works of tenants, free warrens, hawkings, huntings, customs, wreck of the sea, and all other rights, jurisdictions, franchises, liberties, and privileges, profits, commodities, advantages, emoluments and hereditaments whatsoever; with all their rights, members, and appurtenances of what kind, nature, or sort soever they be, or by what names soever they are known, deemed, called, or acknowledged, situate, lying and being, issuing, growing, renewing, happening, or arising in, next, near, or within the lordship or manor aforesaid, or the towns, fields, parishes, places, or hamlets of Higham, otherwise Iham, Winchelsey, St. Thomas and St. Giles, Icklesham, and Bromehill aforesaid, or elsewhere, wheresoever in our said county of Sussex aforesaid, to the lordship or manor, office of bailiff, messuages, lands, tenements, and other the premises above by these presents granted, or mentioned to be granted, or to either or any of them in any wise howsoever belonging, appertaining, incident or appendent, or being or had, accepted or reputed member, part or parcel of the same lordship or manor, office of bailiff, and other the premises above by these presents granted, or mentioned to be granted, and of every part or parcel thereof: And which lordship or manor of Higham, otherwise Iham, and all and singular other the premises above mentioned, with their and every of their appurtenances, by the letters patent of the Lord James, late King of England, our most dear grandfather of pious memory, deceased, under the great seal of England, bearing date at Westminster the tenth day of April, in the eighth year of his reign, were given and granted to Sir Henry Guldeford, Knt., and the heirs male of his body lawfully begotten or to be begotten; and for default of such issue, remainder to the heirs male of the body of Sir Richard Guldeford, Knt., deceased, lawfully begotten, in fee farm for ever, as by the same letters patent, remaining of record, amongst other things is more fully manifest and appears. And further we give, and for us, our heirs and successors, for the consideration aforesaid, grant by these presents to the aforesaid Edward Guldeford, his heirs and assigns, all and singular other the lordships, manors, messuages, lands, tenements, profits, commodities, advantages, emoluments, and hereditaments whatsoever, with their and every of their appurtenances, which by certain letters patent of the Lord Henry the Seventh, late of England, our ancestor, under his great seal of England, bearing date at Westminster the sixth day of October, in the second year of his reign; or by certain other letters patent of the same Lord Henry the Seventh, late king of England, under his great seal of England, bearing date at Westminster the seventeenth day of January, in the twenty-first year of his reign, were given and granted, or mentioned to be given and granted, to the aforesaid Sir Richard Guldeford, Knt., and the heirs male of his body, lawfully begotten, or which by the aforesaid letters patent of our most dear grandfather the Lord James, late king of England, were given and granted, or mentioned to be given and granted, to the aforesaid Sir Henry Guldeford,

Knt., and the heirs male of his body lawfully begotten: and, for default of such issue, to the heirs male of the body of the aforesaid Sir Richard Guldeford, Knt., deceased. And also the reversion and reversions, remainder and remainders whatsoever of all and singular the lordships, manors, office of bailiff, messuages, lands, tenements, hereditaments, and other the premises aforesaid, with the appurtenances by these presents above granted, or mentioned to be granted, and of every part and parcel thereof, dependent or expectant upon the estate tail aforesaid, or either or any of them, or upon any other estates tail, or upon any demise or grant, demises or grants, gift or gifts, for term or terms of life, lives, or years, or otherwise, of the premises aforesaid, or of any part thereof heretofore made, being of record or not of record. And also all and every rent and rents; and all and every payment and payments, and sum and sums of money whatsoever reserved upon the several gifts and grants thereof aforesaid, in form aforesaid made and granted, or in or upon either or any of them, or in or upon any other gifts, demises, and grants, of the premises or any part thereof, in any wise howsoever made; to have, hold, and enjoy, exercise and occupy all and singular the aforesaid lordships, manors, office of bailiff, messuages, lands, tenements, hereditaments, and other the premises aforesaid above by these presents granted, or mentioned to be granted, with all their appurtenances; and our reversion and reversions, remainder and remainders whatsoever of all and singular the same premises and of every of them, and of every part and parcel thereof, to the aforesaid Edward Guldeford, his heirs and assigns; to the only and proper use and behoof of the said Edward Guldeford, his heirs and assigns, in fee farm for ever, as fully, freely, and entirely, and in as ample manner and form as all and singular the same premises above by these presents granted, or mentioned to be granted, or any part or parcel thereof came or ought to have come to our hands or to the hands of any of our progenitors or predecessors, late kings or queens of England, or to the hands of them or any of them by reason or pretext of any dissolution or surrender of either or any late monastery or priory, chantry, college, or hospital, or by reason or pretext of any exchange or purchase of any gift or grant or of either, or any attainder or forfeiture, or by reason or pretext of any act or acts of parliament, or by reason of escheat, or by any other lawful manner, right, or title whatsoever, and as the same premises now are or ought to be or to have been in our hands; to hold of us, our heirs and successors, as of our manor of East Greenwich, in the county of Kent, in free and common socage and not in chief, nor by knight's service; yielding and paying therefore yearly to us, our heirs and successors, twenty pounds of lawful money of England at the receipt of our exchequer at Westminster at the feasts of Easter and St. Michael the Archangel, payable by equal portions every year for ever for all rents, services, and demands whatsoever, for the same to us, our heirs and successors, in anywise howsoever to be rendered, paid, or done, and without account or any other thing, to us, our heirs or successors, for the said to be rendered, paid, or done, provided nevertheless always and by these presents of our more abundant special grace and of our certain knowledge and mere motion, we will, and by these presents for us, our heirs and successors, grant to the aforesaid Edward Guldeford, his heirs and assigns, that these our letters patent, or anything in the same contained, or any other letters patent by us or by any of our progenitors and predecessors of and in the premises, or of any part or parcel thereof heretofore made, or anything in the same, or any of them contained, shall in nowise extend themselves to charge the aforesaid Edward Guldeford, his heirs or assigns, or the aforesaid lordships, manors, office of bailiff, and all and singular other the premises above by these presents granted or mentioned to be granted, or any part or parcel thereof, with the payment of any double rent, or with a double tenure for the premises above by these presents granted, or mentioned to be granted, or any part or parcel thereof, nor that by reason or pretext of any other former letters patent by us or by any of our progenitors out of the aforesaid premises above by these presents granted, or mentioned to be granted, or of any part thereof made, or of these our letters patent, any other yearly rent than one yearly rent, or only one sum of twenty pounds shall be hereafter yearly to us, our heirs or successors, for the premises or any of the premises payable. And that from time to time hereafter, so often as the aforesaid Edward Guldeford, his heirs and assigns, or either of them, shall pay or cause to be paid yearly to us, our heirs and successors, at the receipt of the exchequer of us, our heirs and successors, one rent or sum of twenty pounds of lawful money of England out of it for the premises with the appurtenances by these presents reserved. That then and so often the same Edward Guldeford, his heirs and assigns, and every of them, shall be discharged and acquitted from the payment of any other rent or sum of twenty pounds, or of any part thereof, or of any sum whatsoever, for the premises with the appurtenances for the said year for which such payment shall have been made as aforesaid. And that no other rent or service or sum of money than the aforesaid single rent of twenty pounds shall be hereafter to us, our heirs or successors, by reason or pretext of these our letters patent, or of the aforesaid other letters patent above mentioned, or of any other the letters patent of us or of any of our progenitors or predecessors heretofore made due, reserved, or to be made for or in respect of the aforesaid lordships, manors, office of bailiff, messuages, lands, tenements, and other the premises above by these presents granted, or mentioned to be granted, or of any part or parcel thereof. Also we will, and by these presents for us, our heirs and successors, grant to the aforesaid Edward Guldeford, his heirs and assigns, that if and so often as any doubts or questions shall happen to arise or be moved within the space of ten years next following after the date of these presents, concerning the validity of these our letters patent, or of the estate, title, or interest of the said Edward Guldeford, his heirs or assigns, of, in, or to the premises aforesaid, or any part thereof, or otherwise in any manner howsoever, whereby our true intention may be the less fulfilled to the greatest advantage of the aforesaid Edward Guldeford, his heirs and assigns. That then and so often within the time aforesaid, upon the humble petition of the aforesaid Edward Guldeford, his heirs or assigns, to us, our heirs or successors, by the Attorney General of us our heirs and successors, for the time being, of the defects thereof required to be amended. We, our heirs and successors, at the proper costs and charges in the law of the aforesaid Edward Guldeford, his heirs or assigns, will graciously condescend to grant other letters patent of the premises, or of any part or parcel thereof, to the same Edward Guldeford, his heirs and assigns, with such and the like amendment, explanation, and addition, as by the Attorney General aforesaid in this behalf shall be reasonably advised and devised. And further, of our more ample special grace and of our certain knowledge and mere motion, we will, and by these presents grant to the aforesaid Edward Guldeford, his heirs and assigns, that these our letters patent, or an enrolment of the same, shall be in and by all things firm, valid, good, sufficient, and effectual, in the law towards and against us, our heirs and successors, as well in all our courts as elsewhere wheresoever within our kingdom of England, without any confirmations, licences, or tolerations of us, our heirs or sucessors, by the aforesaid Edward Guldeford, his heirs or assigns, to be procured or obtained notwithstanding the misnaming or not naming, misreciting or not reciting the aforesaid lordships, manors, office of bailiff, messuages, lands, tenements, meadows, feedings, pastures, and other the premises above by these presents granted, or mentioned to be granted, or any part or parcel thereof: and notwithstanding the not finding or misfinding the office or offices, inquisition or inquisitions, of the premises above by these presents granted, or mentioned to be granted, or any part or parcel thereof, by which our title ought to have been found before the making of these our letters patent, or of the yearly rent reserved of, in, and upon the premises, or of, in, and upon any part or parcel thereof, in these our letters patent expressed and contained: and notwithstanding any defect or defects in the nonreciting or misreciting any demise or demises, grant or grants, gift or gifts, of or concerning the premises, or of or concerning any part or parcel thereof, or of any profit thereof, being of record, or not of record, in any wise howsoever heretofore made: and notwithstanding the misnaming or not naming any town, hamlet, parish, place, or county, in which the premises, or any part or parcel thereof are or is: and notwithstanding that if the names of the tenants, farmers, or occupiers of the lands, tenements, and hereditaments aforesaid, or of any of the premises, or of any part or parcel thereof, or of the yearly rent reserved of, in, and upon the premises, or of, in, and upon any part or parcel thereof in these our letters patent expressed and contained, true, full, and certain mention is not made: and notwithstanding any variance, distinction, and difference in any thing, matter, name, or form, between these our letters patent and any particular or survey of the premises, or of any part thereof, heretofore made, or between these our letters patent and any record or records in anywise howsoever touching or concerning the accompt or accompts of the premises aforesaid, or of any part thereof: and notwithstanding any defects of the certainty or computation or declaration of the true yearly value of the premises, or of any part or parcel thereof, or of the yearly rent reserved of, in, and upon the premises, or of, in, and upon any part thereof in these our letters patent expressed and contained: and that notwithstanding that the same premises or any part thereof ever were of a better or greater yearly value than in these our letters patent or in any particular of the premises, or of any part thereof is specified: and notwithstanding the statute made and passed in the parliament of the Lord Henry the Sixth, late King of England, our ancestor, in the eighteenth year of his reign: and notwithstanding the statute made and framed in the parliament of the Lord Henry the Fourth, late King of England, in the first year of his reign: and notwithstanding any other defects in the not naming or not rightly naming the natures, kinds, sorts, quantities and qualities, metes, and bounds of the premises, or of any part thereof, or either or any, who heretofore were or was seized of the premises, or either or any of them, or any estate tail to us or any of our progenitors or ancestors heretofore made: and notwithstanding the mis-reciting or non-reciting or not fully mentioning our estate or estates of freehold or inheritance of or in the premises, or any part thereof, to which we are or were entitled by reason of any attainder, escheat, conveyance, or assurance whatsoever: and any other act, statute, ordinance, provision, thing, or matter whatsoever to the contrary thereof in anywise notwithstanding. Also we will, and by these present declare our royal will, that if it shall happen that the yearly rent to us, our heirs and successors, by these presents in form aforesaid reserved, shall be in arrear and unpaid in part or in whole by the space of forty days after either of the feasts on which it ought to be paid; that then and so often the aforesaid Edward Guldeford, his heirs and assigns, shall forfeit and pay to us, our heirs and successors, forty shillings of lawful money of England, in the name of a pain, beyond the aforesaid yearly rent above by these presents reserved for every feast on which the same rent, or any part thereof, shall so be in arrear and unpaid in manner and form aforesaid: and if the aforesaid Edward Guldeford, his heirs or assigns, shall not enroll or cause to be enrolled these our letters patent in due manner in our exchequer, at Westminster, within the space of six months next following after the date of these presents, that then the aforesaid Edward Guldeford, his heirs and assigns, shall forfeit and pay to us, our heirs or successors, five pounds of lawful money of England in the name of a pain; and so thereafter for every six months, to begin from the date of these presents, until these our letters patent shall be enrolled in manner and form aforesaid: and that thenceforth from thence from time to time, so often as the case shall thus happen, it may and shall be lawful to us, our heirs and successors, by the receiver-general of us, our heirs and successors, of the aforesaid premises for the time being, or by his sufficient deputy or deputies into the premises aforesaid, or into any part or parcel thereof, to enter and distrain: and the distresses there found or to be found to take and retain until we, our heirs and successors of the aforesaid rent above reserved, together with the arrearages thereof, if any be, and of the several forfeitures in the name of a pain aforesaid, as well for the non-payment of the rent aforesaid as for the non-enrolment of these our letters patent shall be fully satisfied and paid, anything in these presents contained to the contrary thereof notwithstanding. Also we will, and by these presents grant to the aforesaid Edward Guldeford, that he may have and shall have these our letters patent under our great seal of England in due manner made and sealed without fine or fee, great or small, to us in our hanaper or elsewhere to our use for the same in anywise howsoever to be rendered, paid, or done; although express mention of the true yearly value, or of the certainty of the premises, or either of them, or of other gifts or grants heretofore made by us or by any of our progenitors or predecessors to the aforesaid Edward Guldeford is not made in these presents or any statute, act, ordinance, provision, proclamation, or restriction, to the contrary thereof, heretofore had, made, passed, ordained, or provided, or any other thing, cause, or matter whatsoever in anywise notwithstanding. In testimony whereof we have caused these our letters to be made patent. Witness ourself, at Westminster, the eighth day of January, in the thirteenth year of our reign.

" By writ of privy seal. HOWARD."

The grant above recited seems to have given to Edward Guldeford all the lands in the manor of Iham, in which was situated the present town of Winchelsea. It ran over all those lands which were partially left or to be left by the sea in the several parishes of St. Thomas and St. Giles, in the town of Winchelsea, of Icklesham, and of Broomhill. No mention is made of the parish of Guldeford, all the waste lands of the latter having probably been already granted to the family, as reference is made to former grants, one made by Henry VII, dated 1486, to Sir Richard Guldeford, knt., and another in 1610 to Sir Henry Guldeford, knt. The fee-farm rent of £20 a year, which was reserved to the King by the grant, is now the property of the Honorable Mr. Herbert (a relative of the Earl of Caernarvon), and is paid by the under-mentioned persons in the following proportions, viz.:—

	£	s.	d.
Mr. William Longley, Camber Farm, in the parish of Winchelsea	6	12	0
Rev. T. S. Curteis	2	18	0
Mrs. Curteis	1	10	0
Do.	3	8	4
Devisees of the late Mr. William Croughton	2	4	0
Mrs. Curteis Mr. John Stonham Mr. Mortimer Mr. Thos. Mills	3	7	8
	£20	0	0

It may seem strange, but there does not appear to be any part of the rent payable from lands on the west side of the Rother, although the greater part of the parish of Icklesham lies here, and but very little on the east side; and when it is considered, also, that the greater part of the Castle Farm must have been then uninclosed.

The next thing we shall introduce is Lord Clarendon's Decree, dated June 26th, 1666, which—

" SHEWETH—That, in 1604, Thomas Fane and others exhibited their bill of complaint into the Court of Chancery, against Sir Edward Hales and others, to the effect that they (the complainants) are owners of lands in Wittersham Level—and that the said Level hath, for the last forty years and upwards, consisted of 1000 acres, or thereabouts, of high marsh land, and of 1500 acres, or thereabouts, of low marsh land; all which said high lands, about thirty-seven years ago, were good summer and winter lands, and all the said low lands were then also good summer lands, and for the most part good winter lands; and that the said Level is governed by a particular Commission of sewers: and that the Upper Levels, for the last forty years, did consist of 5000 acres, or thereabouts, of marsh adjoining to the said Wittersham Level, the greatest part of which were, about thirty-six years since, drowned and lost, yielding no benefit, and the residue were then decaying, and in danger of being lost also: that the said Upper Levels were governed by another particular Commission, and that the owners (having fruitlessly spent about £20,000 about the draining and preserving the said marsh, by the old circular way of sewing by Appledore) took into consideration a new course or channel, which might be made through Wittersham Level in a direct line, and five miles in ten nearer to the sea than the former old circular way; but, as the same could not be effected but by sewing through Wittersham Level, they made several propositions to the owners of the said marsh to obtain their consent. The parties having agreed—the owners of the two Levels petitioned the Lord Keeper, the owners of the Upper Levels, that they and the owners of Wittersham Level might be governed by one Commission, and the owners of Wittersham Level that they might be governed by their own particular Commission as formerly. And, upon hearing of counsel on both sides, Nov. 17th, 1629, his Lordship ordered—That there should be six indifferently chosen of the owners of the Upper Levels, who had no lands in Wittersham Level, and six owners of Wittersham, who had no lands in Upper Levels, and these twelve, or major part, should consider of some means for the draining of Upper Levels, without prejudice to Wittersham, or, if they should receive prejudice, then they might be secured out of the lands of the said Upper Levels. In pursuance whereof, Sir George Fane, knt., and five others were chosen for the Wittersham Level, at Robertsbridge; and Sir Edward Hales, knt., and five others, were chosen for the Upper Levels, at Maidstone. That, after the space of two years or so, upon February 15th, 1631, these twelve made an agreement for completing certain works for the recovery and preservation of the Upper Levels, and also for securing and indemnifying Wittersham Level. The agreement was as follows, viz.:

That the Wittersham Level be governed by its own particular Commission, and that the Wittersham Commission, in return, join in making such decrees as may be necessary to maintain the works to be done.

That the Upper Levels shall, at their cost, procure the King's licence to turn the navigable river of Rother into the new channel. By the Upper Levels hereafter are intended all the lands sewing into the river of Rother and channel of Appledore, between Udiham Oak and Oxney Ferry.

That the new channel running from Kent Wall to the lands of Mr. Howden and Mr. Michelbourn, and so through them to the sea, be fifty feet wide at bottom, and in proportion thereunto at the top, and of the same depth as the present Wittersham sewer, which is to be accounted part of the said fifty feet.

That good and sufficient walls be made on each side to prevent both salt and fresh water from getting into the land.

That the low lands between Kent Wall and Knell's Dam, shall be laid out for an indraught.

That any owner of lands in Wittersham Level having land injured be indemnified by a jury.

That every owner of land in Wittersham Level, who shall have any land taken for the indraught, shall, for every £20 a year, have made over to him, as security, £30 a year in fee-simple lands, and so in proportion.

That every owner giving up lands for indraught have, besides the above security, 2s. per acre, in consideration of their loss of hay.

That the owners and occupiers of indraught lands may take slut and sleech from their own lands, and may fish and fowl in the waters thereof.

That Upper Levels pay the tithes and all taxes on indraught lands as at present charged.

That Upper Levels also pay all future tithes and taxes.

That a free ferry be made at Kent Wall, and maintained by Upper Levels; and that the consideration of a bridge at Blackwall (so much insisted on by the country) be referred to a view in the country.

That they make two private sewers, one in Sussex and one in Kent side, to drain Wittersham high lands below Kent Wall, with such number of bridges as shall be requisite for the owners, at the charge of Upper Levels.

That all lands taken from Wittersham for indraught be measured and plotted, as far as the upland hedges, so that when the ditches and bounds be swarved up, the owners may, in after times, recover their several possessions, at the charge of Upper Levels.

That owners of indraught land may inclose any part of their lands on giving up a proportionate part of their rent. That no owner of Upper Levels shall have power so to inclose indraught lands from the sea until it is worth 13s. 4d. per acre, except such as Wittersham owners shall say can receive no further benefit.

That all lands required for new cut be paid for three months before the work is begun.

That as soon as composition is made, the cut may be commenced, provided that neither fresh nor salt water be let into Wittersham Level until all articles for their security be performed.

That if any Wittersham high lands be damaged, bailiffs and expenditors, and sworn men of Wittersham shall value such damage, and when such valuation is ratified by two Commissioners not interested in Upper Levels, the same shall be delivered to clerk or expenditor of Upper Levels for payment, and, on refusal, Wittersham expenditor may distrain within one month after notice, on any of the fee-simple lands of Upper Levels.

That a jury of Kent and Sussex do find that the Upper Levels cannot be preserved without the intended new cut.

The Commissioners to view and decree the works, and satisfaction to indraught land owners, and also to owners of high lands.

That this Decree be confirmed in Chancery, with the royal assent, if thought needful.

That a bill in Chancery, to be preferred by owners of Wittersham Level against Upper Levels, suggesting the damage that may happen to them by the new works, and that the defendants who have the benefit thereby, suppose their estates not liable thereunto, nor themselves bound thereby.

That defendants submit to the Decree of Court.

That defendants' estate given for recompence be fee-simple.

That the lands decreed for security of indraught lands lie between Farn-hill Wall and Bodiham Bridge; for security of high lands in Wittersham, there shall be as much land secured as is worth £500 per annum above all charges, and at this time so let.

This Decree further sheweth—that all these articles were agreed to and benefit reaped therefrom by Upper Levels; but, before all things were accordingly accomplished, the sea and dead waters of the Upper Levels broke in upon above 1500 acres land in Wittersham Level, and that great danger threatened the rest: whereupon the aforesaid Lord Keeper, in September 1635, ordered (on complaint made to him) that the waters broken in should there remain, and Sir Edward Hales and others should enter into covenants to Sir George Fane and others, to make satisfaction for damage which was, or should be, sustained by the owners of Wittersham Level, by reason of the continuing the sea and letting of the river of Rother into the said indraught until such securities as formerly mentioned should be perfected; or otherwise Knell Dam should be made up at the charges of the said Upper Levels. In pursuance whereof, about February 1636, the said Sir Edward Hales and others entered into certain articles of agreement, as follows:

That as a breach has been made in Knell Dam, preventing the works (formerly agreed to be done) to be perfected, the parties renew the former contract, unless altered by the Decree of Commissioners of Sewers.

Agree to pay the rent to indraught landowners half-yearly, at the church porch in the town of Rye, and to make good all damages done.

That the Upper Levels Commissioners shall finish their works so as to let the sea into the new channel before Michaelmas, 1636, if the Wittersham Commissioners think it fit.

That, within one year after letting in the sea, the Upper Levels Commissioners shall make a stop or dam upon and across the Rother, between the lands of Sir George Fane and the lands of Mr. Howden, and shall keep the same in repair.

That if Upper Levels have not completed all the intended works by Michaelmas, 1636, then they shall repair Knell's Dam, and keep it in repair for one whole year, or make compensation for damages.

That Upper Levels may make one or more stops in the new sewer of Wittersham, above the pond of the indraught, to convey Rother waters into the sea at the new gut.

That Upper Levels repair and keep Kent Bridge until a sufficient ferry be made, as before agreed.

That Upper Levels put in sluice, or sluices in the sea wall near the lands of Sir George Fane, to let out Rother waters.

That Wittersham Levels owners may cut down timber or wood growing on low lands for their own use.

That all these articles be fulfilled.

That, in consequence of the works agreed on being done, the Upper Levels lands increased in value from being well drained, and became worth 20*s*. per acre, therefore Wittersham Levels expected to have their rents paid, as they had performed their part of the agreement, and that Upper Levels had paid the same rents and damages for near thirty years (amounting to £2500 per annum); but that, owing to some differences among themselves about apportioning the same, they have not been paid, and many have suffered in consequence; of all which Sir E. Hales and others taking advantage, and combining to deprive them of their dues, the said rents, &c. have increased to £2879, and they refuse to pay, and thus Wittersham Levels prayed the Court for redress. That the Court did grant a Commission of Sewers, when these differences were settled, and the major part agreed to pay the money due to Wittersham Levels; but still Sir Edward Hales and others refused to pay, on account of some informality in securities, when the Wittersham Levels again petitioned the Court that the arrears might be paid, and all the original articles performed, and defendants subpœnaed into Court, which process being granted, and the defendants served therewith, they appeared and made answer that they acknowledged the articles originally agreed to; that they had been at great expense; that they got in arrear; that differences arose between them about apportioning scots; that, in 1662, they petitioned Court to end these differences; that the Court referred the differences to the Lord Chief Justices, who made their Report July 2d following (i. e. 1663); and a Commission was issued, according to that Report, to several persons at a Session of Sewers, held at Maidstone, September 3, 1663, when it was ordered that Sir Nathaniel Powell and Thomas Herlackenden, Esquire, should end all differences; who reported that all arrears, future rents, and damages be provided for by a scot on Upper Levels, during the continuance of such indraught, and for all general works, whenever the same shall be required: one scot yearly to be of 6*d*. per acre, paid on all lands between Udiam Oak and Knock, in the Isle of Oxney, and the foot of Appledore Windmill, and all other scots yearly to be 2*d*. per acre; for all winter lands or high lands lying in the Levels of Shirley Moor, Redhill, and Appledore, unto and as far as the foot of the windmill thereof, 4*d*. per acre; for all the lands anciently reputed to be scotted, as summer lands above Farn-hill Wall, 5*d*. per acre; for all the other summer lands lying below Farn-hill Wall, 6*d*. per acre; for the casual summer lands in the Levels of Measham, Ewhurst, and Bodiham, 1*s*. per acre; and that all other lands heretofore scotted to the said works and indraught do pay in proportion. That Upper Levels attend both to old sewer of Appledore and new sewer of Wittersham, for the convenience of different lands sewing by either. That this Report was consented unto; and, at another Session of Sewers at Maidstone, ordered and decreed to be performed by all parties, and several times after confirmed by several other orders and decrees made by Commissioners of Upper Levels; and afterwards a day was by this Court appointed for the hearing of the said cause, upon bill and answer, on which day, having been argued by counsel, and defendants being willing to settle all differences, and submit to such order as this Court shall direct, the Court was satisfied that the said several articles, orders, agreements, and decrees made between the parties ought to be ratified, confirmed, and observed by all parties. It is, therefore, this present Term of Easter, (that is to say,) on Saturday, May 6th, 1665, by the Right Honorable Edward, Earl of Clarendon, Lord High Chancellor of England, and by the High Court of Chancery, and the power and authority of the same Court, thought fit, and so ordered, adjudged, and decreed, that the said several articles, orders, agreements, and decrees do stand ratified and confirmed.

CLARENDON,

26 Juni, j665."

About the year 1695, the Commissioners of the Upper Levels made a shut, or bank, called Nichols' Last Shut, from a place called Craven Sluice, quite across Appledore Channel, whereby the river, which was before half a mile abroad, was shut off and secured from the sea, and a small channel only about twenty feet wide was left to sew off the fresh water.

The next matter, in chronological order, bearing the date of 1701, is the following:

"The Case of the Owners of the Upper Levels, relating to a Bill depending in Parliament about the Harbour of Rye.

The Upper Levels contain ten thousand acres of land adjacent to the river Rother, and always sewed their waters into the said river, which anciently passed into the sea, through Romney Marsh, several miles distant from Rye, towards the north-east; but having lost passage, about the year 1610, was turned into the Channel of Appledore, which channel had, at that time, no communication with the ancient or present harbour of Rye, but passed into the sea, through Guildford Marsh, at the distance of two miles from Rye, to the north-east; and, in the year 1623, upon the petition of the inhabitants of Rye, was turned over from the Guildford side, into a small channel on the Rye side, falling into the sea, at the distance of one mile from Rye, towards the north-east.

The Upper Levels, having suffered very much by the inland floods and stoppage of the river Rother; and, after several expensive but unsuccessful attempts, finding it impracticable to drain their lands by their ancient sewer—

They bought and purchased from the owners of Wittersham Level, in Anno Domini 1636, a large new channel, to be cut through Wittersham Level, thereby to sew the Rother through the same into Appledore Channel; and having finished the same soon after (viz. Anno Domini 1644), by the outrage of the sea their banks and walls were broke down, and the whole Level of Wittersham, with great part of the Upper Levels, were drowned.

The true and natural harbour of Rye, in the said year 1644, and always before, lay on the south-west side of the town of Rye, towards Winchelsea; but the sea at that time breaking into a small creek, lying between Guildford Marsh and some low brook lands adjacent to the town of Rye, on the north-east side, flowed several miles up the country, and by its continual and violent flux and reflux so far into the land, in a short time an accidental place, in the nature of a harbour, was formed on the north-east side of the town of Rye; but the inhabitants of Rye and Winchelsea, regarding their present profit more than the preservation of the harbour, seized upon the ground of the old harbour, inning and embanking the derelict lands as their own, whereby the sea, being repelled on the western shore, drove up the eastern channel with greater violence.

Thus, while the country lay under water (and not before) the Channel of Appledore, and the new channel in Wittersham Level, and the accidental channel on the east side of Rye, became navigable by small vessels.

The owners of the Upper Levels, to relieve themselves from the insupportable burthen of scots and taxes assessed upon their lands for the payment of the rents of Wittersham Level, and other ways, amounting to £3000 per annum, and upwards, have at length, at the vast charge of £200,000, drained and recovered these drowned lands from the sea, by inning and embanking Wittersham Level, (and not any derelict lands), and by erecting several slips and sluices in Wittersham Channel and the Channel of Appledore, all which were done by the presentment of juries and decrees of the Commissioners of Sewers, and have restored the lands to the particular proprietors.

Yet now the town of Rye have brought in a bill for the declaring and removing the said stops and sluices as nuisances, and for the opening the passage of the Rother and Appledore, whereby a large country, containing 10,000 acres of ancient lands, saved from the sea at a vast expense, and for which the proprietors have paid above three times the value, will be unavoidably laid under water, to the utter ruin and impoverishment of a great number of families, destruction of several jointures, mortgages, purchases, marriage-settlements, to the great abatement of the king's taxes, and the just fear of all proprietors of land on the sea-coasts, in other counties, of such a dangerous precedent, and yet the accidental harbour of Rye cannot be made a safe or secure harbour.

Upon the whole matter, since the accidental harbour of Rye had anciently no communication with the Rother or Appledore, nor had the inhabitants of Rye any navigation up the same; since the town of Rye have no right to a harbour in the place where it now lies, since the said stops and sluices were made and set down by legal authority, and are not nuisances in law; or, if so, are remediable in the proper and ordinary methods of law; since the town of Rye have it in their own power to restore themselves to their ancient and rightful harbour on the southwest side, by opening and delivering up to the sea the derelict lands they have embanked, and thereby spoiled the same; since the passing of this bill will be so dangerous and destructive to the country, by taking away their property and abandoning them to the sea, the owners of the Upper Levels do humbly hope the bill will be rejected."

To understand the bearings of this case, we must beg our readers to retrace their steps, and recollect that, when the course of the Rother was turned, in 1334, from Romney more to the westward, this river had no well-defined debouchure into the sea, its mouth, properly speaking, might be said to be at Appledore, where all the fresh waters from the Upper Levels were concentrated, when, from this point, they spread at high water over the whole expanse of land still unembanked, between Fairfield, Brookland, and Broomhill on the east, and Winchelsea and Fairlight Cliff on the west; at low water, the stream of the Rother, as well as that of the Brede and Tillingham, found its way through various channels into the sea. In the course of the sixteenth century, Guldeford rose into existence, and a considerable quantity of land was inclosed on the east, north, and south, but more particularly on the former, side of the church. In the early part of the seventeenth century, a new cut was made in the Wittersham Level, between this place and Iden, having a sluice at its mouth, from whence, joining the Appledore Channel, they together still spread over the surface below, though this surface had now become contracted particularly towards Winchelsea, between which town and Rye, their joint harbour, called the Camber, had heretofore existed; for the sea had now considerably receded from it, leaving the harbour of Rye in the miserable state described in the petition of the mayor and jurats in 1618, and again in their brief of 1627. Under the authority of the grant made to Edward Guldeford, Esq., in 1661, a great deal of land was doubtless inclosed, particularly to the southward of Guldeford Church; for Camber Farm was thus rescued, as is clear from its being charged with nearly one third of the rent-charge reserved to the crown in this grant, while the greater part of the remainder is still payable from other lands in that locality. Thus, in 1701, the lands uninclosed were very nearly the same as those which have lately been embanked by the act of 1833; the exceptions are an immense creek, called Wenway Creek, lying on the south-west side of the church, and some marshes on the north-east. The harbour of Rye, previously to 1644, had no connexion with the Rother; and the streams of the Brede and Tillingham not being sufficient to keep it open, it swarved up, and was lost; but in this year it seems the sea forced its way through a bank of some kind, which heretofore prevented the river from flowing nearer to Rye than the westernmost bank in Guldeford parish, which was not far from the church. Rye, thus deprived of its old harbour, naturally was desirous of creating a new one; and this was the object of its inhabitants in applying to Parliament, in 1701, for an Act of Parliament to enable them to have one; but at this period their endeavours were frustrated.

Finding their town decaying from the want of a harbour, the inhabitants of Rye again exerted themselves, and succeeded in obtaining an Act of Parliament, in 1722, enabling them to make a new harbour, the mouth of which was to be near Cliff End, a little to the eastward of Fairlight, to make which a channel was cut from the strand into which the waters of the Tillingham were turned, while those of the Brede were let into it near Winchelsea. These streams not supplying a sufficient volume of water, after a great expenditure of time and money, it was determined, in 1769, that the Rother should also be turned into the same channel, to keep it open. Now the Rother at this time, after flowing from Wittersham Level about, as it now does, to Pollard's Wharf, immediately under the mills on Playden Cliff, turned to the south-west, and passed out to sea through the North Channel, and at this wharf many vessels unloaded, while others passed by the Gun Garden Channel to the strand, and now, to effect the object they had in view, the commissioners put in a dam at the last-named passage at once, leaving all the ships coming to Rye to unload at Pollard's Wharf. In 1787 the North Channel was stopped by the erection of a dam across it, under the superintendence of Mr. John

Pinkerton, from whom it received the name of Pinkerton's Dam, while the event was celebrated, on June 4th, by the roasting of an ox whole upon it.

All efforts proved vain. In this same year the landowners complained their land was not sewed in consequence of the erection of these dams, when, on November 7th, it was ordered that the dam at the Gun Garden Rocks should be cut, and a channel made 130 feet wide at top, with a suitable slope to the bottom. This gave the *coup de grâce* to the new harbour, when the present, commonly called the Old Harbour, became, and still remains, with some few alterations, the harbour of the town. Upwards of sixty years elapsed from the commencement of the work, and nearly £200,000 had been expended in the construction of the New Harbour, and all to no useful purpose.

It now remains to say a few words on the Act of 1833, which was passed to enable the commissioners of Rye Harbour to embank certain salt marshes adjoining the harbour, over which the commissioners claimed right of the flow of the tide, and the owners of lands adjoining a right of feeding their sheep on the herbage. Within a few years previous to 1833 the lands had greatly swarved, so that they were not overflowed, except at very high spring tides.

It has invariably been the case that, as the sea has left the salts, the owners of the lands adjoining have inclosed them, and as the salts in question were in a fair way of being so left in a very few years, when the commissioners could derive no benefit from them, either as regarded the waters which had overflowed them, or from the sale of them, when their right over them should have ceased with the recession of the tide, it is clear that the harbour commissioners acted wisely, and in the way most likely to be beneficial to the harbour funds.

By this Act the commissioners inclosed 742 ac. 2 r. 11 p. of land, for which the several landowners paid £10,630 12s. 11½d., and, after paying all the expenses of the embankment, they have the sum of £3256 10s. 6½d. left, which is secured to them by mortgages on the lands of certain of the owners, who availed themselves of the clause in the Act which empowered them to give such mortgages in lieu of payment.

In the course of the year 1838 this embankment was completed, and the last hand was put to the vast work of the inclosure of lands which constitute that immense tract of rich alluvial soil generally known by the name of Romney Marsh. And thus this great task, which was commenced by the Romans, has (after a lapse of eighteen hundred years,) been finally accomplished by the Commissioners of Rye Harbour.

SECT. VII.

Conclusion and Summary.

WE now approach the concluding scene of our labours,—a summary of the present state of Romney and the adjoining Marshes.

The district which we have been surveying, and which is generally comprehended under the common name of Romney Marsh, consists, in fact, of several different marshes or levels, known by the several names of Romney Marsh, Denge Marsh, Walland Marsh, Kent and Sussex Rother Levels, Guldeford Level, and Brede Level, besides Tillingham Level, and various other spots, which, not being under any commission, are not included in those above enumerated.

Romney Marsh (properly so called) occupies the eastern extremity of the district extending from New Romney by the sea-coast to Hythe, having the Kentish hills, almost to Appledore, for its inland or upper boundary; while the Marsh Wall, running in a south-east direction from Appledore to Romney, constitutes its boundary on that side. This Marsh contains within it fifteen parishes, viz.: New Romney, Old Romney, Hope, Orgerswyck, St. Mary's, Blackmanstone, Dymchurch, Burmarsh, West Hythe, Eastbridge, Newchurch, Snave, Snargate, Brenzett, and Ivy Church. The population of these several parishes, according to the census of 1831, was as under, viz.:

New Romney	983
Old Romney	113
Hope	24
Orgerswyck	8
St. Mary's	111
Blackmanstone	4
Dymchurch	521
Burmarsh	105
West Hythe	168
Eastbridge	16
Newchurch	241
Snave	93
Snargate	76
Brenzett	262
Ivy Church	198
Total	2923

Besides these entire parishes, there are several parts of the adjoining hill parishes which run into this Marsh, but have no part of their population residing in it.

The total contents of Romney Marsh at the last inspection, in the year 1824, was 24,049½ acres, the greater part of which sews out at Dymchurch, at which place stands that immense work known by the name of Dymchurch Wall, the maintenance of which is attended with a vast expense, while the removal of it would expose the Marsh to all the evils of an inundation.

This Marsh is still governed by that celebrated ordonnance which was framed by Henry de Bathe in the year 1257, which placed it under the management of twenty-four lords and one bailiff. The twenty-four lords are the owners, for the time being, of certain manors situate in and adjoining to the Marsh. This seems all very clear; but when we come to enumerate the manors, there is some complexity in the business, inasmuch as we only find twenty-three manors mentioned. On inquiry, I am informed, by parties likely to know, that the jurats and bailiffs together have one vote, which makes up the twenty-four. Each lord has the power of appointing a deputy for the manor which he possesses, and I now subjoin the names of the respective manors, of their owners, and of the deputies, where any are appointed:

MANOR.	OWNER.	DEPUTY.
Aldington	William Deedes, Esq.	—
Blackmanstone	John Finn, Esq.	—
Bilsington, Supr.	Lady Cosway	Mr. Thomas Pilcher.
Bilsington, Infr.	Do.	Mr. Thomas Pilcher.
Bonnington	Thos. Papillon, Esq.	—
Burmarsh	Sir Ed. C. Dering, Bart.	Mr. Wm. Coates.
Craythorne	James Taylor, Esq.	Thos. Twisden Hodges, Esq.
Eastbridge	Sir Ed. C. Dering, Bart.	Mr. John Russell.
Eastwell	Earl of Winchelsea and Nottingham	David Denne, Esq.
Fawknerhurst	Dr. Henry Carter	—
Horton	Hon. Henry Montague	Mr. John Neame.
Honychild	Sir Ed. C. Dering, Bart.	Mr. Odiarne Coates.
Kenardington	Thomas Breton, Esq.	Mr. Jesse Pilcher.
Newington (Fee)	Rev. Wm. Brockman	Fred. Brockman, Esq.
Orlestone	Thomas Thornhill, Esq.	Rt. Hon. Sir Edward Knatchbull, Bart.
Packmanstone	Archibald Stoakes, Esq.	—
Ruckinge	Dean and Chapter of Canterbury	Edward Drake. — Brockman, Esq.
Snave	John Marsh, Esq.	Mr. James Watts.
Street	Sir John E. Honeywood, Bart.	—
Tinton	Sir Ed. C. Dering, Bart.	Edward Russell, Esq.
Warehorne	Earl of Thanet	Rev. Wm. Brockman.
Week, alias Court-a-Week	Francis Dashwood, Esq.	Mr. Thos. Daws.
Willop	Earl of Romney, Wm. Hughes, Esq., and Representatives of Alexander Evelyn, Esq.	Mr. Thomas Butler.

It appears by this, that the lords are the virtual possessors of all the powers relating to the management of Romney Marsh at the present time, so far as the surveying the walls and watercourses, and keeping them in proper repair, is concerned; but whether their power was hereditary, so far as the possession of the particular manors goes, at their original appointment, may well be questioned, seeing that no mention of such power is to be found in the celebrated ordonnance of Henry de Bathe.

I have said above, that the power of the lords is paramount over the repairs of the Marsh; but there is another body in the Marsh, which, with one exception, is independent of the lords, and this is the corporation called by the name of the "Bailiff, Jurats, and Commonalty of the Liberty of Romney Marsh." On reference to page 132, the reader will find that the charter for this corporation was granted by Edward IV, Feb. 23, 1461; and the duties of this body are confined to taking cognizance of all criminal acts and of all offences triable at quarter sessions, but have nothing to do with the works of the Marsh. The bailiff is elected annually, at Whitsuntide, by the lords of the Marsh, the offices of bailiff of the court and bailiff of the Marsh being united in the same person. Besides the bailiff, who presides over the court, the corporation consists of twenty-four jurats and the commonalty, the jurats being elected by the latter, whose only qualification is residence within the Marsh. The bailiff and jurats are justices of the peace; and these appoint a coroner, a clerk of the peace, and an assessor, the duties of which last are similar to those of a recorder, the only difference being, that the bailiff always occupies the chair. The justices hold a petty sessions once a month. All the business falling on the lords and on the members of the corporate body, is transacted at Dymchurch.

NEW ROMNEY MARSH.

This is a small marsh, not included in the former, lying to the eastward of New Romney, between the town and the sea, containing only 398 acres, which sew out near Little Stone Watchhouse. It is under a commission of sewers. This marsh was formed by the stopping up of the old mouth of the river.

OLD BED OF THE ROTHER.

Between the Marsh Wall which constitutes the south-west boundary of Romney Marsh, and the Ree Wall, which is the north-east boundary of Walland Marsh, lies the old bed of the Rother, when it flowed from Appledore to Romney, and hence out to sea. This was granted (as we have seen) by Queen

Elizabeth to the corporation of New Romney, and contains 61 acres up to Brenzett, the part now possessed by them, and if we allow 40 acres more for the remainder part, we shall have 101 acres.

DENGE MARSH

lies to the south and south-west of Romney Marsh, occupying the southernmost extremity of the district we have been describing. It contains 2910½ acres, and sews out near Lydd Lighthouse.

In this marsh are situate the town and part of the parish of Lydd, containing a population of 1410 souls in 1831.

This marsh is governed by commissioners, whose qualification in former times was the possession of land in it of the annual value of forty marks, that is, £26 13s. 4d.; but by a recent act of parliament it has been fixed at £150 per annum. The owner of land to the value of £300 per annum may appoint a deputy. A freeman of a corporation, without regard to the quantity of land he may hold, is also qualified to act as a commissioner.

It is from the southern point of this marsh that remarkable bank of beach, known by the name of Dungeness, commences, and on which stands the lighthouse called Dungeness or Lydd Light, and which extends to the distance of three miles and a half from the town of Lydd, which originally stood on the sea-shore. This bank forms the division between the two bays of Rye and Romney, the former lying on the west, and the latter on the east side of it. In consequence of the continued extension of Dungeness Beach, the sea retires on either side of it, and the land increases. On the eastern side, within the memory of many old sailors, vessels of considerable draught of water could anchor where the sands have now accumulated, and the water is become shallow; and I suppose so long as the respective points of Fairlight, of Dungeness, and of Folkestone Cliffs prevent the great stream of the tides, whether setting up or down the Channel, from sweeping into the lower part of these bays, the land will still continue to be left by the sea.

By way of showing the immense quantity of beach which has accumulated in and about Dungeness, I will here give the measurement of Lydd parish.

	ac.	r.	p.
Arable (including gardens)	811	0	22
Pasture	5848	1	6
Beach	5062	2	12
	11,722	0	0

JURY'S GAP MARSH

lies to the westward of Denge Marsh, has the sea on the south, Guldeford Level on the west, and Walland Marsh on the north. It contains 3009 acres, sews out at Jury's Gap, and is not in any commission. Broomhill is in this marsh, and has a population of 80 souls.

WALLAND MARSH.

This marsh lies on the south-west side of the Ree Wall, but does not extend down to the sea. It is about four miles from east to west, and five miles from north to south. The Kent and Sussex Rother Levels lie to the north, and Guldeford Level to the west of it. It occupies all the land in this direction, that is, in the county of Kent. It contains 12,848 acres, all of which sew into the Rother through the Union Sluice, which stands at a short distance below Scot's Float Sluice.

The several parishes of Fairfield, Brookland, and Medley are in this marsh, and their population at the last census was as follows, viz,:

Fairfield	48
Brookland	434
Medley	52
Total	534

Here are also parts of the parishes of Appledore, Snargate, Ivychurch, Old Romney, New Romney, and Lydd.

This marsh is under the authority of Commissioners, whose qualification is the possession of £100 per annum landed property, according to the Act of 3d and 4th of William IV, c. 22.

APPLEDORE DOWLES

are a low swampy piece of land, continually liable to be flooded, lying to the north-east of Walland Marsh, and containing about 500 acres. The waters are pumped out into Walland Marsh, and then pass out through the Union Sluice.

GULDEFORD LEVEL

is situate to the westward of Walland Marsh, and occupies the whole of the land between that marsh and Rye Harbour, with the exception of the salt marshes belonging to Rye, inclosed by the Rye Harbour Embankment Act of 1833. This level contains 3244 acres, of which 3062 acres sew through the Union Sluice, and 182 acres through North Salts Gut.

The parish of Guldeford is in this Level, and it contains 126 inhabitants.

The present commission was formed in 1831; the qualification is the possession of land in the Level, without regard to the amount; each owner being named in the commission, which lasts twenty-one years; and during this term no new proprietor can become a commissioner, but must wait until a new commission is formed.

MARSHES
INCLOSED UNDER THE RYE HARBOUR EMBANKMENT ACT OF 1833, EAST OF THE ROTHER.

These marshes lie between Guldeford Level and Rye Harbour, extending from a little above Scot's Float Sluice to the north, down to the North Salts Gut to the south. They contain 540 ac. 1 r. 32 p.

IDEN AND PLAYDEN MARSHES.

On the south-east side of the Rother, adjoining to Walland Marsh, lies a narrow strip of land which, as the tide left it, has been inclosed, but is in no commission; it extends from the Willow Farm, in the parish of Iden, down to the northern extremity of the Salt Marshes, which were inclosed under the Rye Harbour Embankment Act of 1833. These marshes contain about 150 acres.

ECHINGHAM.

If we go to the source of the Rother and descend the stream, we shall first come to a parcel of marsh land at Echingham, containing about 150 acres, not in any commission.

ROBERTSBRIDGE MARSH.

Between Robertsbridge and Udiham Oak, the western boundary of the Kent and Sussex Rother Levels, lies a spot of marsh land containing about 150 acres, not under any commission. Udiham Oak stands on the boundary line of the parishes of Salehurst and Ewhurst. An old oak did stand there, which, being decayed, another was planted in its place.

KENT AND SUSSEX ROTHER LEVELS.

These levels extend down the Rother from Udiham Oak to Scot's Float Sluice; they now have the Wittersham Level united with them, including the Wet Level and Shirley Moor. Their united contents are as follows, viz:

	acr.
Upper Levels	6296
Wittersham and Wet Level	2850
Total	9146

These marshes all sew out through Scot's Float Sluice.

The qualification of a commissioner is the possession of land in these levels to the value of £100 a year.

RAYTON SALTS.

In these I include the Salt Marsh so called, and two or three small pieces besides, which lie below Scot's Float Sluice, on the western side of the Rother, containing together 41 ac. 1 r. 17 p. These sew out principally through a drain near to Scot's Float.

TILLINGHAM LEVEL

reaches from the parish of Brede down to Tillingham Sluice, through which its waters sew; it forms a valley, having the high lands of Beckley and Peasmarsh on the north, and those of Brede, Udimore, and part of Rye, on the south. It contains 1080 acres, but is not in any commission.

RYE BOROUGH MARSHES.

The town of Rye is surrounded by marshes, the property of the borough. Those on the north-east and west sew out through Tillingham Sluice. Including a few small pieces belonging to private individuals, this division contains 67 acres.

Added to these are two pieces on the south side of the town, one the property of the borough, the other of a private individual. These last two contain 7½ acres, thus making together 74⅜ acres.

BREDE LEVEL

extends from the neighbourhood of Battle down to the Brede Sluice, through which its waters are sewed into Rye Harbour. It forms a large valley lying in the following parishes, viz. Battle, Seddlescomb, Whatlington, Brede, Udimore, and Rye, on one side, and in Westfield, Brede, Guestling, and Icklesham, on the other. It contains about 2000 acres, and the river Brede runs through the midst of it until it reaches the foot of Winchelsea Hill, when from hence to Brede Sluice it forms its south-east boundary. This level is under the jurisdiction of the Pevensey Level Commission.

PETT LEVEL

extends from the eastern foot of Fairlight Cliff to the Castle Estate on the west, and from the sea on the south, to the high lands of Pett, Icklesham, and Winchelsea, on the north. It contains 1000 acres, and sews out through the Brede Sluice. This level is in the same commission as Brede.

THE CASTLE ESTATE

is situated to the eastward of Pett Level, and contains 720 acres of land, which, together with the Castle Salts, inclosed by the Rye Harbour Embankment Act of 1833, containing 137 ac. 25 p., makes a total of 857 ac. 25 p.

These lands sew out partly into the Rock Channel and partly into Rye Harbour, below the Holm Bush.

Besides the lands above mentioned there are some others, amounting to about 200 acres, which sew out through the Oyster Creek; and these, added to the above, make 1057 ac. 25 p.

Having got through all the different marshes, let us put them together and sum up their contents, which are as under, viz.:—

	ac.	r.	p.
Romney Marsh, Proper	24,049	2	0
New Romney Marsh	398	0	0
Old bed of the Rother	101	0	0
Denge Marsh	2910	2	0
Jury's Gap Marsh	3009	0	0
Walland Marsh	12,848	0	0
Appledore Dowles	500	0	0
Guldeford Level	3244	0	0
Rye Harbour, Embankment Level	540	1	32
Iden and Playden Marshes	150	0	0
Echingham Level	150	0	0
Robertsbridge Level	150	0	0
Kent and Sussex Rother Levels	9146	0	0
Rayton Salts	41	1	17
Tillingham Level	1080	0	0
Rye Borough Marshes	74	2	0
Brede Level	2000	0	0
Pett Level	1000	0	0
Castle Estate	1057	0	25
Total	62,449	1	34

In summing up the contents of the several marshes, we will proceed to show what is the aggregate amount of the population residing in them. To the parishes already mentioned I think I shall be justified in adding those of the Isle of Oxney and Appledore: they are so intimately connected with our history, and have sprung so completely out of the marsh, that it may be rather a question whether I should leave my work in a complete state without their insertion; therefore I shall offer no apology for setting them down in my list of marsh parishes. The amount of population will then stand thus, viz.:—

The fifteen parishes in Romney Marsh	2923
Lydd, in Denge Marsh	1410
Broomhill, in Jury's Gap Marsh	80
The three parishes in Walland Marsh	534
Appledore	600
Guldeford, in Guldeford Level	126
Wittersham, Stone, and Ebony, in the Isle of Oxney, in the Kent and Sussex Rother Levels	1640
Icklesham and Pett, in Pett Level, and on the Castle Estate	62
Rye within the Liberty	4000
Winchelsea	800
Total	12,175

Whether I ought to insert Rye and Winchelsea here I must leave my readers to decide.

Having now arrived at the end of our journey, let us cast a retrospective glance at the length of time we have been travelling together, and at the mighty changes which, during that time, have been effected.

Two thousand years ago the district we have been describing was one immense sea, and for many ages subsequent thereto was nothing better than a low, wet, swampy morass, abounding in malaria, the ever-fruitful source of disease. So insalubrious and so uncongenial for the habitation of man was it considered, that many successive sovereigns granted and confirmed various privileges and immunities to the district, with the view of inducing persons to come and settle there; and even so late as the latter part of the sixteenth century, a writer describes it as being " bad in winter, noisome in summer, and good at no time." Such was its state: but we have watched the quiet recession of the water, and have marked the gradual embankment of the land, until, in the place of a sea, we now behold a large tract of rich pasture, extending over a surface of more than sixty thousand acres, affording sufficient food, in genial years, for more than half a million of sheep, besides numerous herds of cattle. And, in consequence of the improved method of grazing, and the generally better management of the land, combined with the excellent state of the drainage, the insalubrity of the marsh is in a great measure done away with, and we accordingly find upwards of twelve thousand persons constantly residing here, the duration of whose lives is fully equal to the general average of that of the inhabitants of the adjoining districts.

I feel that I can add nothing more to illustrate the subject, and therefore, with these few remarks, I shall close my book, and bid the reader farewell.

THE END.

PRINTED BY C. AND J. ADLARD
BARTHOLOMEW CLOSE.

LIST OF SUBSCRIBERS.

	COPIES.
Attree, William Wakeford, Esq., Recorder of Rye	1
Ayerst, Mr. Thomas, Newenden, Kent	1
Ayerst, Mr. Samuel, Do.	1
Aylward, Mr. Thomas, Rye	1
Baden, Mr., Brookland, Kent	1
Barnard, Mr. John, Rye	1
Bishop, Mrs., Lossenham House, Newenden	3
Breeds, Mr. Boykett, Hastings	1
Brocket, Stanes B., Esq., Spain's Hall, Essex	1
Brockman, Rev. Tatton, Beachboro', Kent	1
Burkett, Mr. John, Rye	1
Butler, George Slade, Esq., Rye	1
Butler, Thomas, Esq., Ivychurch, Kent	1
Chapman, Mr. Samuel Herbert, Playden	1
Chatterton, Mr. William Holt, Rye	1
Clarke, George, Esq., New Romney, Kent	1
Collins, Mr. George, Rye	1
Cooper, Rev. Henry, Vicar of Rye	1
Cooper, William Durrant, Esq., London	1
Colquhoun, Daniel, Esq., Collector of Customs, Rye	1
Curteis, Edward B., Esq., Leesam House	4
Curteis, Rev. Thomas, Sevenoaks	1
Collett, Mrs., The Jungle, Lincolnshire	1
Croughton, William P., Esq., Tenterden, Kent	1
Dering, Sir Edward C., Bart., Surrenden Dering	1
Edwards, Mr. George, Rye	1
Elliott, Mr. James, sen., Playden	1
Elliott, Mr. James, jun., Dymchurch, Kent	1
Espinett, Mr. David, Salehurst, Sussex	1
Finn, Mr. Thomas, Lydd	1
Frewen, Thomas, Esq., Brickwall House, Northiam	5
Ginner, Mr. William, Hastings	1
Green, Mr. William, Lydd, Kent	1
Hastings Literary Society	1
Hicks, Charles, Esq., Alderman of Rye	1
Hilder, Mr. Edward, jun., Rye	1
Holmes, Mr., Rye	1
Horton, Mr., Peasmarsh	1
Hutchings, Mr. C. P., Hastings	1
Jenner, Thomas, Esq., Rye	1
Kenrick, Mrs., Barnet's Place	1
Kenrick, William, Esq., St. Clare, Walmer, Kent	1
Kinglake, A. William, Esq., London	1
Langford, Frederick, Esq., Udimore	1
Langham, James George, Esq., Hastings	1

LIST OF SUBSCRIBERS.

	COPIES.
Lardner, John Haddock, Esq., Rye	1
Larking, Rev. L. B., Ryarsh Vicarage, Kent	1
Legg, Mr., London	1
Legg, Mr. Thomas R., London	1
Lord, Mr. James, Rye	1
Meryon, Edward, Esq., M.D., London	1
Moore, Rev. Edward, Frittenden, Kent	1
Neame, John, Esq., Selling Court, Kent	1
Pilcher, Mr. Charles, Rolvenden, Kent	1
Pix, Thomas Smith, Esq., Rye	1
Plater, Rev. Charles E., Rector of Newchurch, Kent	1
Plomley, Mr. James, Rye	1
Pomfret, Virgil, Esq., Tenterden	1
Pomfret, Richard, Esq., Rye	1
Powell, James, Esq., Chichester	1
Prosser, Rev. James, Rector of Thame, Oxfordshire	1
Puling, Rev. William, Rector of Dymchurch, Kent	1
Ramsden, William, Esq., Rye	1
Ross, Mr. Thomas, jun., Hastings	1
Russell, Mr. James, Rye	1
Sandys, Charles, Esq., Canterbury	1
Shadwell, W. D. Lucas, Esq., Fairlight, Hastings	1
Smith, Jeremiah, Esq., Mayor of Rye	5
Smith, Benjamin, Esq., Hastings	1
Smith, Miss Barbara Leigh, Hastings	1
Smith, Mr. Charles, Rye	1
Smith, Charles Roach, Esq. Liverpool Street, City	1
Stoakes, Archibald, Esq., Newchurch, Kent	1
Strickland, Mr. George, Hastings	1
Stringer, William, Esq., New Romney, Kent	1
Thorpe, Mr. Thomas, Rye	1
Tomkins, Mr., Wittersham, Kent	1
Tress, Mrs., Gate Court, Northiam, Sussex	1
Twopeny, William, Esq., Temple	1
Vennall, Mr. Thomas, Rye	1
Vidler, John, Esq., Alderman of Rye	1
Walker, William, Esq., New Romney	1
Watson, Mrs., Rye	1
Way, Albert, Esq., Nonham, Reigate	1
Wright, Mr. Daniel, Playden, Sussex	1
Woodforde, Thomas, Esq., St. Leonard-on-Sea	1
Woodhams, William, Esq., Udimore, Sussex	1

Kent, Sussex, and Surrey.

Preparing for Publication,
And will be put to Press when the Names of 200 Subscribers are received,
In 1 Vol. 8vo,
ILLUSTRATED WITH ENGRAVINGS,

Price, to Subscribers, 15s.,

A

COMPARATIVE LIST

OF

THE CHURCHES,

MENTIONED IN

Domesday Book,

AND THOSE OF MORE RECENT DATE,

IN THE

COUNTIES OF KENT, SUSSEX, AND SURREY,

WITH NOTES ON THEIR

Architecture, Sepulchral Memorials,

AND OTHER ANTIQUITIES.

BY THE
REV. ARTHUR HUSSEY, M.A.

Subscribers' names will be received by the Publisher, JOHN RUSSELL SMITH, 4, Old Compton Street, Soho, London, or by the Rev. A. HUSSEY, Rottingdean, near Brighton.

[For Specimen of the Work, see over.]

Part of Kent.

Modern Names.	Domesday Names.	Churches in D. B.	A.D. 1291.
(237) Oxney near Deal			*
(238) Paddlesworth			
(239) Ditto near Snodland	Pellesorde	1	
(240)	Palestrei	1	
(241) Peckham, East	} Pecheham	1	*
(242) Ditto West			*
(243) Pembury			*
(244) Penshurst			*
(245) St. Peter's, Thanet			*
(246) Petham	Piteham	2	*
(247)	Piventone	1	

EXPLANATION.

The first column contains the present names; the second, those by which the several places are described in Domesday Book. In the third column, the figures opposite the names denote the Churches mentioned in Domesday Book, as then existing at those places; and the asterisk in the last column signifies that the Churches so marked are alluded to in the Taxation of Pope Nicholas IV, taken A.D. 1291.

NOTES.

(237) OXNEY NEAR DEAL.—"Ecclia de Oxne et de Popyshall." Valor Ecclesiasticus. In A.D. 1291 Popeshall Chapel is annexed to Colred, in which parish it stood, and which see. Valor Ecclesiasticus declares Oxney Church to have belonged to the Canons of Langdon; wherefore both this and Langdon Churches were probably suppressed at

the same period. It is omitted in the Clergy List. "The walls" of Oxney Church " still remain; it has a roof, and is now made use of as a barn."—Hasted's Hist. of Kent.

(238) PADDLESWORTH.—A Chapel to Liminge. The Church is described as having a round chancel arch, "with Saxon ornaments," and two very small round-headed doors.—Hasted. A Priory here, belonging to the Abbey of Beaulieu, in Normandy, by foundation of John de Pratellis, temp. King John, was suppressed by King Henry V.—Kilburne's Survey of Kent.

(239) PADDLESWORTH NEAR SNODLAND.—The Church was long since destroyed, but the name of this place appears in Val. Eccl. as a rectory, though not in the Clergy List. The Textus Roffensis states this to have been esteemed a Chapel to Birling. Compare the list of Churches in the Diocese of Rochester, extracted from that work, under Rochester.

(240) PALESTREI.—Now Palster Court, a manor farm in Wittersham. Hasted says, that the manor extends into Ebeney; therefore the Church may have stood in either parish. Kilburne, however, speaks of "Aeton chancel, or more truly, Palster chancel," in the Church of Wittersham, and mentions the manor of Palster, along with Wittersham, being given to Christ's Church, Canterbury, in 1032 and 1035. From which circumstances it would appear, that Palestrei was an important property in ancient times; wherefore the Church, though described as belonging to Palestrei, within the limits of which manor it might stand, not improbably perhaps occupied the site of the existing parish Church of Wittersham.

(241) THE PECKHAMS.—Domesday Book estimates one portion of Peckham manor as belonging to the monks of the Archbishop, the other as the property of the Bishop of Bayeux. The former, which possessed a Church, is easily recognised as East Peckham, which benefice is at this day in the gift of the Dean and Chapter of Canterbury. *East Peckham.*—Brasses: Richard Ecclesley, rector (consecrating a chalice), 1526.—Man and woman.—Registrum Roffense.

(242) PECKHAM WEST.—Brass: Elizabeth, wife of William Culpeper (the husband is lost), 1460.—Reg. Roff. Val. Eccl. notices a Preceptory, then existing at West Peckham; which was founded A.D. 1408, according to Kilburne.

(243) PEMBURY.—The Church consists of western tower, nave with south porch, and chancel. The south door is perfectly plain Norman, and there is one small very plain Norman window in the south wall of the nave, partly cut off by the roof of the Church. The chancel and tower are decorated, the former early, but with only one original window. Harris, in his History of Kent, broaches the absurd supposition, that the name of this parish, "Pepenbury, Pipingbury," came "very likely from the quantity of pepins which anciently grew here, and for which formerly this place hath been famous." Perhaps the last assertion is a gratuitous assumption of the worthy D.D.; beside that orchards are recorded to

have been first introduced into England during the reign of Henry VIII. See the note below, on Teynham. The Pimpes were a family of much consideration in early times, who gave their name to more than one residence in the neighbourhood (Pimpe's Court), though not in Pembury; and property called "Pinpa" is mentioned in Domesday Book in Twyford Hundred, which brings it very near Pembury. It is far more probable than the above conjecture, that the place, when first cleared and settled, might have been "Pimpe's Bury," and so denominated.

(244) PENSHURST.—This parish is not named in Domesday Book, and in A.D. 1291 it is styled "Penecestre." We learn from Reg. Roff., pp. 460, 469, that A.D. 1239, John Belemeyns, canon of St. Paul's, and lord of the manor of Penshurst, founded a Chapel upon his domain, but, as it is expressly stated, within the parish of Leigh. Hasted notices this Chapel in his account of Penshurst parish, but describes it under that of Leigh, there intimating, through a confused use of his authority shortly to be pointed out, that it existed before the erection by Belemeyns in 1239, and asserting plainly that it was suppressed in the first year of Edward VI; but he produces no evidence for his statements, neither does he assign any locality for his suppressed Chapel. On the contrary, the old deeds preserved in Reg. Roff. seem to testify, that Penshurst originally formed part of Leigh parish; that Belemeyns's Chapel was the prototype of the existing parish Church of Penshurst; and that it was at first considered only a Chapel of Ease to Leigh, though in process of time it acquired all the privileges of a distinct parish. The first document "Of the foundation of a Chapel within the parish of Leghe," granting the patronage to the founder and his heirs, contains the following expressions: "We, having inspected the deed of lord John Canucus, patron of the Church of Leghe, and of Richard, rector of the same Church, and of Alan, vicar of the said Church, concerning a certain Chapel situated below the court-house of lord John Belemeyns, *in the parish of the said Church*, also the indemnity of the mother Church of Leghe being altogether provided for, have confirmed to the aforesaid lord John Belemeyns and his successors," &c., A.D. 1239: John Belemeyns being named, as above, canon of St. Paul's, and lord of the manor of Penshurst. Next we have an Indulgence, dated 1249, which speaks of "the Chapel erected in the court (curia) of the manor of Penshurst," dedicated to St. Thomas. In the confirmatory charter, also dated in 1249, the patron of Leigh, the parson, and the vicar grant to Thomas of Penshurst a Free Chapel for ever, in his manor of Penshurst, to be served by his own chaplain, with reservation of certain payments to Leigh; especially the yearly oblations from the mansion of Penshurst, wholly at the four holy seasons; also all confessions, baptisms, &c. And if at Easter Mass should not be celebrated in the said Chapel, the whole family should receive "Christ's body" in the mother Church of Leigh. Again; we find an authorized encroachment upon the above reservations about one hundred and fifty years from the foundation by John Belemyns; for licence to hear confessions and enjoin penance in the "great Chapel" of Penshurst "*from all and singular persons inhabiting the said manor*," was granted by the Bishop, A.D. 1393, "on account of the distance from the parish Church of Leigh." Hasted, disregarding the date, quotes the confirmatory charter as that of the original foundation,

Valuable and Interesting Books

Philology,

Early English Literature,

Heraldry,

Topography,

&c.

Archaeology,

Numismatics,

Literary History,

Biography,

&c.

PUBLISHED OR SOLD BY

JOHN RUSSELL SMITH,
4, OLD COMPTON STREET, SOHO SQUARE, LONDON.

Philology and Early English Literature.

A Dictionary of Archaic and Provincial Words, Obsolete Phrases, Proverbs, and Ancient Customs, from the reign of Edward I. By JAMES ORCHARD HALLIWELL, F.R.S., F.S.A., &c. 2 vols. 8vo, containing upwards of 1000 pages, *closely printed in double columns, cloth,* 2l. 2s.

This work, which has occupied the Editor some years, is now completed; it contains above 50,000 words (embodying all the known scattered glossaries of the English language) forming a complete key for the reader of the works of our old Poets, Dramatists, Theologians, and other authors whose works abound with allusions, of which explanations are not to be found in ordinary Dictionaries and books of reference. Most of the principal Archaisms are illustrated by examples selected from early inedited MSS. and rare books, and by far the greater portion will be found to be original authorities.

"This promises to be a very useful work, and is evidently the result of extensive research, and of great labour judiciously applied. The want of a work of this description has long been felt, and several attempts have been made to supply the deficiency, but for some reason or other they have all hitherto failed. The Glossary of Archdeacon Nares is not only imperfect, but professedly restricted to a comparatively narrow scope, embracing terms used by the writers chiefly of the Elizabethan era; it is now, besides, a rare and costly book. Boucher's Glossary miscarried because it was begun in an inconvenient form, and on too expensive a scale. The work now before us, of which the first two parts alone have been published, appears to be much more complete than Boucher's, and has the advantage of being printed in a convenient form for reference, while its price is very moderate. It forms a most comprehensive Glossary to all our Old English writers, from the beginning of the fourteenth century to the time of the Stuarts, including the earlier Chroniclers, the writings of Wycliffe, and a long range of Poets, from Piers Ploughman, Chaucer, Gower, Lydgate, &c., to Spenser and his contemporaries, with Shakespeare and the Dramatists of that age. In addition to the obsolete portion of our language, this work may be said to be a complete Dictionary of the local dialects of the present day, and is one which will be an acceptable addition to every library."—*Morning Herald.*

"Mr. Halliwell is, we must acknowledge, as well qualified, by industry, ability, and previous study, to be the editor as any man living. We could indeed easily name a dozen persons, each of whom would be better qualified for particular departments, but not one who, including the whole range embraced by the title would have the ability and energy to go through all the drudging duties of the office more satisfactorily. It is a work, however, that, in the first instance, must be imperfect. We hold, therefore, that every English scholar should have an interleaved copy, that he may contribute a something towards improving a second edition. The first number appears to have been carefully compiled; but we are not inclined to seek very curiously for faults in a work of such obvious difficulty, when, even if it be imperfect, it cannot fail to be useful."—*Athenæum.*

Essays on the Literature, Popular Superstitions, and History of England in the MIDDLE AGES. By THOMAS WRIGHT, M.A., F.S.A. 2 stout vols. post 8vo, *elegantly printed, cloth,* 16s.

Contents: Essay I. Anglo-Saxon Poetry. II. Anglo-Norman Poetry. III. Chansons de Geste, or Historical Romances of the Middle Ages. IV. On Proverbs and Popular Sayings. V. On the Anglo-Latin Poets of the Twelfth Century. VI. Abelard and the Scholastic Philosophy. VII. On Dr. Grimm's German Mythology. VIII. On the National Fairy Mythology of England. IX. On the Popular Superstitions of Modern Greece, and their connexion with the English. X. On Friar Rush, and the Frolicsome Elves. XI. On Dunlop's History of Fiction. XII. On the History and Transmission of Popular Stories. XIII. On the Poetry of History. XIV. Adventures of Hereward the Saxon. XV. The Story of Eustace the Monk. XVI. The History of Fulke Fitzwarine. XVII. On the Popular Cycle of Robin-Hood Ballads. XVIII. On the Conquest of Ireland by the Anglo-Normans. XIX. On Old English Political Songs. XX. On the Scottish Poet Dunbar.

Guide to the Anglo-Saxon Tongue: on the basis of Professor Rask's Grammar, to which are added Reading Lessons in verse and prose, with Notes for the use of learners. By E. J. VERNON, B.A., Oxon. 12mo, *cloth*, 5s. 6d.

The student is furnished with a cheaper, easier, more comprehensive, and not less trustworthy guide to this tongue, than has hitherto been placed within his reach.

"The author of this Guide seems to have made one step in the right direction, by compiling what may be pronounced the best work on the subject hitherto published in England."—*Athenæum.*

"Mr. Vernon is a laboriously accurate Anglo-Saxon scholar, as is seen in his attention to the quantity of words: a branch of Anglo-Saxon grammar in which later scholars have done much by comparing the forms of roots as they are found in the different Teutonic dialects."—*Gent.'s Mag. for Feb.*

Reliquiæ Antiquæ. Scraps from Ancient Manuscripts, illustrating chiefly Early English Literature, and the English Language, edited by WRIGHT and HALLIWELL, 2 vols. 8vo. cloth, 2l. 2s.—REDUCED to 1l. 4s.

Containing communications by Ellis, Madden, Hunter, Bruce, Turnbull, Laing, Nichols, &c. But very few copies remain. Odd numbers may be had to complete sets, at 2s. each.

It contains a large number of pieces in Anglo-Saxon, Anglo-Norman, and Early English; it will be found of use to future Philologists, and to all who take an interest in the history of our language and literature.

Popular Treatises on Science, written during the Middle Ages, in Anglo-Saxon, Anglo-Norman, and English. 8vo. Edited by THOS. WRIGHT. *Cloth*, 4s. 6d.

Contents:—An Anglo-Saxon Treatise on Astronomy of the TENTH CENTURY, now first published from a MS. in the British Museum, with a translation; Livre des Creatures, by Phillippe de Thaun, now first printed with a translation, (extremely valuable to the Philologist, as being the earliest specimens of Anglo-Norman remaining, and explanatory of all the symbolical signs in early sculpture and painting); the Bestiary of Phillippe de Thaun, with a translation; Fragment on Popular Science from the Early English Metrical Lives of the Saints, (the earliest piece of the kind in the English language.)

An Introduction to Anglo-Saxon Reading; comprising Ælfric's Homily on the Birthday of St. Gregory, with a copious Glossary, &c. By L. LANGLEY, F.L.S. 12mo, *cloth*, 2s. 6d.

Anecdota Literaria: A Collection of Short Poems in English, Latin, and French, illustrative of the Literature and History of England in the XIIIth Century; and more especially of the Condition and Manners of the different Classes of Society. By T. WRIGHT, M.A., F.S.A., &c. 8vo, *cloth*. Only 250 printed. 7s. 6d.

Philological Proofs of the original Unity and recent Origin of the Human Race, derived from a Comparison of the Languages of Asia, Europe, Africa, and America. By A. J. JOHNES. 8vo, *cloth*. REDUCED from 12s. 6d. to 6s.

Printed at the suggestion of Dr. Pritchard, to whose works it will be found a useful supplement.

Early Mysteries, and other Latin Poems of the XIIth and XIIIth centuries. Edited from original MSS. in the British Museum, and the Libraries of Oxford, Cambridge, Paris, and Vienna. By THOS. WRIGHT, M.A., F.S.A. 8vo, bds. 4s 6d.

"Besides the curious specimens of the dramatic style of Middle-Age Latinity, Mr. Wright has given two compositions in the Narrative Elegiac Verse (a favorite measure at that period), in the Comœdia Babionis and the Geta of Vitalis Blesensis, which form a link of connexion between the Classical and Middle-age Literature; some remarkable Satirical Rhymes on the people of Norfolk, written by a Monk of Peterborough, and answered in the same style by John of St. Omer; and lastly, some sprightly and often graceful songs, from a MS. in the Arundel Collection, which afford a very favorable idea of the Lyric Poetry of our clerical forefathers."—*Gentleman's Mag.*

The Early History of Freemasonry in England, Illustrated by an English Poem of the XIVth Century, with Notes. By J. O. HALLIWELL. Post 8vo, SECOND EDITION, *with a facsimile of the original MS. in the British Museum, cloth,* 2s. 6d.

"The interest which the curious poem of which this publication is chiefly composed has excited, is proved by the fact of its having been translated into German, and of it having reached a second edition, which is not common with such publications. Mr. Halliwell has carefully revised the new edition, and increased its utility by the addition of a complete and correct glossary."—*Literary Gazette.*

Torrent of Portugal; an English Metrical Romance, *now first published*, from an unique MS. of the XVth century, preserved in the Chetham Library at Manchester. Edited by J. O. HALLIWELL, &c. Post 8vo, *cloth, uniform with Ritson, Weber, and Ellis's publications,* 5s.

"This is a valuable and interesting addition to our list of early English metrical romances, and an indispensable companion to the collections of Ritson, Weber, and Ellis."—*Literary Gazette.*

"A literary curiosity, and one both welcome and serviceable to the lover of black-letter lore. Though the obsoleteness of the style may occasion sad stumbling to a modern reader, yet the class to which it rightly belongs will value it accordingly; both because it is curious in its details, and possesses philological importance. To the general reader it presents one feature of interest, viz. the reference to Wayland Smith, whom Sir W. Scott has invested with so much interest."—*Metropolitan Magazine.*

An Essay on the Origin, Progress, and Decline of Rhyming Latin Verse, with many specimens. By Sir ALEX. CROKE. Post 8vo, *cloth*, 7s. 6d., reduced to 3s.

"This is a clever and interesting little volume on an attractive subject, the leisure work of a scholar and a man of taste."—*British Critic.*

On the Origin and Formation of the Romance Languages; containing an examination of M. Raynouard's Theory on the Relation of the Italian, Spanish, Provençal, and French, to the Latin. By GEO. CORNEWALL LEWIS. 8vo, *cloth*, 12s. REDUCED to 7s. 6d.

The Harrowing of Hell, a Miracle
Play, written in the Reign of Edward II., now first published from the Original in the British Museum, with a Modern Reading, Introduction, and Notes. By JAMES ORCHARD HALLIWELL, Esq., F.R.S., F.S.A., &c. 8vo, *sewed*, 2s.

This curious piece is supposed to be the earliest specimen of dramatic composition in the English language; vide Hallam's Literature of Europe, Vol. I.; Strutt's Manners and Customs, Vol. II.; Warton's English Poetry; Sharon Turner's England; Collier's History of English Dramatic Poetry, Vol. II. p. 213. *All these writers refer to the Manuscript.*

Nugæ Poeticæ; Select Pieces of Old
English Popular Poetry, illustrating the Manners and Arts of the XVth Century. Edited by J. O. HALLIWELL. Post 8vo. *Only 100 copies printed*, cloth, 5s.

Contents:—Colyn Blowbol's Testament; the Debate of the Carpenter's Tools; the Merchant and his Son; the Maid and the Magpie; Elegy on Lobe, Henry VIIIth's Fool; Romance of Robert of Sicily, *and five other curious pieces of the same kind.*

Rara Mathematica; or a Collection
of Treatises on the Mathematics and Subjects connected with them, from ancient inedited MSS. By J. O. HALLIWELL. 8vo, Second Edition, *cloth*, 3s. 6d.

Contents: Johannis de Sacro-Bosco Tractatus de Arte Numerandi; Method used in England in the Fifteenth Century for taking the Altitude of a Steeple; Treatise on the Numeration of Algorism; Treatise on Glasses for Optical Purposes, by W. Bourne; Johannis Robyns de Cometis Commentaria; Two Tables showing the time of High Water at London Bridge, and the Duration of Moonlight, from a MS. of the Thirteenth Century; on the Mensuration of Heights and Distances; Alexandri de Villa Dei Carmen de Algorismo; Preface to a Calendar or Almanack for 1430; Johannis Norfolk in Artem progressionis summula; Notes on Early Almanacs, by the Editor, &c. &c.

Reliques of Irish Jacobite Poetry,
with Interlinear Translations, and Biographical Sketches of the Authors, and Notes by J. DALY, also English Metrical Versions by E. WALSH. 8vo. Parts 1 and 2 (all yet published,) 2s.

Popular Errors in English Grammar,
particularly in Pronunciation, familiarly pointed out. By GEORGE JACKSON. 12mo, Third Edition, *with a coloured frontispiece of the " Sedes Busbeiana."* 6d.

Provincial Dialects of England.

Bibliographical List of all the Works
which have been published towards illustrating the Provincial Dialects of England. By JOHN RUSSELL SMITH. Post 8vo, 1s.

'Very serviceable to such as prosecute the study of our provincial dialects, or are collecting works on that curious subject. We very cordially recommend it to notice."—*Metropolitan.*

The Vocabulary of East Anglia,
an attempt to record the vulgar tongue of the twin sister Counties, *Norfolk* and *Suffolk*, as it existed in the last twenty years of the Eighteenth Century, and still exists; with proof of its antiquity from Etymology and Authority. By the Rev. R. FORBY. 2 vols. post 8vo, *cloth*, 12s. (original price 1l. 1s.)

An Historical Sketch of the Provincial
Dialects of England, illustrated by numerous examples. Extracted from the " Dictionary of Archaic and Provincial Words." By JAMES ORCHARD HALLIWELL. 8vo, sewed, 2s.

Westmorland and Cumberland
Dialects. Dialogues, Poems, Songs, and Ballads, by various Writers, in the Westmorland and Cumberland Dialects, now first collected, to which is added, a Copious Glossary of Words peculiar to those Counties. Post 8vo, pp. 408, *cloth*, 9s.

This collection comprises, in the *Westmorland Dialect*, Mrs. ANN WHEELER'S Four Familiar Dialogues, with Poems, &c.; and in the *Cumberland Dialect*, I. Poems and Pastorals by the Rev. JOSIAH RELPH; II. Pastorals, &c., by EWAN CLARK; III. Letter from Dublin by a young Borrowdale Shepherd, by ISAAC RITSON; IV. Poems by JOHN STAGG; V. Poems by MARK LONSDALE; VI. Ballads and Songs by ROBERT ANDERSON, the Cumbrian Bard (*including some now first printed*); VII. Songs by Miss BLAMIRE and Miss GILPIN; VIII. Songs by JOHN RAYSON; IX. An Extensive Glossary of Westmorland and Cumberland Words.

" Among the specimens of Cumberland Verse will be found some true poetry, if not the best ever written in the language of rural life this side the Scotch Borders. The writers seem to have caught in their happiest hours inspiration from the rapt soul of Burns. Anderson's touching song of wedded love, 'The Days that are geane,' is a worthy answer for a husband to Burn's 'John Anderson my Jo.'"—*Gent's. Magazine.*

" No other two counties in England have so many pieces, both in prose and verse, illustrative of the manners and customs of the inhabitants, and written in their own native dialect. The philologist will find numerous examples of words and phrases which are obsolete in the general language of England, or which have been peculiar to Westmorland and Cumberland from time immemorial. Nor are the pieces uninteresting in other respects. Some of the *patois* verses are rich in the true spirit and vigour of poetry."—*Metropolitan.*

" A charming volume: it contains some beautiful poetical effusions, as well as characteristic sketches in prose."—*Archæologist.*

The Yorkshire Dialect, exemplified
in various Dialogues, Tales, and Songs, applicable to the County, with a Glossary. Post 8vo, 1s.

" A shiling book worth its money; most of the pieces of composition are not only harmless, but good and pretty. The eclogue on the death of 'Awd Daisy,' an outworn horse, is an outpouring of some of the best feelings of the rustic mind; and the addresses to riches and poverty have much of the freedom and spirit of Burns."
Gent's Magazine, May 1841.

Specimens of Cornish Provincial
Dialect, collected and arranged by Uncle Jan Treenoodle, with some Introductory Remarks and a Glossary by an Antiquarian Friend, also a Selection of Songs and other Pieces connected with Cornwall. Post 8vo, *with curious portrait of Dolly Pentreath, cloth,* 4s.

Exmoor Scolding and Courtship
in the Propriety and Decency of Exmoor (Devonshire) Language, *with Notes and a Glossary.* Post 8vo, 12th edition, 1s. 6d.

" A very rich bit of West of Englandism."—*Metropolitan.*

Valuable and Interesting Books on Sale by

Grose's (Francis, F.S.A.) Glossary
of Provincial and Local Words used in England, with which is now first incorporated the SUPPLEMENT by SAMUEL PEGGE, F.S.A. Post 8vo, *elegantly printed, cloth, 4s. 6d.*

The utility of a Provincial Glossary to all persons desirous of understanding our ancient poets is so universally acknowledged, that to enter into a proof of it would be entirely a work of supererogation. Grose and Pegge are constantly referred to in Todd's "Johnson's Dictionary."

Poems of Rural Life, in the Dorset
Dialect, with a Dissertation and Glossary. By WILLIAM BARNES. SECOND EDITION *in the press.*

A fine poetic feeling is displayed through the various pieces in this volume; according to some critics nothing has appeared equal to it since the time of Burns; the 'Gent.'s Magazine' for Dec. 1844, gave a review of the volume some pages in length.

A Glossary of Provincial Words
and Phrases in use in Wiltshire, showing their Derivation in numerous instances from the Language of the Anglo-Saxons. By JOHN YONGE AKERMAN, Esq., F.S.A. 12mo, *cloth, 3s.*

A Collection of Fugitive Pieces
in the Dialect of Zummerzet. Edited by J. O. HALLIWELL. Post 8vo, *only 50 printed, 2s.*

Dick and Sal, or Jack and Joan's
Fair, a Doggrel Poem, in the Kentish Dialect. 3d edition, 12mo, 6d.

Jan Cladpole's Trip to 'Merricur
in Search for Dollar Trees, and how he got rich enough to beg his way home! written in Sussex Doggerel. 12mo, 6d.

John Noakes and Mary Styles,
a Poem, *exhibiting some of the most striking lingual localisms peculiar to Essex*, with a Glossary. By CHARLES CLARK, Esq. of Great Totham Hall, Essex. Post 8vo, *cloth, 2s.*

"The poem possesses considerable humour." *Tait's Mag.*—"A very pleasant trifle." *Lit. Gaz.*—"A very clever production." *Essex Lit. Journal.*—"Full of rich humour." *Essex Mercury.*—"Very droll." *Metropolitan.*—"Exhibits the dialect of Essex perfectly." *Eclectic Review.*—"Full of quaint wit and humour." *Gent's Mag. May* 1841.—"A very clever and amusing piece of local description." *Archæologist.*

Heraldry, Topography, Numismatics, and Archæology.

The Curiosities of Heraldry, with Illustrations from Old English Writers.
By MARK ANTONY LOWER, Author of "Essays on English Surnames;" *with Illuminated Title-page, and numerous Engravings from designs by the Author.* 8vo, cloth, GULES, appropriately ornamented, OR, 14s.

This work is one of the principal authorities made use of by the compiler of Parker's recently published "Glossary of Heraldry," which is printed uniformly with it, and similarly illustrated. The two works should accompany each other. For the student of the "Noble Science," a treatise like Parker's is necessary for matters of detail, while one who wishes for a copious, continuous, and philosophical view of Heraldry, and its connexion with the history and manners of the middle ages, will be amply gratified by a perusal of the "Curiosities of Heraldry."

"The present volume is truly a worthy sequel (to the 'SURNAMES') in the same curious and antiquarian line, blending with remarkable facts and intelligence, such a fund of amusing anecdote and illustration, that the reader is almost surprised to find that he has learnt so much, whilst he appeared to be pursuing mere entertainment. The text is so pleasing that we scarcely dream of its sterling value; and it seems as if, in unison with the woodcuts, which so cleverly explain its points and adorn its various topics, the whole design were intended for a relaxation from study, rather than an ample exposition of an extraordinary and universal custom, which produced the most important effect upon the minds and habits of mankind."—*Literary Gazette.*

"Mr. Lower's work is both curious and instructive, while the manner of its treatment is so inviting and popular that the subject to which it refers, which many have hitherto had too good reason to consider meagre and unprofitable, assumes, under the hands of the writer, the novelty of fiction with the importance of historic truth."—*Athenæum.*

English Surnames. A Series of Essays on Family Nomenclature, Historical,
Etymological, and Humorous; with Chapters on Canting Arms, Rebuses, the Roll of Battel Abbey, a List of Latinised Surnames, &c. By MARK ANTONY LOWER. The *second edition, enlarged,* post 8vo, pp 292, *with 20 woodcuts, cloth, 6s.*

To those who are curious about their patronymic, it will be found a very instructive and amusing volume— mingling wit and pleasantry, with antiquarian research and historical interest.

"An instructive and amusing volume, which ought to be popular. Perhaps no subject is more curious than the history of proper names. How few persons are there who have not on one occasion or other been struck with the singular names which have fallen under their own observation, and who have not sought for information as to their origin? Yet we know of no work of any value, much more a popular work, which treats on the subject. Mr. Lower has written a very good and well-arranged book, which we can with confidence recommend to our readers."—*Archæologist.*

A Genealogical and Heraldic History of the Extinct and Dormant
Baronetcies of England, Ireland, and Scotland. By J. BURKE, Esq. and J. B. BURKE, Esq. Medium 8vo SECOND EDITION. 638 *closely printed pages*, in double columns, with about 1000 arms engraved on wood, *fine portrait of* JAMES I, *and illuminated title-page*, extra cloth, 1l. 8s. REDUCED TO 10s.

This work, which has engaged the attention of the Authors for several years, comprises nearly a thousand families, many of them amongst the most ancient and eminent in the kingdom, each carried down to its representative or representatives still existing, with elaborate and minute details of the alliances, achievements, and fortunes, generation after generation, from the earliest to the latest period. The work is printed to correspond precisely with the last edition of Mr. Burke's Dictionary of the Existing Peerage and Baronetage; the armorial bearings are engraved in the best style, and are incorporated with the text as in that work.

Pedigrees of the Nobility and Gentry of Hertfordshire. By WILLIAM BERRY, late and for fifteeen years Registering Clerk in the College of Arms, Author of the "Encyclopædia Heraldica," &c. &c. Folio (only 125 printed), bds. 3l. 10s. REDUCED to 1l. 5s.

"These Collections of Pedigrees will be found of great utility, though not of sufficient proof in themselves to establish the claims of kindred set forth in them: but affording a ready clue to such necessary proof whenever it should be required, by pointing out the places of nativity, baptism, marriages, and burials, and such other legal documents, as localities will otherwise afford, and the modern entries in the Herald's College, are of no better authority, requiring the very same kind of proof for legal purposes. This observation will perhaps silence the ill-natured remarks which have emanated from that quarter: and it is self-evident that the printing of 250 copies is a much safer record than one manuscript entry there, which might easily be destroyed."—*Preface.*

History and Antiquities of the Ancient Port and Town of Rye in Sussex, compiled from Original Documents. By WILLIAM HOLLOWAY, Esq. Thick 8vo, cloth, 1l. 1s.

History and Antiquities of Dartford, in Kent, with Incidental Notices of Places in its Neighbourhood. By J. DUNKIN, Author of the "History of the Hundreds of Bullington and Ploughley in Oxfordshire; "History of Bicester;" "History of Bromley," &c. 8vo, 17 plates, cloth. Only 150 printed. 21s.

Historic Sites and other Remarkable and Interesting Places in the County of Suffolk. By JOHN WODDERSPOON, with Prefatory Verses by BERNARD BARTON, Esq., and a Poetical Epilogue by a "SUFFOLK VILLAGER." Improved edition, *fine woodcuts*, post 8vo, pp. 232, *closely printed, and containing as much matter as many 12s. volumes,* cloth, ONLY 4s. 6d.

Principal Contents:—Framlingham Castle; Staningfield; Rookwood; Mrs. Inchbald; Aldham Common; the Martyr's Stone; Westhorpe Hall, the residence of Charles Brandon, Duke of Suffolk; Ipswich; Wolsey's Gate and Mr. Sparrow's House; Rendlesham; Redgrave; Bury St. Edmunds, the Abbey; David Hartley; Bp. Gardiner; George Bloomfield; Wetheringset; Haughley Castle; Grimstone Hall; Cavendish, the Voyager; Framlingham Church, the burial-place of Surrey, the Poet; Bungay Castle; Dunwich; Aldborough; Wingfield, and the Old Halls of Suffolk.

The Local Historian's Table-Book of Remarkable Occurrences, Historical Facts, Traditions, Legendary and Descriptive Ballads, &c. &c., connected with the Counties of NEWCASTLE-ON-TYNE, NORTHUMBERLAND, and DURHAM. By M. A. RICHARDSON. Royal 8vo, profusely illustrated with woodcuts, *now Complete in 8 vols. royal 8vo,* cloth, 9s. each, or the Divisions sold separately as follows: HISTORICAL DIVISION, 5 vols. LEGENDARY DIVISION, 3 vols.

The legendary portion will be found very interesting volumes by those who take no interest in the Historical portion.

"This chronology of local occurrences, from the earliest times when a date is ascertainable possesses an especial interest for the residents of the Northern Counties; but, inasmuch as it records Historical events as well as trivial incidents, and includes Biographical notices of men whose fame extended beyond their birth-places, it is not without a value to the general reader. The work is divided into two portions, the larger consisting of the chronicle, and the lesser of the traditions and ballads of the country. Some of these are very characteristic and curious; they invest with poetic associations almost every ruin or plot of ground; and the earlier legends of moss-troopers and border-strifes afford an insight into the customs and state of society in remote periods. The handsome pages are illustrated with woodcuts of old buildings and other antiquities."—*Spectator*.

History of Banbury, in Oxfordshire, including Copious Historical and Antiquarian Notices of the Neighbourhood. By ALFRED BEESLEY. Thick 8vo, 684 *closely printed pages, with 66 woodcuts, engraved in the first style of art,* by O. Jewitt, *of Oxford*, (pub. at 1l. 5s.) NOW REDUCED to 14s.

"The neighbourhood of Banbury is equally rich in British, Roman, Saxon, Norman, and English Antiquities, of all which Mr. Beesley has given regularly cleared accounts. Banbury holds an important place in the history of the Parliamentary War of the Seventeenth Century, and was the scene of the great Battle of Edghill, and of the important fight of Cropredy Bridge. Relating to the events of that period, the author has collected a great body of local information of the most interesting kind. By no means the least valuable part of Mr. Beesley's work, is his account of the numerous interesting early churches, which characterize the Banbury district."—*The Archæologist.*

J. R. SMITH having bought the whole stock of the above very interesting volume, invites the Subscribers to complete their copies in parts without delay, the price of which will be (for a short time) 1s. 6d., instead of 2s. 6d.

History and Topography of the Isle of Axholme, in Lincolnshire. By the Rev. W. B. STONEHOUSE. Thick 4to, FINE PLATES, REDUCED from 3l. 3s. to 15s.

The Druidical Temples of the County of Wilts. By the Rev. E. DUKE, M.A., F.S.A., Member of the Archæological Institute, &c., Author of the "Hall of John Halle," and other works, 12mo, *plates,* cloth, 5s.

"Mr. Duke has been long honourably known as a zealous cultivator of our local antiquities. His collections on this subject, and on the literature of Wiltshire, are nowhere surpassed; while his residence on the borders of the Plain, and within reach of our most interesting remains, has afforded scope to his meritorious exertions. The work before us is the fruit of long study and laborious investigation."—*Salisbury Journal.*

A Critical Dissertation on Professor Willis's "Architectural History of Canterbury Cathedral." By C. SANDYS, of Canterbury. 8vo, 2s. 6d.

"Written in no quarrelsome or captious spirit: the highest compliment is paid to Professor Willis, where it is due. But the author has certainly made out a clear case, in some very important instances, of inaccuracies that have led the learned Professor into the construction of serious errors throughout. It may be considered as an indispensable companion to his volume, containing a great deal of extra information of a very curious kind."—*Art-Union.*

The Visitor's Guide to Knole House, near Seven Oaks in Kent, with Catalogue of the Pictures contained in the Mansion, a Genealogical History of the Sackville Family, &c. &c. By J. H. BRADY, F.R.A.S. 12mo, 27 *woodcuts by Bonner, Sly, &c.* cloth, 4s. 6d. *Large Paper*, 10s.

Illustrations of Knole House, from Drawings by KNIGHT, engraved on wood by Bonner, Sly, &c. 8vo, 16 *plates, with descriptions*, 5s.

Greenwich; its History, Antiquities, and Public Buildings. By H. S. RICHARDSON. 12mo, *fine woodcuts by Baxter.* 1s. 6d.

The Folkestone Fiery Serpent, together with the Humours of the DOVOR MAYOR; being an Ancient Ballad full of Mystery and pleasant Conceit, now first collected and printed from the various MS. copies in possession of the inhabitants of the South-east Coast of Kent, with Notes. 12mo, 1s.

The History of the Town of Gravesend in Kent, and of the Port of London. By R. P. CRUDEN, late Mayor of Gravesend. Royal 8vo, 37 *fine plates and woodcuts, a very handsome volume*, cloth, 1843, REDUCED FROM 1l. 8s. to 10s.

Bibliotheca Cantiana, a Bibliographical Account of what has been published on the History, Topography, Antiquities, Customs, and Family Genealogy of the COUNTY OF KENT, with Biographical Notes. By JOHN RUSSELL SMITH. In a handsome 8vo volume, pp. 370, *with two plates of fac-similes of Autographs of 33 eminent Kentish Writers.* 14s. REDUCED TO 5s.—*large paper*, 10s. 6d.

A Journey to Beresford Hall, in Derbyshire, the Seat of CHARLES COTTON, Esq. the celebrated Author and Angler. By W. ALEXANDER, F.S.A., F.L.S., late Keeper of the Prints in the British Museum. Crown 4to, *printed on tinted paper, with a spirited frontispiece, representing Walton and his adopted Son Cotton in the Fishing-house, and vignette title-page*, cloth, 5s.

Dedicated to the Anglers of Great Britain and the various Walton and Cotton Clubs, only 100 printed.

A Brief Account of the Parish of Stowting, in Kent, and of the Antiquities lately discovered there. By the Rev. F. WRENCH, Rector. 8vo, *three folding plates, etched by the author.* 2s. 6d.

History of Portsmouth, Portsea, Landport, Southsea, and Gosport. By HENRY SLIGHT, Esq. 8vo, Third Edition, bds. 4s.

The Hand-Book to Leicester. By JAMES THOMPSON. 12mo, SECOND EDITION, enlarged, *plates*, bds. 2s.

A Hand-Book to Lewes in Sussex, Historical and Descriptive, with Notices of the Recent Discoveries at the Priory. By MARK ANTONY LOWER. 12mo, *many engravings*, cloth, 2s.

Chronicles of Pevensey in Sussex. By M. A. LOWER. 12mo, *woodcuts*, 1s.

Historia Collegii Jesu Cantabrigiensis à J. SHERMANNO, olim præs. ejusdem Collegii. Edita J. O. HALLIWELL. 8vo, *cloth*, 2s.

History and Antiquities of the Hundred of Compton, Berks, with Dissertations on the Roman Station of Calleva Attrebatum, and the Battle of Ashdown. By W. HEWITT, Jun, 8vo, 18 *plates*, cloth. Only 250 printed. 15s. REDUCED TO 9s.

The Archæologist and Journal of Antiquarian Science. Edited by J. O. HALLIWELL. 8vo, Nos. I. to X. COMPLETE, with Index, pp. 490, *with 19 engravings*, cloth, *reduced from* 10s. 6d. *to* 5s. 6d.

Containing original articles on Architecture, Historical Literature, Round Towers of Ireland, Philology, Bibliography, Topography, Proceedings of the various Antiquarian Societies, Retrospective Reviews, and Reviews of Recent Antiquarian Works, &c.

Newcastle Tracts; Reprints of Rare and curious Tracts, chiefly illustrative of the History of the Northern Counties; *beautifully printed in* crown 8vo, *on a fine thick paper, with fac-simile Titles, and other features characteristic of the originals.* Only 100 *copies printed.* Nos. I. to XLI, 4l. 2s.

Purchasers are expected to take the succeeding Tracts as published.

Coins of the Romans relating to Britain, Described and Illustrated. By J. Y. AKERMAN, F.S.A., Secretary to the Numismatic Society, &c. Second edition, greatly enlarged, 8vo, *with plates and woodcuts*, cloth, 10s. 6d.

The 'Prix de Numismatique' has just been awarded by the French Institute to the author for this work.

"Mr. Akerman's volume contains a notice of every known variety, with copious illustrations, and is published at very moderate price: it should be consulted, not merely for these particular coins, but also for facts most valuable to all who are interested in the Romano-British history."—*Archæological Journal.*

Ancient Coins of Cities and Princes, Geographically arranged and described, HISPANIA, GALLIA, BRITANNIA. By J. Y. AKERMAN, F.S.A. 8vo, *with engravings of many hundred coins from actual examples*, cloth, 18s.

Numismatic Illustrations of the Narrative Portions of the New Testament. *fine paper, numerous woodcuts from the original coins in various public and private collections.* 1 vol. 8vo, *cloth*, 5s. 6d.

Lectures on the Coinage of the Greeks and Romans, delivered in the University of Oxford. By EDWARD CARDWELL, D.D., Principal of St. Alban's Hall, and Professor of Ancient History. 8vo, *cloth*, reduced from 8s. 6d. to 4s.

A very interesting historical volume, and written in a pleasing and popular manner.

Essay on the Numismatic History of the Ancient Kingdom of the East Angles. By D. H. HAIGH. Royal 8vo, 5 *plates, containing numerous figures of coins*, sewed, 6s.

Notitia Britanniæ, or an Inquiry concerning the Localities, Habits, Condition, and Progressive Civilization of the Aborigines of Britain; to which is appended a brief Retrospect of the Result of their Intercourse with the Romans. By W. D. SAULL, F.S.A., F.G.S., &c. 8vo, *engravings*, 3s. 6d.

A Verbatim Report of the Proceedings at a Special General Meeting of the British Archæological Association, held at the Theatre of the Western Literary Institution, 5th March, 1845, T. J. Pettigrew in the Chair. With an Introduction, by THOMAS WRIGHT. 8vo, *sewed*, 1s. 6d.

A Hand-Book of English Coins from the Conquest to Victoria. By L. JEWITT. 12mo, 11 plates, cloth, 1s.

British Archæological Association. A Report of the Proceedings and Excursions of the Members of the British Archæological Association, at the Canterbury Session, Sept. 1844. By A. J. DUNKIN. Thick 8vo, with many engravings, cloth, 1l. 1s.

"The volume contains most of the papers entire that were read at the Meeting, and revised by the Authors. It will become a scarce book as only 120 were printed; and it forms the first yearly volume of the Archæological Association, or the Archæological Institute."

Popular Poetry, Stories, and Superstitions.

The Nursery Rhymes of England, collected chiefly from Oral Tradition. Edited by J. O. HALLIWELL. The Fourth Edition, enlarged, with 38 Designs by W. B. SCOTT, Director of the School of Design, Newcastle-on-Tyne. 12mo, in very rich illuminated cloth, gilt leaves, 4s. 6d.

"Illustrations! And here they are; clever pictures, which the three-year olds understand before their A, B, C, and which the fifty-three year olds like almost as well as the threes."—Literary Gazette.

"We are persuaded that the very rudest of these jingles, tales, and rhymes, possess a strong imagination-nourishing power; and that in infancy and early childhood a sprinkling of ancient nursery lore is worth whole cartloads of the wise saws and modern instances which are now as duly and carefully concocted by experienced litterateurs, into instructive tales for the spelling public, as are works of entertainment for the reading public. The work is worthy of the attention of the popular antiquary."—Tait's Mag.

The public are cautioned against other works with imitative titles, which have been published since the second edition of the above, and which are mostly pirated from it. Mr. Halliwell's is the largest collection of these odd ditties ever formed, with explanatory notes, &c. &c.

An Essay on the Archæology of our Popular Phrases and Nursery Rhymes. By H. B. KER. 2 vols. 12mo, new cloth, 4s. (pub. at 12s.)

A work which has met with great abuse among the reviewers, but those who are fond of philological pursuits will read it now it is to be had at so very moderate a price, and it really contains a good deal of gossiping matter. The author's attempt is to explain everything from the Dutch, which he believes was the same language as the Anglo-Saxon.

The Merry Tales of the Wise Men of Gotham. Edited by JAMES ORCHARD HALLIWELL, Esq. F.S.A. Post 8vo, 1s.

These tales are supposed to have been composed in the early part of the sixteenth century, by Dr. Andrew Borde, the well-known progenitor of Merry Andrews. "In the time of Henry the Eighth, and after," says Ant.-à-Wood, "it was accounted a book full of wit and mirth by scholars and gentlemen."

The Noble and Renowned History of Guy, Earl of Warwick, containing a full and true account of his many famous and valiant actions. 12mo, new edition, with woodcuts, cloth, 2s. 6d

Saint Patrick's Purgatory; an Essay on the Legends of Purgatory, Hell, and Paradise, current during the Middle Ages. By THOMAS WRIGHT, M.A., F.S.A., &c. Post 8vo, cloth, 6s

"It must be observed, that this is not a mere account of St. Patrick's Purgatory, but a complete history of the legends and superstitions relating to the subject, from the earliest times, rescued from old MSS. as well as from old printed books. Moreover, it embraces a singular chapter of literary history, omitted by Warton and all former writers with whom we are acquainted; and we think we may add, that it forms the best introduction to Dante that has yet been published."—Literary Gazette.

"This appears to be a curious and even amusing book on the singular subject of Purgatory, in which the idle and fearful dreams of superstition are shown to be first narrated as tales, and then applied as means of deducing the moral character of the age in which they prevailed."—Spectator.

Trial of the Witches at Bury St. Edmunds, before Sir M. HALE, 1664, with an Appendix by CHARLES CLARK, Esq. of Totham, Essex. 8vo, 1s.

"The most perfect narrative of anything of this nature hitherto extant."—Preface.

Wonderful Discovery of the Witchcrafts of Margaret and Philip Flower daughters of Joan Flower, near Bever (Belvoir), executed at Lincoln for confessing themselves actors in the destruction of Lord Rosse, son of the Earl of Rutland. 1618. 8vo, 1s.

One of the most extraordinary cases of Witchcraft on record.

Account of the Trial, Confession, and Condemnation of Six Witches at MAIDSTONE, 1652; also the Trial and Execution of Three others at Faversham, 1645. 8vo, 1s.

These transactions are unnoticed by all the Kentish historians.

Biography, Literary History, and Criticism.

England's Worthies, under whom all the Civil and Bloody Warres, since Anno 1642 to Anno 1647, are related. By JOHN VICARS, Author of "England's Parliamentary Chronicle," &c. &c. Royal 12mo, reprinted in the old style, (similar to Lady Willoughby's Diary,) with copies of the 18 rare portraits after Hollar, &c. half morocco, 9s.

Copies of the original edition have been sold from 16l. to 20l.

The portraits comprise, Robert, Earl of Essex; Robert, Earl of Warwick; Lord Montagu, Earl of Denbigh, Earl of Stamford, David Lesley, Gen. Fairfax, Sir Thomas Fairfax, O. Cromwell, Skippon, Col. Massey, Sir W Brereton, Sir W. Waller, Col. Laughorne, Gen. Poyntz, Sir Thos. Middleton, Gen. Brown, and Gen. Mitton.

Bibliotheca Madrigaliana, a Catalogue of Musical and Poetical Works, published in England in the 16th and 17th Centuries, under the titles of 'Madrigals,' 'Ballets,' 'Ayres,' 'Canzonets,' &c. By E. F. RIMBAULT, LL.D. F.S.A. 8vo, *cloth, 7s. 6d.*

Autobiography of Joseph Lister, of Bradford, in Yorkshire, to which is added a contemporary account of the Defence of Bradford, and Capture of Leeds by the Parliamentarians in 1642. Edited by THOMAS WRIGHT. 8vo, only 250 copies printed, *cloth, 4s.*

Love Letters of Mrs. Piozzi, written when she was Eighty, to the handsome Actor, William Augustus Conway, aged Twenty-seven, 8vo, *sewed, 2s.*

"—— written at three, four, and five o'clock (in the morning) by an Octogenary pen, a heart (as Mrs. Lee says) twenty-six years old, and as H. L. P. feels it to be, *all your own.*"—*Letter V.* 3d Feb. 1820.

On the Character of Falstaff, as originally exhibited by Shakespeare in the two parts of King Henry IV. By J. O. HALLIWELL. 12mo. *cloth,* (only 100 *printed,*) *2s.*

Collection of Letters on Scientific Subjects, illustrative of the Progress of Science in England temp. Elizabeth to Charles II. Edited by J. O. HALLIWELL. 8vo, *cloth, 3s.*

Shakesperiana, a Catalogue of the Early Editions of Shakespeare's Plays, and of the Commentaries and other Publications illustrative of his Works. By J. O. HALLIWELL. 8vo, *cloth, 3s.*
"Indispensable to everybody who wishes to carry on any inquiries connected with Shakespeare, or who may have a fancy for Shakespearian Bibliography."—*Spectator.*

A Rot among the Bishops; or a Terrible *Tempest* in the *Sea* of Canterbury, set forth in lively emblems to please the judicious Reader, in Verse. By THOMAS STIRRY, 1641. 18mo, (*a satire on Abp. Laud,*) *four very curious woodcut emblems, cloth, 3s.*
A facsimile of the very rare original edition, which sold at Bindley's sale for 13l.

An Introduction to Shakespeare's Midsummer Night's Dream. By J. O. HALLIWELL. 8vo, *cloth (only 250 printed), 3s.*

An Account of the only known Manuscript of Shakespeare's Plays, comprising some important variations and corrections in the Merry Wives of Windsor, obtained from a Playhouse copy of that Play recently discovered. By J. O. HALLIWELL. 8vo, *sewed, 1s.*

Miscellanies.

Illustrations of Eating, displaying the Omnivorous Character of Man, and exhibiting the Natives of various Countries at feeding-time. By a BEEF-EATER. Fcap. 8vo, *with woodcuts, 2s.*

Elements of Naval Architecture, being a Translation of the third part of CLAIRBOIS' "Traité Elémentaire de la Construction des Vaisseaux." By J. N. STRANGE, Commander, R.N., 8vo, *with 5 large folding plates, cloth, 5s.*

Lectures on Naval Architecture, being the substance of those delivered at the United Service Institution. By E. GARDINER FISHBOURNE, Commander R.N. 8vo, *plates, cloth, 5s. 6d.*
Both these works are published in illustration of the "WAVE SYSTEM."

Poems, partly of Rural Life (in National English). By WILLIAM BARNES, Author of "Poems in the Dorset Dialect." 12mo, *cloth, 5s.*

Waifs and Strays (a Collection of Poetry). 12mo. *only 250 printed, chiefly for presents, sewed, 1s. 6d.*

Vestiges of the Antiquities of Derbyshire, and the Sepulchral Usages of its Inhabitants, from the most remote Ages to the Reformation. By THOMAS BATEMAN, Esq., of Yolgrave, County of Derby. 8vo, *illustrated with 80 wood engravings, cloth, 15s.*

An Archæological Index, serving as a Guide to the Antiquities of the Celtic, Romano-British, and Anglo-Saxon Periods. By J. Y. AKERMAN, F.S.A. 8vo, *with numerous engravings, comprising upwards of 500 objects, cloth, 15s.*

A New Life of Shakespeare, including many particulars respecting the Poet and his Family, never before published. By J. O. HALLIWELL, F.R.S., &c. *In one handsome volume,* 8vo, *illustrated with 76 engravings on wood of objects, most of which are new, from drawings by* FAIRHOLT, *cloth, 15s.*
This work contains upwards of forty documents respecting Shakespeare and his Family *never before published,* besides numerous others indirectly illustrating the Poet's biography. All the anecdotes and traditions concerning Shakespeare are here for the first time collected, and much new light is thrown on his personal history, by papers exhibiting him as selling Malt and Stone, &c. Of the seventy-six engravings which illustrate the volume, *more than fifty have never before been engraved.* It is the only Life of Shakespeare to be bought separately from his works.

The Anglo-Saxon Version of the Life of St. Guthlac, Hermit of Croyland, with a Translation and Notes by C. W. GOODWIN, M.A. 12mo, *cloth, 5s.*

Sussex Archæological Collections, illustrating the History and Antiquities of the County, published by the SUSSEX ARCHÆOLOGICAL SOCIETY. 8vo, *plates and woodcuts, cloth,* 10s. (VERY FEW FOR SALE.)

J. R. S. will be happy to publish on Commission any Historical, Antiquarian, or Topographical work, and will give it all possible publicity through the medium of his Catalogues, &c. without cost to the Proprietor.

DOES NOT CIRCULATE

Lightning Source UK Ltd.
Milton Keynes UK
UKOW010127010312

188134UK00016B/2/P